Concrete Jungle

edited by Mark Dion and Alexis Rockman

Juno Books

new york city

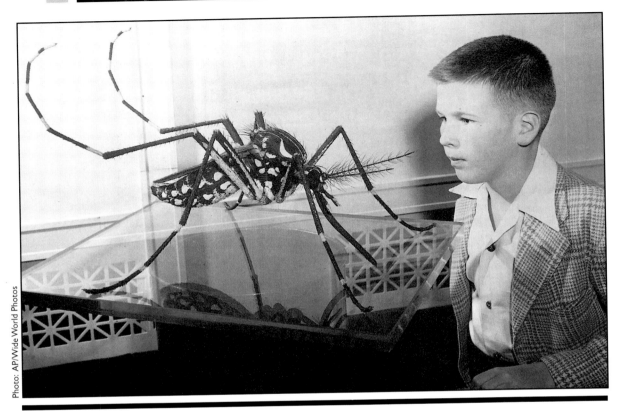

Photo: AP/Wide World Photos

Copyright ©1996 by Mark Dion and Alexis Rockman
ISBN: 0-9651042-2-2

Concrete jungle / edited by Alexis Rockman and Mark Dion.
     p.   cm.
   Includes bibliographical references.
   ISBN 0-9651042-2-2 (pbk.)
   1. Environmentalism. 2. Environmental degradation. 3. Ecology.
  4. Nature--Effect of human beings on. I. Rockman, Alexis, 1962-
. II. Dion, Mark.
  GE195.C66   1966
  304.2'09173'2--dc21   96-45940
                                  CIP

BOOKSTORE DISTRIBUTION
   U.S.: Consortium, 1045 Westgate Drive, Saint Paul, MN 55114-1065, orders 800-283-3572,
     tel. 612-221-9035, fax 612-221-0124;
   UK & EUROPE: Airlift Book Co., 8 The Arena, Mollison Avenue, Enfield Middlesex, England EN3-7NJ
     tel. 181-804-0400, fax 181-804-0044;
   AUSTRALIA & NEW ZEALAND: Peribo Pty Ltd, 58 Beaumont Road, Mount Kuring-gai, NSW 2080, Australia,
     tel. 61-2-457-0011, fax 61-2-457-0022.
For a catalog, send SASE to: JUNO BOOKS, 180 Varick Street, 10th Floor, New York, NY 10014;
tel. 212-807-7300, fax 212-807-7355, toll free 800-758-5238.

Typesetting by Quadright, NYC
Printed in Germany

10 9 8 7 6 5 4 3 2 1

Cover art: *Concrete Jungle III*, Alexis Rockman (1991)
Back cover art: *Concrete Jungle Diorama II*, Bob Braine, Mark Dion, Alexis Rockman (1995)
First page photo: Negative #243009, Courtesy Department of Library Services, American Museum of Natural History
Back page photo: "Rats in Moscow," AP/Wide World Photos

Acknowledgements

We would like to thank the staff at Juno Books, especially Shireen R.K. Patell and Sarah E. Carnevale, for making the experience of editing this book a pleasure and a labor of love as opposed to a task. We would also like to thank the following people and institutions for their invaluable support: Jill Rowe, Katherine Dunn, Gary Leib, Anthony Bregman of Good Machine, J. Morgan Puett, Mike Chiodo of the Rat and Mice Club, Lou Sorkin of the American Museum of Natural History, Diane Shapiro of the Photographic Library, New York Zoological Society/Wildlife Conservation Society, the courteous and efficient staff at the American Museum of Natural History Picture Collection and the Civitella Ranieri Center. Thanks to the staff at Jay Gorney Modern Art, especially Beth Harbottle, and American Fine Art Co. Extra thanks to Bob Braine and Jocko Weyland for their resourcefulness in obtaining images.

For reasons of space, deadline, continuity and redundancy, a number of contributors could not be included. However, the ideas expressed in these pieces were crucial to the development of this book: Tom Zummer, Peter Ward, Miwon Kwon, Cathy Clarke, Claire Pentecost, Paul Towell, Tim Collins and Reiko Goto, Paul Schneider, Richard Smith, Stephen Lack, Marina McDougall, Tom Kazo, Ph.D., and Donna McVicker Cannon of the Wildlife Research Team, Florida.

We would also like to thank Klaus Ottmann for providing the opportunity for an early version of this project at Wesleyan University.

Special thanks to Jon Reiss. And, of course, special thanks to Andrea Juno for her keen insight and judgment every step of the way.

Editors-at-large:	Mark Dion
	Alexis Rockman
Contributing Editors:	Michael Crewdson
	Margaret Mittelbach
Photo Editor:	Bob Braine
Associate Photo Editor:	Jocko Weyland

JUNO BOOKS STAFF

Editor-in-Chief:	Andrea Juno
Managing Editor:	Shireen R.K. Patell
Designer/Production Manager:	Sarah E. Carnevale
Proofreader/Copy Editor:	Rebecca Godfrey
Front Cover Designer:	Susan B.A. Somers-Willett

Contents

Contents

Introduction

by editors Mark Dion and Alexis Rockman

In fact, the whole idea of nature as something separate from human experience is a lie. Humans and nature construct one another. Ignoring that fact obscures the one way out of the current environmental crisis—a living within and alongside of nature without dominating it.

—Alexander Wilson, *The Culture of Nature*

Welcome to *Concrete Jungle.*

As the second millennium approaches and increasing numbers of humans are waking up to the seriousness of the environmental devastation that has been wrought in the name of progress and prosperity, this volume brings together a diverse array of perspectives from artists, writers and scientists, who examine the question of "Nature" at the end of the 20th century. What, in particular, can "Nature" mean for those who live in urban environments?

If the word *Nature* appears in quotation marks in the above paragraph, it is because by this time, it is generally agreed upon that at least some part of Nature is culturally or socially constructed. The idea of the social construction of Nature does not mean to obliterate the obvious fact that there is a reality upon which we can all agree. However, the shifting meaning of Nature throughout history and the various values associated with and ascribed to it, point to the different social and political aims to which its concept has been submitted. Nature has always been both a source for the imagination and a projection of our imagination. In the Middle Ages, it symbolized religion; in the Renaissance, science and in the Baroque, politics. In the modern era, Nature has designated a site of contestation for different groups with various, sometimes conflicting, political aims.

Concrete Jungle functions as a kind of resource book, a select survey of some of the deeply conflicting ideas about what "Nature" means at a particular moment for particular groups of people. We regard natural areas as integral parts of the health of the planet as well as important markers of identity for the people who live in them, around them or

Photo: Kranefuss/Voller Ernst, Ostereier

deeply love and identify with them. It might seem that a society such as ours can afford the luxury of wilderness. However, when those who concern themselves with nature focus on unspoiled wilderness alone, they tend to leave out the concerns of a large number of people, who, like ourselves, live in urban areas. What does Nature mean to us? Where do we find it? Furthermore, the impulse to environmental protection may sometimes be at odds with social justice. Where do we put the waste, the dumps, the incinerators? Who will have access to unspoiled wilderness, and how?

The status of animals is a fundamental part of our investigation, for while fewer and fewer people have direct contact with animals, other than pets, they remain an important part of our everyday lives. While flesh and blood experience with the animal world is diminishing, we are inundated with surrogates broadcast over every imaginable media, configured in every shape, and made out of every imaginable material from blue plastic to polyester fur to gold. What child of the West does not grow up with a crib and toy chest lined with anthropomorphic beasts? Animals do not speak back to us, either from the other side of the television screen, or from behind the bars of the zoo or through the button eyes of the teddy bear. Rather, they are often ciphers bearing our own anxieties, fantasies, and assumptions about ourselves and the natural world. It is extremely difficult to chart precisely how this symbolic use of animals impacts in very real ways the ecology of the Alaskan tundra or the river front alley. We are interested in charting some of the consequences of an anthropomorphic relation with Nature that fails to take into account what a complex, dynamic cosmos an ecosystem can be. And we humans do not stand outside of Nature; we too are animals, a part of the very thing that we have tried to control, whether to exploit it, or now, to protect it. However, it may be that anthropomorphization is ineluctable, a permanent feature of our relation to Nature and the language we use to describe it. As Andrew Ross has written in *The Chicago Gangster Theory of Life*: "...ideas that draw upon the authority of Nature nearly always have their origin in ideas about society." Just as humanity does not stand outside of Nature, our conception of Nature cannot be said to stand outside of culture or society.

Our anthropomorphic common taxonomy of animals has been based largely on utility. Thinking about animals has been broadly divided into categories such as destructive/pests, useful/domestic, or useless/wild. Each of these positions have become unstable. The latter category is clearly one in transition as eco-tourism, the sustainable product market and wildlife conservation organizations prove that "the wild" is indeed not only marketable, but extremely profitable. In this context, wilderness is a luxury and, for many nations, eco-tourism is sometimes the only viable economic model other then clearcutting, mining and monoculture agriculture. However, it is rarely without some socially destructive price. In some countries (Kenya, for example) eco-tourism has become the single largest industry in the nation.

For both practical as well as conceptual reasons, pests—what biologists call r-selected species, such as the cockroach, rat and pigeon—are that dangerous class of animals, who are rarely appreciated with the sentimental eye we reserve for pets. Seen as emblems of decay and contamination, as potentially chaotic elements, these animals are symptomatic of our inability to control all the variables in nature. It is difficult to deny the power of their adaptability. These persistent organisms, to our great anxiety, remind us of our part in the biological contract: they remind us that we, like all animals, are part of a complex web of relations that is not always in our favor. In the same way that advanced urban society refuses to acknowledge shit, distances itself from food production, and denies the process of aging, these animals remind us that we too are animals, and therefore, mortal. The cockroach and rat can shake the foundations of civilization to the core and us to the marrow. Against the general impetus to protect and preserve Nature, pests are seen as that which must be destroyed, lest they destroy us.

In this way, the notion of the pest also shows to what extent we humans, even in the preservationist, conservationist mode, determine what is and is not a healthy or viable part of Nature. Even our best attempts to preserve or represent Nature for those who might not otherwise have access to our zoos and museums bear the mark of a particular culture. A recent trip to the museum of natural history in Salzburg, Austria revealed that the room titillatingly labeled "mutations and freaks" was an exhibition of mounted specimens of cross-bred domesticated animals. The museum's concept of deviation was the transgression of the pure breed. What

Photo: AP/Wide World Photos

Guarded Possum: Policeman has unusual assignment of guarding an opossum for 45 minutes after it nipped the heels of a passerby.

does that reveal about Austrian culture? This was a provocative experience, since we in the U.S. find ourselves in a similar situation, which is the result of a long colonial process in which Nature is continually reordered. In terms of a conservation model, we are always in the process of deciding which species is to be preserved and which is expendable. What does that selection process indicate about us?

In this *Concrete Jungle*, the limited ability of humans to control Nature and circumscribe the effects of our interventions is a starting point, not a dead-end. ∎

chapter 1

Wild in the City

Concrete Jungle Diorama I, Bob Braine, Mark Dion, Alexis Rockman (1993)

A Warning

As the 20th century draws to a close, humanity faces the daunting prospect of supporting its population without inducing catastrophic and irreversible destruction on Earth's life-support systems. Human and agricultural fertility are on a collision course: the stork is threatening to overtake the plow. By 1999, the human population will surge past 6 billion in number and will still be skyrocketing. United Nations demographers project continuing expansion for another century or so to nearly 12 billion.

The struggle merely to support today's population at today's standards of living is causing environmental destruction on a scale and at a pace unprecedented in human history. Accelerating degradation and deforestation of land, depletion of groundwater, toxic pollution, biodiversity loss, and massive atmospheric disruption are wrecking the planet's machinery for producing the basic material ingredients of human well-being.

Alarm in the international scientific community regarding the seriousness of this dilemma is widespread and mounting. Yet the very existence of the dilemma is largely unappreciated by the general public and the politically oriented and ecologically important pundits of the TV/radio talk-show circuit. A student can get all the way through a major university and still not be aware of its existence. Presidents and prime ministers overlook it. Vatican policies and the exhortations of fundamentalists of various religions make it worse.

This set of circumstances prompted over 600 of the world's most distinguished scientists, including a majority of the living Nobel laureates in the sciences, to issue the "World Scientists' Warning to Humanity" in 1993. It reads, in part:

> The earth is finite. Its ability to provide for growing numbers of people is finite. And we are fast approaching many of the earth's limits. Current economic practices which damage the environment, in both developed and underdeveloped nations, cannot be continued without the risk that vital global systems will be damaged beyond repair....
>
> Pressures resulting from unrestrained population growth put demands on the natural world that can overwhelm any efforts to achieve a sustainable future. If we are to halt the destruction of our environment, we must accept limits to that growth....
>
> No more than one or a few decades remain before the chance to avert the threats we now confront will be lost and the prospects for humanity immeasurably diminished....A great change in our stewardship of the earth and the life on it is

by
Paul R. Ehrlich,
Anne H. Ehrlich
and
Gretchen C. Daily

Biodiversity resources are being lost at an accelerating rate that may cause the disappearance by 2025 of one quarter of all the species now existing on Earth.

World Population Projections, 1990-2100 (billions)

Impact of varying fertility assumptions on population growth

YEAR	LOW 1.8 children per woman by 2025; 1.7 by 2100	MEDIUM 2.3 children per woman by 2025; 2.1 by 2100	HIGH 2.8 children per woman by 2025; 2.5 by 2100	INSTANT REPLACEMENT-LEVEL FERTILITY Were fertility to have dropped in 1990 to 2.1 children per woman	CONSTANT FERTILITY Fertility stays at 1990 level of 4.3 children per woman until 2025
1990	5.3	5.3	5.3	5.3	5.3
2000	6.1	6.3	6.4	5.8	6.5
2025	7.6	8.5	9.4	7.1	11.0
2050	7.8	10.0	12.5	7.7	21.2
2075	7.1	10.8	15.7	7.9	46.3
2100	6.0	11.2	19.2	8.1	109.4

Source: *Long Range World Populations: Two Centuries of Population Growth, 1959-2150* (United Nations, NY, 1992)

While overpopulation in poor nations tends to keep them poverty-stricken, overpopulation in rich nations tends to undermine the life-support capacity of the entire planet.

required, if vast human misery is to be avoided and our global home on the planet is not to be irretrievably mutilated. The developed nations are the largest polluters in the world today. They must greatly reduce their overconsumption, if we are to reduce pressures on resources and the global environment. The developed nations have the obligation to provide aid to the developing nations, because only the developed nations have the financial resources and technical skills for these tasks.

Acting on this recognition is not altruism, but enlightened self-interest: whether industrialized or not, we all have but one lifeboat.

Biotic diversity is the most irreplaceable component of our resource capital, and the least understood and appreciated. Plants, animals, and microorganisms are organized, along with the physical elements of the environment with which they interact, in ecosystems. These organisms thus help to provide indispensable, free ecosystem services, which support civilization. Many of these services are essential to agriculture, including:

■ Maintenance of the gaseous composition of the atmosphere
■ Moderation of climate

- Control of the hydrologic cycle (which supplies fresh water)
- Detoxification and disposal of wastes
- Cycling of nutrients and replenishment of soil
- Control of the great majority of pests and diseases that could attack crops
- Pollination of crops and wild plants
- Maintenance of a vast "genetic library" containing many millions of kinds of organisms, from which humanity has "withdrawn" all manner of benefits, including all the crop and livestock species on which agricultural systems were built. And if preserved, the genetic library potentially could provide enormous benefits in the future.

Yet biodiversity resources are being lost at an accelerating rate that may cause the disappearance by 2025 of one quarter of all the species now existing on Earth. Every species that disappears is a marvel gone forever—often without humanity ever knowing what potential direct economic value it might have possessed, much less its role in providing ecosystem services. Every genetically distinct population that is exterminated reduces precious living capital and potentially weakens nature's ability to support humanity. Even if the evolutionary process that creates diversity continued at rates comparable to those in the geologic past, it would take tens of millions of years for today's level of diversity, once seriously depleted, to be restored.

We see no choice but for Americans who recognize the predicament to become heavily involved in politics, to take voting very seriously, and to pay attention to fundamental issues rather than the crime, petty politics, accidents, and nonsense that pass for news in most of the media. Rising carbon dioxide in the atmosphere is infinitely more important than rising prices on the stock market. The current decline of biodiversity is a truly cosmic issue, an "event" that will mark the planet for millions of years after the breakup of the former Soviet Union is totally forgotten. The changing evolutionary and ecological relationships between *Homo sapiens* and the viruses, bacteria, and fungi that feed upon it will almost certainly affect many more human lives than the changing relationships between Israel and the PLO or between Catholics and Protestants in Northern Ireland. Rapid population growth, which threatens the future of everyone in our already overpopulated nation, should be much bigger news than which politician is trying to get elected by promising tax cuts or a war on drugs. ■

No more than one or a few decades remain before the chance to avert the threats we now confront will be lost and the prospects for humanity immeasurably diminished. Biotic diversity is the most irreplaceable component of our resource capital.

This piece was excerpted from their 1995 book The Stork and the Plow, *a Grosset/Putnam Book published by G.P. Putnam's Sons. Paul and Anne were also the authors of* The Population Bomb.

Interview with Andrew Ross

interview
by
Mark
Dion

Andrew Ross is professor and Director of the Graduate Program in American Studies at New York University. He is the co-editor of the journal Social Text *and author of a number of books, most recently* The Chicago Gangster Theory of Life: Nature's Debt to Society *published in 1994.*

MARK DION: *At the moment, the topic of the future of the natural world is broached with extreme trepidation. When did dread replace our notion of a new and hopeful era?*

ANDREW ROSS: I can tell you exactly when. Tet, 1968, when the U.S. commanding officer in charge of recapturing the Vietnamese provincial capital of Ben Tre told reporters: "We had to destroy the town to save it." This concept sweetly captured the military mentality of the Pax Americana, a mentality responsible for enforcing a violent peace upon "subdominant" species all over the world. I think this phrase also illustrated the finally illogical endpoint of a liberal Enlightenment tradition, if you like, of rationalizing destructive behavior as progressive in some way. You just couldn't endow this kind of behavior with meaning any longer, except as some absurd tough guy psychosis that was a self-parody. What Vietnam brought home to an incredibly insular domestic culture was what most of the rest of the world knew anyway from the history of colonialism.

The Vietnam War, of course, was the last of the old-style colonial campaigns that had reshaped so much of the earth's surface. Its apocalyptic nature, à la Coppola, was a real cultural shock, certainly for the boomers, but also for the generation that fought in the Second World War. By the time of the Gulf War, the stage was then set for all of those grand apocalyptic visions of the world's end that had become Hollywood disaster movie clichés, and could now be acted out for real. No wonder Werner Herzog had one of his morbid orgasms in touring the burning oil lakes with his camera. The point of view he chose was that of a visiting alien species, trying to make sense of these catastrophic scenes. This is a favored perspective of some of the deep Greens, implying that our problems are caused by an irrational species—humankind—at war with its environment. It's irresponsible in my view. I subscribe more to social ecology's view that the roots of the domination of nature lie in the social domination of some groups over others. In other words, some hands are really dirtier than others.

MD: The landscape of the future as seen through the last 20 years of Hollywood has been a dystopia based on ecological catastrophe: Planet of the Apes, Soylent Green, Silent Running, Mad Max, Blade Runner, Waterworld. *Are these films simply analogous to the anxiety expressed in the 1950s atomic monster films or is something else occurring?*

> **"We had to destroy the town to save it." This concept sweetly captured a mentality responsible for enforcing a violent peace upon "subdominant" species all over the world. It rationalized destructive behavior as progressive in some way.**

Photo: Bob Braine

Concrete tyrannosaur menaces passing Winnebago.

AR: Now you are talking. Forget Herzog. This is the real political unconscious speaking—at least for the American Empire. The first thing to be said is that dystopias are entertaining; utopias are not. So, from decade to decade, there will be attempts to provide the most appropriate dystopian vehicle for the overriding concerns of the day. Like the 1950s monster genres, the "alien" genre of the 1980s was a multipurpose vehicle for carrying the anxieties generated by Reagan's out-of-control Cold War fantasies. The eco-dystopian films you mentioned have been consistently appealing since the early 1970s, but the apocalyptic strain seems to have been on the decline for some time now. Consequently, *Waterworld* was a bit of a joke, really, at the expense of the genre's conventions at least. By contrast, the important films of the mid-1990s are about risk consciousness, like Todd Haynes' *Safe* which portrays the social and psychic cost of producing risk-free environments, or its Rabelaisian opposite, Danny Boyle's *Trainspotting*, where risk-free behavior is revealed as a complete and utter luxury for pleasure-seeking youth without much of a future. As for Hollywood, there is the 1990s "virus" genre, which similarly poses the question of risk analysis—how much are you willing to tolerate in the way of losses to save how much? Risk management is very much the institutional face of environmentalism these days—in government policy-making, at the development agencies, and in the military.

MD: I hate to ask, but what about Independence Day? *Is it just a reversed colonial narrative (cowboys and Indians, but this time the Indians are us)? What about the eco-threat in the film?*

AR: Well, it is probably as much a Gulf War movie as anything else. Americans were slightly embarrassed by their technological superiority in the Gulf. The popular wisdom is that the war was won too easily because the Iraqi soldiers didn't put up much of a fight. *Independence Day,* and here I am following Steve Fagin's unimpeachable analysis, presents a version of what Americans would have done if they had been the Iraqi underdogs in the Gulf. They would have used native gusto and basic know-how to outwit the forces that had destroyed their cities with sheer airpower and were intent on sucking their resources out of the earth.

It was quite a treat that the film was immediately followed by the discovery of the Mars bacteria, however. Who would have thought that we could identify ourselves so easily with such elementary life forms— we're not alone!—when we spend so much of our earthly lives demarcating ourselves from other mammals?

MD: The post-1960s progressive Left has been deeply criticized for not producing a motivating blueprint for social change or even a glimmer of utopian sentiment. Economic and environmental organizations tend to foretell doom and gloom scenarios rather than projecting ways to avoid them. The only major exception to the entropic future forecast seems to come from two groups: the New Age culture and information technology freebooters. What do they see that so many of us seem to be missing?

AR: It's not so much what they see that's worth learning from, since each of these cultures recycle familiar utopian discourses—religious and technological, respectively—that have a venerable history in North American culture. What's more important is the personal libertarian energies that they are designed to harness. The last time the Left really had a good fix on these energies was in the early 1970s, before Madison Avenue bought the whole scene out, or, to a much lesser extent, on the Internet and early Web, before the big boys moved in on the virtual real estate. In this respect, environmentalism is still struggling with its puritan soul, ascetically self-denying to the

Located just around the corner from the American Museum of Natural History, this shop provides nostalgic curiosities for the morbid consumer.

Photo: Mark Dion

core. People in this culture—and I don't mean simply consumer culture with its steady promise of increased gratification—don't respond well to the politics of self-denial. They want social fulfillment, and Green politics has to address this liberatory side of things more.

MD: In your recent writing, you discuss a certain suspicion of pleasure and excess found within the Green movement [from the asceticism of Thoreau, to Jimmy Carter's sweater, to the limit-to-growth arguments of today]. Yet, sometimes when I read your characterizations of environmentalists, I don't recognize who you are speaking about. If there is one thing that unites the various individuals I know involved in eco-activism, it is the intense pleasure they derive from nature. Regardless of whether they are bird watchers, conservation biologists, city parks planners, urban gardeners, social ecologists or vacant lot naturalists, many different people have become politicized through a passionate pleasure derived from their interaction with the natural world. None of these folks are essentialists or purists in their understanding of what gets to stand for Nature. Perhaps, because you are admittedly not a nature-lover, you sometimes underplay the political potential generated by the pleasure that motivates these individuals?

AR: Yes and no. My arguments are in no way directed at or against the pleasure people take in natural environments, but rather at the advocacy of sacrifice and collective self-denial urged by many environmentalist polemics in the movement. Many of these polemics do appeal to guilt and self-reform in the Puritan mold, and have a limited, local meaning (i.e. the Northern tier of countries). When I suggest that Green politics has to offer more in the way of social fulfillment than coercive self-limitation, I am drawing attention to the uses that have been made, historically, of manufactured scarcity to impose austerity on vulnerable populations.

The rage for limitation often has dangerous social consequences, and in many cases is underscored by neo-Malthusian currents that run strong in certain quarters of the Green movement. By now, you would think that most people would be aware of the eugenic connotations of the arguments about overpopulation, or that the concept of "wilderness preservation" only makes sense in Northern countries where purification has often depended upon a powerful link between social Darwinism and ideas about the natural order. The American practice of evacuating indigenous peoples in order to create wilderness is now being exported to those parts of the non-Western world where eco-tourism is beginning to flourish.

On the other hand, the pleasure people take in nature is far from

In the mid–19th century, the mania for natural history collections brought nature into the domestic setting. Stores like Evolution in New York's SoHo are a throwback to this era.

Photo: Mark Dion

For an increasingly urban population, **Nature** is encountered in the marketplace.

Photo: Mark Dion

innocent, and not unrelated to some of these concerns. This is why it's a little dodgy to build a politics solely upon pleasure, although a politics without pleasure is not worth having. When I say that I am not a nature-lover, I mean that I don't have any of the bona fide credentials conventionally required of environmentalist writers. I get my quota of countryside trips, but I don't hike on trails regularly. I don't live in the Adirondacks, like nature writer Bill McKibben (although if everyone followed his example there wouldn't be an Adirondacks), and my leisure time is not driven by the pursuit of nature. I say that upfront to preempt being called on it, although saying it always partially undercuts any authority one might claim to speak about environmental matters. Quite frankly, I am just as much interested in urban ecology, and in the kinds of questions relating to environmental justice that are not ordinarily associated with trees, rivers, and mountains.

MD: You and I use a kind of shorthand. When we say "the Greens," we are talking about a social movement roughly called environmentalism. It has its own complex history and ideology, both left and right, which includes aspects of ecology (the science of the study of living organism's relation to their non-living environment) and conservation (the notion that the natural world must be wisely managed in order to continue to exist). But maybe we don't mean exactly the same thing. For example, I was just in Europe and had a difficult time explaining how the animal rights movement, which supports individual animal welfare, differs from conservation biology's stress on biodiversity, or the rights of animal species. Who are the Greens to you, and how is it possible to lump them all together?

AR: I'm not sure that there's significantly more disagreement, or lack of common ground, among environmentally-minded people than in other social movements, but it often feels that way. Nature, after all, is the consummate people-pleaser—it is serviceable to anyone who wants to speak in its name (viz. the Wise Use movement, which borrowed the moniker of early century Conservationists in order to camouflage their backlash campaigns with Green rhetoric). Nature can always be wheeled in to ventriloquize support for a social claim about environmental matters. It's more difficult to do that within social movements of disenfranchised peoples. They have their own voices, after all, which Nature lacks. This is the fundamental problem of Green politics. Nature cannot speak for itself, but everyone else is all too willing to do the job. Now this perception is often caricatured and sleazily dismissed as a belief that the natural world is entirely socially constructed and doesn't really exist. In fact, it's a very important point to acknowledge, and goes a long way to explaining the difficulties you allude to in your question.

MD: One of the most invaluable aspects of your writing is a relentless scrutiny of the more sinister flaws in the history of America's environmental movement. You have examined its relation to eugenics, its pervasive social Darwinism, its obsession with self-denial and scarcity and its anti-urbanism and machismo. A number of ecological organizations and environmental studies programs maintain a deeply romantic relationship to this grimly checkered past. Of course, there are other models. After all, for every gun-toting, neo-colonial, patriarchal, conservationist like Teddy Roosevelt, there is a socially insightful ecologist, compelled to translate science into environmental activism, like Rachel Carson. But, why is serious eco-criticism such a late bloomer?

AR: There has always been a body of criticism devoted to nature writing, landscape art and wilderness appreciation. By "serious," I assume that you mean a critical approach that does not take Nature for granted, but interrogates its representation. Well, most of the reasons have to do with the distance between environmentalism and other social movements related to race, gender and sexuality. First, environmentalism has been pursued under the aegis of scientific authority, and so there has been a tradition of deference to natural, as opposed to social or cultural, criteria in building a critical body of ethics. It has taken a while for cultural critics to catch up, and there's still a long way to go. Second, the other social movements I mentioned have developed schools of cultural criticism that are largely based upon "liberating" unheard voices in literature or history or art. Movements in critical writing have been the point of entry for identity politics on the part of women, queer, post-colonial and minority thinkers. This has been accompanied by a certain degree of empowerment and representation in public life. As I said before, Green politics does not necessarily carry this liberatory air. By this criterion, of course, the predominantly white, middle-class stewardship of the ecology movement does not make it a great candidate for the empowerment of marginalized persons or communities, at least not in the pastoral mode of its perceived stereotype. Another major difference is that cultural critics do not respond well to narratives of self-restraint. More often they favor a hermeneutic that uncovers that which is hidden. Liberating the voice of the planet doesn't count in the same way. More attention to urban ecology and environmental justice will change this view.

MD: Some have characterized your critique of the Greens as too harsh.

"If Mother Earth shops anywhere, it's here [SoHo, New York City]. But she better have good credit —nontoxic things have other ways of burning a hole in your pocket."
—Andrew Ross, *The Chicago Gangster Theory of Life*

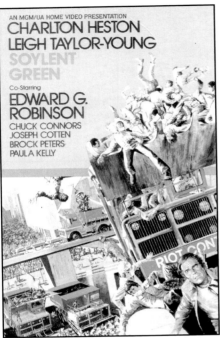

Soylent Green by director Richard Fleischer (1973).

Clearly you would not waste so much energy on the environmental movement if you didn't think it had some powerful potential.

AR: My criticisms are strategic rather than constitutional, and they emerge out of the tensions within the ecology movement that are well-known: basically, the antagonism between the social justice and wilderness wings of the movement. If my criticisms are a little zealous at times, it's because I do think that ecological consciousness is one of the most important bulwarks against the ravages of capitalism, at all levels—economic, political, cultural. And the value of Green politics is that there is little that cannot and should not be subsumed under its banner. To limit the definition of ecological concerns to one sector of our political life is to balkanize our ability to respond in a concerted fashion, or to think in terms of coalitions. Look at "quality of life" issues in the cities. Where do you draw the line between issues that relate to toxic dumping, or the location of incinerators, and those that relate to the uneven distribution of resources like education, housing, parks, transportation, and clinics? All of these factors affect our environment, not just the former.

MD: When we spoke about utopias you mentioned Madison Avenue's buy out of the progressive culture of the 1970s. Since the reappearance of popular environmentalism in the late 80s, we have seen the same spectacle. Corporations from the Body Shop to Georgia Pacific to the various oil conglomerates "Greenwash" or pay lipservice to ecological sensitivity. It is also outrageous to have to witness the parties competing to out-Greenwash each other. Don't you find it absurd and frustrating to watch Washington buying out the Greens today?

AR: There is no question that this is a central story in the politics of our times. By inviting representatives of the big ten environmentalist groups into the corridors of power, Clinton and Gore gained more access to the movement than the movement gained access to real power. The result was that the mainstream groups chose to stay mute for two years while the Democrats retreated on almost every legislative front. It was only when the public interest was roused over the Gingrich Congress's fierce assault against the whole edifice of environmental law that the retreat was halted. It was widely perceived, rightly or wrongly, that public commitment to health, safety and environmental preservation provided the impetus to draw the line and rebuff the Contract with America. Environmentalism is a very strong element of the property-owning middle-class anxiety about quality of life, and it has now penetrated the non-urban areas that are the Republican electoral base. Hence the sick spectacle of the parties vying to be the Greenest guys on the block, at least in an election year. My own assumption is that the Contract with America was resisted for all sorts of other reasons, economic for the most part. In addition, it's necessary to realize the switching role of someone like Gore, who played Jolly Green Giant before 1992. Since then he has functioned primarily as the pointman for information and telecommunications industries within the Administration, guaranteeing the overhaul of the state in the transition of sectors of the economy towards the new media industries. The biggest conundrum to me, however, has been the Greening of the military, or if you like, the militarization of the Greens. The Pentagon's investment in "environmental security" which I have written a little about ("A Few Good Species"), is one of the most extraordinary stories of these times.

MD: Do you conclude that the armed forces can spend the next 50 years cleaning up the mess they have made over the last 50, in which they have been the nations largest single polluter?

AR: They will need a good bit longer than 50 years, especially if they are going to tackle the decontamination of nuclear weapons complexes like Hanford, Rocky Flats, and Savannah River. On the one hand, we might be happy to see our military tax dollars being put to good use for once. On the other hand, we're likely to see these allocations being used to build environmental considerations into new weapons systems on a cradle-to-grave (production to disassembly) basis. Is it too much of a contradiction in terms to see the same defense budget fund hard-energy weapons production and environmental programs? I believe there is something wrong with that scenario. The larger picture, however, is one in which environmental security provides a doctrinal framework for the Pentagon's new global mission after the Cold War. For the first half of the 1990s, the concept of "environmental security" (introduced at the 42nd session of the UN General Assembly in 1987) was touted as one of the most likely successors to the "Communist threat" as an organizing principle of military-industrial policy. With the evaporation of Communism, all the talk was of threats without enemies. Increasingly, security overviews and wargame scenarios focus on the new tensions and conflicts caused by environmental threats: shortages of natural resources, water, and oil; cross-border pollution, including radioactivity and acid rain; the environmental underbelly of North-South trade—resource degradation; and population control in the new migrant economy generated by

NATURE FOR SALE: Stores such as this one evoke nature on one hand while devastating local ecosystems on the other.

Photo: Mark Dion

Photo: AP/Wide World Photos

THE GREENING OF THE MILITARY: Italian army engineers use flamethrowers to eradicate poisonous snakes in suburban Florence (1965).

economic restructuring. Ecology always took for itself a planetary perspective. Now the masters of the New World Order are learning how to use it.

MD: What you are describing is important: the amalgamation of the military, research science, industry and corporate investment. I'm always astounded to hear people pretend that "hard science's" white tower of pure research stands tall. We all know it is a ruin, since corporate university sponsors, like DuPont and United Technologies call the shots. The paper tiger which covers that ruin is the powerful generator of a mythology called "scientific journalism" where New York Times *science pages resemble the covers of 1960s* Popular Mechanics *magazines.*

AR: Yes, they do. The same romantic quest narratives are employed. The difference is that the press plays an increasingly important role in the funding game. As the state cuts science funding, and corporate-academic contracts are normalized, scientists are increasingly likely to go directly to the press with the results of their research, often circumventing the apparatus of peer reception, and generating publicity in the bargain. The reason why so many critics of science talk of technoscience is that it is no longer possible to distinguish between science—as the enlightened production of public knowledge—and technology—as the commercial application of that knowledge. Where secrecy and competition thrive, and where the patent system is all-powerful, one cannot preserve that distinction in a meaningful way. And as far as its division of labor goes, science has been a heavily proletarianized activity for over a hundred years. Most scientists don't do publishable research; they perform technical tasks to meet commercial needs.

MD: What is the meaning of the title of your recent book: The Chicago Gangster Theory of Life? *Is it just a warmed-over and Americanized version of social Darwinism?*

AR: Yes, although it's fair to say that social Darwinism was pretty Americanized to begin with, if you consider the grand reception the robber barons gave to Herbert Spencer and his ideas. At any rate, the basic thesis of the Chicago Gangster Theory—to which I am inveterately opposed—is that natural phenomena often are invoked to support social agendas; evolutionary biology is not only asserted as an explanatory guide to social behavior, but also as an authority for social action. The term comes from an analogy Richard Dawkins draws in his controversial book *The Selfish Gene,* where he compares survivor genes to successful Chicago gangsters. The fundamental move behind such sociobiological assertions is to take descriptions of social behavior and find some derivation for them in the natural world, such as selfish genes. They then re-apply this description to the social world as if it had always existed in nature and carried the authority of nature as a result. You can see the theory in action in any piece of science journalism which informs us that a gene has been found for arrogance, shyness, adventurousness, you name it. Which only affirms that ideas about nature always originate in ideas about society. Ultimately, the Chicago Gangster Theory imagines biological limits to our social potential. The alternative is to emphasize that our large evolved brains make us capable of building societies that do not have to be ruled by natural necessity. That is the response offered by folks like Stephen Jay Gould, which seem to me to be remarkably sane.

The new sociogenetic paradigm that we are heading into is a profound makeover of the thinking about nature and culture which has prevailed for much of this century—the period from the New Deal onwards which banished social Darwinism and the eugenics science with which it was associated. Many commentators see the new biologism as a revival or continuation of eugenics by other means, where genetics predisposition will be the basis of social discrimination and hierarchies. The air is thick with talk about genetic underclass and genetic redlining and the like. It takes a scandal like *The Bell Curve* to awaken people to the fact that this kind of stuff is much closer to policymaker's hearts and minds than we are prepared to believe. ∎

The predominantly white, middle-class stewardship of the ecology movement does not make it a great candidate for the empowerment of marginalized persons or communities.

Standard Exterminating

interview by
Alexis
Rockman

Gil Bloom is vice-president of Standard Exterminating in Brooklyn, NY and teaches entomology at Queensboro Community College.

ALEXIS ROCKMAN: How long have you been working as an exterminator?

GIL BLOOM: I'm the third generation of my family's business, Standard Exterminating, which was established in 1929. I'm the technical director and vice-president, and I also teach pest control and entomology at Queensboro Community College. I have a lot of experience. I've been dealing with pests and people for over 20 years. It's a great job, though I didn't intend to head out in this direction.

AR: You didn't want to continue the family legacy?

GB: In high school, I really shied away from it. I wanted to be a lawyer. Until I realized, I'd just be dealing with pests anyway. Another pivotal moment for me occurred when New York State started requiring certification. I got really turned on. I saw there was real science behind pest control, both chemistry and entomology. It's not just spraying.

AR: No, absolutely not. How did you get involved with the Staten Island ferry?

GB: I was attending a pest control conference in Atlantic City when I heard news reports about roaches infesting the Staten Island Ferry. I

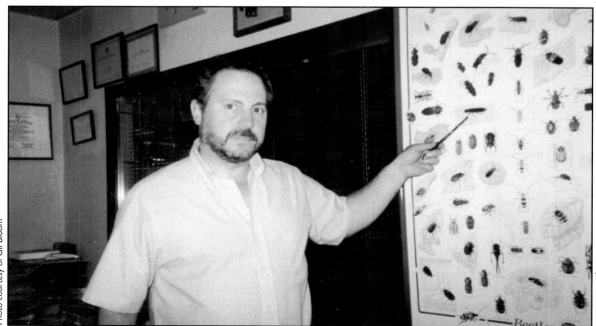

Gil Bloom, president of Standard Exterminating, Brooklyn, NY.

thought it would be a really good idea—

AR: Great photo op.

GB: Actually, photos were a bit of a problem because the DOT [Department of Transportation] did not want to advertise its problem. I contacted the city, the Giuliani administration, and said, "We're a New York-based company, we'd like to lend a hand, and take care of the roaches on this particular severely infested ferry boat." The boat was named the *Barberi*.

AR: How many cockroaches were on that vessel at its most infested moment?

GB: Easily over 2,000-3,000 German cockroaches on the boat.

AR: Would they be territorial, and not allow American cockroaches to exist in the same site?

GB: It's not so much territorial. There's an actual ecological niche that these roaches can exploit.

AR: What made the Staten Island Ferry so attractive?

GB: The problem was largely caused by people creating a tremendous environment with their food and garbage. Already, you have constant moisture and temperature on the boat. People just come along and supply the food. This completes the triangle of life roaches need: food, shelter and water.

AR: Did the roaches come from Manhattan or Staten Island?

GB: I wouldn't want to answer that, and actually, that was the most frequently asked question.

AR: Everyone wanted to point a finger across the water?

GB: Well, let's put it this way. The people commuting are living on one side or the other and going back and forth.

AR: Was there a dominant sex or was it a complete roach community?

GB: The majority were female, which was one of the reasons we had problems controlling them. A female-dominant species can reproduce so rapidly and repeatedly.

AR: What part of the boat were they living in?

GB: They were in the main structure near the food service, but they were also scattered throughout the seats. They had really gotten themselves entrenched under the seats. They were using the life preservers as nests, and they were nesting in garbage. We found everything from beer cans to condoms to hypodermic needles.

AR: Oh, man.

GB: You have to realize, this job was done in 1994, and we found flyers under the seats dating back to sales at Crazy Eddie's, which closed in the early 80s! People would stick food up in the grooves underneath the seats, exactly the cracks where the roaches would love to hide. A lot of the pest control was done with screwdrivers, just flicking that stuff out.

AR: It was really hands-on hard work.

The Menu of the Annual New York Entomological Society Dinner

AT THE BAR

Assorted Crudités with Peppery Delight Mealworm Dip

Oven Crunchy Mix with Mealworms, Wax Worms, and Crickets

BUTLERED HORS d'OEUVRES

Plain, Wax Worm and Mealworm Avocado California Rolls with Tamari Dipping Sauce

Wild Mushrooms in Mealworm Flour Pastry

Cricket and Vegetable Tempura

Mealworm Balls in Zesty Tomato Sauce

Mini Fontina Bruschetta
with Mealworm Ganoush

Wax Worm Fritters with
Plum Sauce

Roasted Australian
Kurrajong Grubs

Sautéed Thai Water Bugs

Thai Water Bug and
Mango Dip

BUFFET DINNER

Chicken Normandy with
Calvados Sauce

Rice Pilaf

Roast Beef with Gravy

Roesti Potatoes

Mediterranean Pasta

Mélange of Vegetable Ragu

Mesclun Salad with
Balsamic Vinegar

Assorted Cricket Breads
with Butter

GB: Right. We were altering the environment.

AR: Besides the baited traps, what other strategies did you use on that job?

GB: We went through the boat and pinpointed some things that needed to be changed. For example, for garbage cans they were using 55-gallon drums with plastic bags inside. That was bad enough, and then six inches above the garbage bags were fire extinguishers. Unfortunately, apparently in New York fire extinguishers grow legs.

In order to stop the theft, the fire extinguishers were encased in wooden boxes with a plexiglass covering.

AR: Why was that a problem?

GB: Roaches love wood because they can attach their fecal material to it. Wood picks up the odor of roaches, the aggregate pheromone which attracts even more roaches. They were nesting in these wood boxes which were placed right above the garbage cans! So our suggestion was, move the garbage cans!

AR: It was as simple as that?

GB: Break up the triangle of life, make it harder for them to have food, water and shelter.

AR: What was the response to your work?

GB: There was an amazing amount of attention. Everyone from the American to the Greek to the Japanese media came. They wanted to say, "See, America is roach-infested!" I do know from speaking with people at the DOT that our job remained successful for a period of over six months.

AR: Wow.

GB: So obviously, we approached the DOT with a proposal to service all the boats. But because there's a certain charge for our services, they weren't interested. I think it went back to a low-bid type scenario. Still, it was a great experience for us in terms of publicity. We also gained confidence in a new technology. In the baits, we were able to use a pesticide which was more ecologically sound. One of the materials used was boric acid.

AR: Isn't boric acid one of the oldest pesticides around?

GB: Yes. Unfortunately, myths have developed around it. People throw mounds of boric acid down in their apartments. I'm not sure whether they're making a display to re-enact the trench warfare of World War I—

AR: The war of attrition.

GB: Roaches won't die that way because they're not going to climb over these mounds. It has to be dusted down and applied in the right areas. The new pesticide we used on the ferry takes traditional boric acid a step further. The roaches ingest it, and then it kills them. So that's an exciting part. It also has virtually no odor. New York City has a lot of asthmatics who have to be careful since some aerosol delivery systems blow pesticides into the air. These passive baiting systems are really just what they need.

AR: This new pesticide is also species specific?

GB: Right. Its toxicity is not as great to non-target organisms, a cat, a dog, or a person.

AR: Great. Well, I think that about covers it, Gil.

GB: If anybody's interested in going into pest control, it's really an exciting job. I've been to every place under the sun, from the World Trade Center to the Federal Reserve Bank to air traffic control towers.

AR: Air traffic control towers?

GB: I went to a large metropolitan airport.

AR: I actually have a significant fear of flying right now and that would just add to my hysterical fear.

GB: It would. They had a problem with fruit flies flying across the radar screens. The controllers ate at their work stations, and kept the garbage nearby. Fruit flies would breed in the decaying matter in the garbage, and dart all around this dark room. They're somewhat attracted to light, so they'd head over to the only source of light: the radar screen.

AR: Were the fruit flies being confused with the actual planes?

GB: I wouldn't say that, but it was annoying for the air-traffic controllers. You're seeing a fly dart across a screen when you're trying to watch for other flying objects. Actually, we were able to solve the problem by utilizing mason jars with holes in the caps and a rotten banana inside. The banana attracted the fruit flies, and lured them away from the screens. We changed the sanitation; the garbage cans were cleaned out, and everything returned to normal relatively quickly.

AR: So-called normal. You mentioned you'd also been to the Federal Reserve?

GB: Their building is in lower Manhattan, and we were brought in to prevent rats.

AR: What problems would rats cause?

GB: They didn't get in, but if they had, they could get into the vaults where money is kept. Gnaw and nest in money. Trigger alarms. We reviewed the current pest control program there, and it was adequate. Pest control is a constantly-changing field, and the government wanted an independent company to ensure that everything was up to snuff, because obviously the Federal Reserve Bank does not have its own

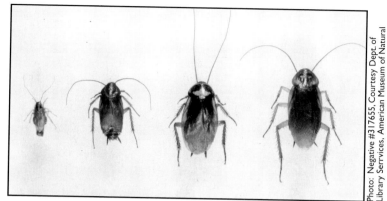

German roach, Oriental roach, Australian roach, and American roach (l. to r.).

Photo: Negative #317655, Courtesy Dept. of Library Serrvices, American Museum of Natural

DESSERT

Lemon Squares

Chocolate Cricket Torte

Mini Canoli

Peach Clafouti

Assorted Insect Sugar Cookies

Honey Pot Ants

(Menu courtesy of Lou Sorkin)

Photo: Bob Braine

Urban La Brea tar pit mouse in glue trap with other elements of the food chain present.

experts in pest control. That's another one of the many interesting sites I've done work in.

AR: Have you ever participated in entomological dinners?

GB: I'm a member of the New York Entomological Society, part of the Museum of Natural History. Six years ago, for their 100th anniversary celebration, they were really looking to do something different. They had a complete dinner of insects. Obviously, these are lab-bred insects, not insects caught in the streets or out in the wild. I took the attitude of: Well, you can only come and do this once. How different is it than sushi...

AR: Or any other arthropod, like lobster —

GB: I don't eat lobster. I spent too much time in labs. As I tell my classes, a lobster is only a pair of antennae and a couple feet away from being a cockroach.

AR: That's right.

GB: You know, if you want to eat it, fine.

AR: I'm allergic to crustaceans, but—

GB: I grew up kosher. There's something about filter feeders that just isn't attractive to me.

AR: What did you eat?

GB: I had the obligatory buffet, the meal worm meat balls and the meal worm tempura. Had one or two of the honey pot ants where you can actually taste the honey from their abdomen. The main course was a large wood grub.

AR: Now Gil, isn't a wood grub a beetle larvae?

GB: Yes. I drew the line there and went with the chicken. During the dinner, I was amazed to see that the number of reporters almost equaled the number of attendees. The humorous part was about a week after the dinner, my son was getting off the school bus, and he comes running over to me saying, "Daddy, Daddy, I'm so proud of you." Of course, that's a real high for any parent. I asked him, "O.K. Why?" He said, "You are on the cover of *Weekly Reader*." There was a whole write-up on the entomological affair. And sure enough, there I was, holding a plate of these little insects. I thought that was pretty funny. ∎

> **I don't eat lobster. As I tell my classes, a lobster is only a pair of antennae and a couple feet away from being a cockroach.**

Mud Season, I'll Fix it Tomorrow

by Michael Paha

Mud Season was produced in the spring of 1993, around the time of the Mississippi River floods. I wanted to create a mud slide—literally. The piece was a record of the action of the force of water over soil and mud, like the alluvial fans and meanders which spread over the landscape.

Much of my work has to do with nature taking over. As much as we like to manipulate and harness the environment, it always does what it needs to do. The installations are not set up to solve problems, but rather to examine the beauty that surrounds us: the poetry of the physical and kinetic forces in the environment.

I often set up my installations to read left to right. However, like traditional sculpture, I would like to read the piece from all directions. There is a sequence of events that takes place. This sequence is dictated by the directional flow of the water and reinforced by the visual elements of plants, props, and architectural structure. The livestock such as birds, fish and other aquatic life give movement which reinforces the constant growth, death, change and balance of (nature) the installation.

The composition of *Mud Season* starts with a broken aquarium. The water spills out of it and then literally leads you through the whole piece. As you encounter the other elements on the tables and shelves, it hints of a moment of neglect, as if you left the faucet running when you went on vacation. Nature left up to its own devices.

As in other works, living organisms play an important part. For example, house plants like the asparagus fern help to miniaturize the setting to give a sense of immensity from afar, like a view from above a jungle canopy.

The library shelves hold books on geology, entomology, botany and animal rearing. From the drawing room through the library, you come across the kitchen area which has the window to look into the flooded yard.

The water is constantly recalculating through the work to keep the life sustained. If the pumps stopped or the water level receded below its intake, the plants and animals would not be able to sustain life very well. There is a certain amount of human intervention required to maintain the installation. It is impossible to reproduce all the variables in nature which sustain life. My work is a celebration of life, not the exhibition of the cruelty of captivity. The flight cage for the finches was developed with the intention of maximum flight freedom and multiple nesting facilities. As time evolved, the birds were able to make nests out of a variety of different materials; they add another dimension to the installation as something which becomes alive. ∎

Photos: Mike Paha

MUD SLIDE (from top): View of slide, view of kitchen, and view of yard.

Michael Paha is an artist who lives and works in Chicago. He is also an exhibition designer for the Field Museum of Natural History.

How to Help Animals Escape from Degraded Habitats

written and
illustrated by
Bill
Burns

These images are from the forthcoming guidebook, *How to Help Animals Escape from Degraded Habitats*. The guide responds to the commonplace notion that ours are challenging times and that, owing to the punitive vastness of environmental destruction within the globalized economy, old rules of wildlife conservation may no longer apply. Using everyday language, the guide explains how to find, rescue, host, and deliver endangered fauna and provides helpful tips as to how to finance such a mission.

Great pains have been taken to make *How to Help Animals Escape from Degraded Habitats* informationally concise and free of technical jargon; however, some problems require complex explanations and even nuance. For example, the guide's claims about animal anxieties and requirements may at first glance seem extravagant, but they are rooted in fact. Rather than unraveling a complicated victimology, the guide advances practical health and safety solutions. While it provides instructions, diagrams, and maps, readers are expected to be motivated self-starters and problem-solvers. They must be eager to travel, hike, improvise, nurse and sometimes incubate. Teamwork and consensus-building are encouraged. The guide's frog team, for instance, consists of a camera repair expert, an experienced rafter and camper, a pharmacist, and a security guard from the local aquarium.

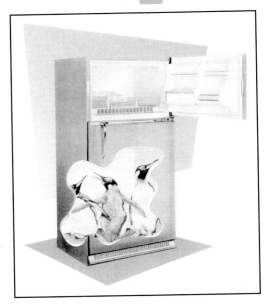

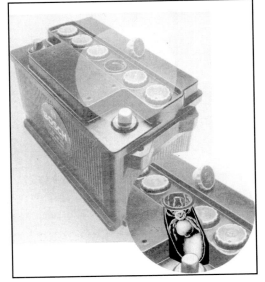

In deference to all parties, the terms "survivor" or "victim" are not used. Instead, animals are referred to as "clients" or "passengers" and those that choose to help them are called "hosts" or "facilitators."

Perforce charged with the commodious conduct of the client, hosts wield frightful power. For this reason they are urged to guard against corruption and to keep their inner child close at hand. ∎

Bill Burns is an artist and nature lover who lives in Montreal. He is also director of the Museum of Safety Gear for Small Animals.

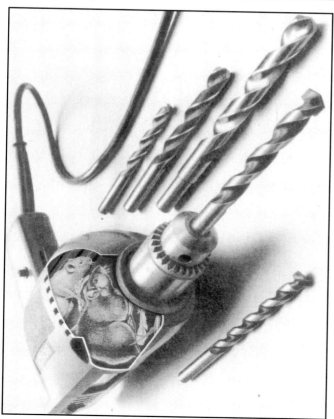

Pigeons: The Smart Bird

by
Boris
Palameta

Most species of pigeons have not benefited from contact with humans. One, the passenger pigeon, has become virtually synonymous with extinction. Nevertheless, one can hardly fail to notice that pigeons are everywhere. Where did they come from and why are they so successful?

Street pigeons comprise a single species (*Columba livia*), descended from domesticated rock doves. Wild populations of rock doves are indigenous to Africa, Europe (mainly Mediterranean and eastern regions, but also Ireland, Scotland, and nearby islands), and Asia (as far as India and Sri Lanka). The range of the species has, however, been greatly expanded by human activity. Everywhere we go, pigeons follow, from north of the Arctic circle to the southernmost tip of Tierra del Fuego in South America. It's almost as though evolution has prepared them especially for human intervention.

In reshaping nature to suit ourselves, we have inadvertently created a pigeon's paradise. Everything they need can be found in our cities and towns in greater abundance than nature provides. As natural seed eaters that prefer to forage on relatively bare ground, rock doves took readily to cultivated grains and deforestation—in other words, pecking at bread crumbs on paved streets. We also provided them with unparalleled nesting opportunities. Structures built by humans supply the sheltered holes and ledges which rock doves require, and which can only be found in caves and on cliff sides in the wild.

In reshaping nature, we have created a pigeon's paradise. Everything they need can be found in our cities and towns in greater abundance than nature provides.

Because of their affinity for things human, rock doves proved easy to domesticated, and the process of domestication prepared them still further for life among us. People who kept pigeons were fascinated by their ability to "home"—to return faithfully to favored roosting sites from great distances. Keeping and racing homing pigeons became a popular pastime. High quality birds were often sold or traded, and breeders selected for qualities that would maximize their profits, such as navigational ability. Generations of selective breeding produced

Photo courtesy of Mark Dion

The regal pigeon.

pigeons that were more sociable, less afraid of humans, and more spatially adept than their ancestors. Research has revealed that the hippocampus, a brain structure responsible for spatial memory, is significantly larger in varieties of pigeons that were bred specifically to home than it is in non-homing breeds. Homing pigeons that escaped their lofts and began to live on the street found themselves armed not only with a naturally evolved sense of direction, but also with an artificiality bred ability to remember subtle details about visual landmarks. Thus, pigeons are prepared to solve problems never faced by rock doves. For example, when a rock dove wants to leave a cave, it merely has to move toward the light. A pigeon wishing to leave the inside of a subway station, on the other hand, is faced with an array of synthetic lights and reflective surfaces. City pigeons, it seems, orient themselves according to memorized "maps" of their surroundings.

Designer pigeon in city park.

Photo: Bob Braine

Researchers who have observed the feeding habits of pigeons in the laboratory have also recorded a variety of remarkable abilities. For example, pigeons can learn where to search for food by observing the relative successes and failures of their peers. There is also some indication that inexperienced pigeons may be able to learn new ways of uncovering concealed food by observing and imitating techniques displayed by expert fellow flock members. On the streets, pigeons often don't have to work so hard to get a good meal. They learn to identify people who habitually feed them, and simply wait for their arrival at the usual time and place.

Ironically, feeding pigeons probably does them more harm than good. Pigeons regulate the number of young they produce according to good availability. Continuous year-round surpluses lead to overpopulation and high rates of infection by disease and parasites. Not many of these infections can be transmitted to humans, but some can. For example, there have been several cases of people suffering severe, even life-threatening allergic reactions to pigeon tick bites. Pigeon droppings may be a more general hazard, as they are known to provide a medium for the growth of the fungus *Cryptococcus neoformans*, which if inhaled can pose serious health risks particularly for people with depressed immune systems. Droppings also cause tens of thousands of dollars

The smart bird?

Photo: Bob Braine

The pigeon is also called the rock dove. Today skyscraper ledges substitute for the stony cliffs of Europe where it evolved.

Feeding pigeons leads to overpopulation resulting in high rates of infection by disease and parasites. There have been several cases of people suffering severe, even life-threatening allergic reactions to pigeon tick bites. Pigeon droppings may be a more general hazard, as they are known to provide a medium for the growth of a fungus which if inhaled can pose serious health risks.

worth of damage to buildings.

Regulating pigeon populations has proved to be a major problem for many cities. Killing large numbers of birds has no lasting effect, as any breeding vacancies that are created are quickly filled by birds that had previously been squeezed out of the mating game due to lack of space. Researchers have tried to develop a pigeon contraceptive pill, with little success. The best solution is the simplest one: convince people to stop feeding them. A concerted campaign to change public attitudes toward feeding pigeons was recently launched in Basel, Switzerland. Pamphlets and posters were distributed, with the aim of convincing people that feeding pigeons, however well-intentioned, is a form of cruelty to animals. The campaign worked. Feeding declined, and thousands of pigeons were trapped and killed to avoid mass starvation. The population was reduced from 20,000 to 10,000 in a little more than four years.

It was never a goal in the Basel campaign to completely eradicate the pigeon population. Many people like to have some pigeons around, as long as their numbers are manageable. For the most part, the relationship between people and pigeons can be characterized as a kind of urban symbiosis. We see to their material needs, and in return we get something indeterminate, something abstract, a kind of peace of mind. People need to see animals, to feel their presence. Maybe after living as hunter-gatherers for 99% of our history, our sense of aesthetics is linked to practical matters such as obtaining food and shelter, so that landscapes that are likely to provide both, landscapes that include free-living animals, are perceived as beautiful. Maybe the sight of pigeons, strolling calmly in our midst, is the closest most of us come to reliving a time when our very survival depended upon daily intimate contact with nature. ■

Dr. Boris Palameta is a professor in the Department of Evolutionary Psychology at the University of New Brunswick in Canada.

Savage Paris

Xavier Japiot and Pascal Bonneau are naturalists and researchers who organized an exhibition on the wildlife of Paris at the Parc Floral in 1993. They speak with Art Orienté Objet, the collaborative artist team of Marion Laurel-Jeantet and Benoit Mangin who live and work in Paris. Their work deals with the social engineering of attitudes toward the environment.

interview by
Art Orienté
Objet

ART ORIENTÉ OBJET: As urban naturalists you must have noted the recent invasion of Paris by foxes, swifts, falcons, blackbirds, seagulls and other wild animals. Are these animals taking refuge in the city because the countryside has become increasingly inhospitable?

XAVIER JAPIOT AND PASCAL BONNEAU: Not exactly, but there has been an interesting development regarding animal issues. Over the last several centuries, wildlife left the city. We assumed they left for good, but today they are slowly reconquering urban space. To do this, they must adapt their behavior. For example, the falcons which roost on Nôtre-Dame have changed their diet. They feed less on shrews, voles and field mice and more on sparrows. The owls in Paris also exploit the vast sparrow population.

AoO: Are some animals arriving in the city because of specific disorders? We heard that the seagulls from the menagerie of the Jardin des Plantes attracted the first wild flocks.

XJ&PB: That may be true, but most of the birds' presence is an adaptation to the effortlessness of city life: lack of predators; the increased food supply due to rubbish; the park's decorative fish which make easy prey and, lastly, the hand-outs. People who feed the gulls and other birds don't realize they are often causing harm. We have autopsied many birds who have overdosed on bread and died from obstructed bowels. However, the city is ideal for many gulls. Buildings function in a fashion similar to their natural nesting cliffs.

AoO: How did the authorities react to this animal invasion?

XJ&PB: In City Hall, there is a secret department, which eradicates rats, pigeons,

The unnatural warmth and light level within the city have disrupted the bird's natural rhythms. Now they reproduce six or seven times a year, regardless of season. Food is also abundant in Paris, making it a competition-free environment.

Photo: Jocko Weyland

The shop window of an exterminator in Paris.

Photo: Jocko Weyland

Rat trap display hanging in exterminator's window in Paris.

People who feed the gulls and other birds don't realize they are often causing harm. We have autopsied many birds who have overdosed on bread and died from obstructed bowels.

cats and other pests.

AoO: Are they secret because they fear public reaction?

XJ&PB: Very much so. When they are obliged to act publicly, they pretend to be doing research, like banding or taking a population census. In fact, it's euthanasia.

AoO: In the early 80s, the campaign to eradicate cats backfired when the rat population exploded. Now there are three rats for every person in Paris. An estimated 20% of the remaining cats have FLV, Feline Leuko-Virus. It's as if the urban ecosystem has broken down.

XJ&BP: Social factors always determine the make-up of the urban ecosystem. For example, I live in the suburb of Avon, where a smokers' league created a campaign to save the tiny subway cricket.

Many believe this insect lives entirely by eating the filters of discarded cigarettes thrown on the tracks. Needless to say, this group of concerned citizens didn't really give a damn about protecting the subway cricket. All they wanted to do was figure out a way to continue to smoke on the subway platform. In the city, we must always be wary about those who claim to speak for nature.

AoO: How much does the city shape animals?

XJ&BP: Let's look at pigeons. The unnatural warmth and light level within the city have disrupted the bird's natural rhythms. Now they reproduce six or seven times a year, regardless of season. Populations are high, due to a lack of predators. Food is also abundant in Paris, making it a competition-free environment. A stunning number of individuals survive to breed. One result is an abundance of malformations such as foot atrophy. Deformed and ill pigeons stay alive and transmit non-lethal diseases indefinitely. People also tend to feed the birds they find the most attractive which might give some birds a slight edge and affect the population coloring. Pollution, however, may become a selection factor for pigeons. More than a thousand chemical components exist in the air of Paris. Thirty of these are very dangerous; their rates are 200 times greater than in rural zones. The respiratory systems of birds are particularly affected by these toxins, especially lead.

AoO: Today, bird populations are higher in density in urban areas than rural areas.

XJ&PB: They're about three times greater in density, in fact, but don't forget that diversity is lower. The success of pigeons is clearly a result of their amazingly diverse nutritional regime. They can eat anything. The city's gulls get over 50% of their diet from people feeding them. They also prefer the city because pollution and agitated water do not freeze in winter. In January, one can see mergansers, eiders and even scoters on the Seine. Mid-winter can also bring lapwings, pewits and thrushes since pollution and higher temperature mean less snowfall. While the birds find many benefits in the city, there is also a cost.

For example, they often do lose their ability to know when to sing. The light pollution has confused them. You hear robins singing at two or three o'clock.

AoO: What do you regard as the most significant animal appearance in the last five years?

XJ&PB: The most significant appearance is an alien species. We have been invaded by the Florida turtle. In the U.S., they are illegal to transport across state lines, but not here. Some time ago, the wildlife service had the bad idea to launch a Minitel site with the Herpetological Society of France. They wanted to collect all of the unwanted pet turtles from around the country. The turtles were to find a new home in the large pond of Bois de Vincennes which also housed a collection of rare aquatic lotus. Within a few weeks, a pond of 60x30 meters was packed with 300 turtles. Every lotus had been destroyed. The gardeners were furious. Since then, the turtles have continued to increase in numbers and range.

Another interesting appearance is a colony of bats which recently settled in an abandoned railway station outside Paris. Our 1991 census placed their number at 861. That's more bats than in the entire forest of Fontainebleau. Fringe areas are appealing to animals. Airports have large populations of rabbits. They have even had to post signs to forbid the hunters from entering the flight zone.

AoO: Do domestic animals take much of a toll on wildlife?

XJ&BP: In Paris, not too much. It's the anonymous city service which tries to limit populations of wild animals. They used to destroy bird eggs, but this merely provoked a second laying. Now they inject formaldehyde into the eggs which preserves them but they never hatch. For some city dwellers, birds are their only joy, but to the authorities they are annoying and destructive. The 33,000 ring-necked doves which live in the Bois de Vincennes, can produce a formidable amount of acidic excrement which can destroy architecture and monuments. Other bird populations are on the increase: the magpies of the city more than doubled their population last year. In general, the wildlife of Paris is more impressive in individual numbers than in species. There are only about 60 species which visit the city parks each winter and only 30 which arrive in the summer. ■

A smokers' league created a campaign to save the tiny subway cricket. Many believe this insect lives entirely by eating the filters of discarded cigarettes thrown on the tracks. Needless to say, this group of concerned citizens didn't really give a damn about protecting the subway cricket. All they wanted to do was figure out a way to continue to smoke on the subway platform.

A Look at the Present Extinction Spasm
and what it means for the future evolution of the species

by
Norman
Myers

> After all, a tree's a tree.
> If you've seen one giant
> redwood, you've seen 'em
> all. What's the big deal?
> —Ronald Reagan

We share the planet with somewhere between 5 and 10 million other species. The number can only be estimated. Some scientists say that there are less than 5 million, and some say there are a good deal more than 10 million. Dr. Terry Irwin, an entomologist at the Smithsonian Institute in Washington, D.C. believes that there may be 30 million insects alone. But let us stay with 5 million as a baseline working figure.

In the mid-1970s, when I was preparing material for my book *The Sinking Ark*, I tried to get a handle on the rate at which species were disappearing. The figure we used to hear was one species per year, but that referred primarily to mammals and birds, and only to species that were actually observed to be disappearing. But because we have identified only about 1/6 of all the existing species on earth anyway, and a multitude exist to which we have not even given names, we can reasonably assume that many more than that are going under. In looking at the distribution of species on the Earth's surface, I soon found that the scientific community believes that at least 2/3 of all existing species live in the tropics. And of those 2/3, at least 1/2 live in the tropical moist forests. We can thus calculate that these tropical moist forests contain nearly 2 million species, even though they extend over a very small part of the Earth's surface, approximately 7% of the land area. Moreover, the tropical forests are taking the biggest beating right now. There are various estimates of the rate at which they are being grossly disrupted or actually destroyed. It is fair to say that by the end of the century, we can expect that somewhere between 1/3 and 1/2 of all our remaining tropical moist forests will be so grossly disturbed or depleted as to have lost much of their capacity to support their current huge array of species. They will not, by a long way, have been destroyed altogether—a few trees will still be standing—but they will not be virgin ecosystems as they are now, able to support a remarkable variety of species.

If we assume that between 1/3 and 1/2 of those forests are going to be degraded for wildlife purposes by the end of the century, it seems reasonable to surmise that by the year 2000, we could lose 1 million species out of the postulated minimum of 5 million.

What about the rate at which this could occur? If we say that 1 million species will disappear in the last 20 years of this century, that averages out to more than 130 species a day. But the big waves of extinction are not expected to occur in the next two or three years, but in the late 1990s, as human populations inexorably build up and generate their enormous impact. It is realistic to suppose that by the end of the 1990s, we could be losing dozens of plant and animal species with every single hour that goes by.

When I worked out these figures, I circulated the arithmetic to several hundred scientific colleagues throughout North America, Western Europe, Japan, and Africa. The consensus was that the current figure of one species a day is probably pretty cautious and conservative. Some people say 500 species a year and some say 1,000. The figure varies. Anyone can make a guess, but there seems to be no doubt that the rate of extinction today is much greater than we would have supposed it to be just a few years ago. The rate is also very much greater than it has been since the first flickering of life arose on the face of this planet some 3-1/2 billion years ago. Apparently, the maximum rate of extinction for the dinosaurs was about one species every 10,000 years—

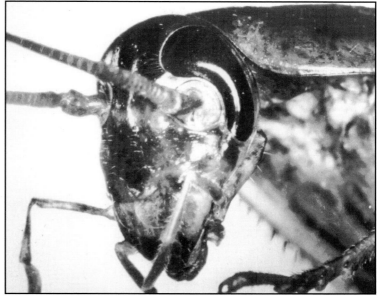
Head of an American cockroach.

Photo: AP/Wide World Photos

a pretty low rate when compared with the current one species per day. What we are facing in the period immediately ahead of us is a biological debacle, a gross impoverishment of our world on a scale greater than at any other time since life began. That is the size of it.

As a practical, hard-nosed conservationist, I would not be inclined to argue that we must try to save each and every existing species on earth— that is just not realistic. It is too late to begin trying to do that. However, suppose we do lose a million species in the next two decades and possibly another million or another 2 million during the first half of the 21st century. After this time, the growth in human numbers might level off, and we might reach some kind of ecological equilibrium with our living space. Is there still another major issue down the road if that happens?

There is. During the whole of the planet's history, there has never before been such a massive and compressed spasm of extinction. If we now precipitate a spasm of that scale, what does it mean for the processes of evolution? Can the processes of evolution pick up the remaining bits over the next thousand or million years and restore genetic diversity? There have been various phases in pre-history when a large proportion of species has disappeared, sometimes as many as 1/4, 1/2, or even 2/3 of the existing species. And in due course, meaning 20 or 30 million years, the processes of evolution have been able to restore the diversity of life and generate new species.

We may need 3 billion dollars a year to sufficiently safeguard tropical forests. Is 3 billion dollars a year such a big sum? If we were to divide that figure up among the citizens of the developed countries, it would amount to less than one martini per month per adult.

Herring gulls *(Larsus argentatus)* are one of the city's most common birds, due to an increased food supply.

But this time, it may not work out like that. In the past, when an outburst of extinction has occurred, the Earth has generally retained some concentrations of biological diversity, or "pools of species," from which the rest of the planet could be colonized after the geologic catastrophe had passed. This occurred on a minor scale just 20,000 years ago when the last glaciation receded, and the Earth was able to restock itself with plants and animals. At that time, the main storehouse from which those plants and animals came was the tropical moist forest, a kind of repository of species that is being most severely disrupted right now. So the next time, when evolution has to try to pick up the bits and restore the situation, it will very likely not have that reservoir of species with which to do the job.

Still these are considerations for the next 5, 15 or 30 million years, and we are not going to be around for quite that length of time. What about the more immediate future, when we shall be in our rocking chairs and our children making their way? If we lose 1 or 2 million species in the near future, does it really matter all that much? I suspect that it does. When a large number of species disappear, the process tends to be counterbalanced by increased speciation, an evolutionary process that throws up new species to occupy vacancies we call the ecological living space. New species can rush in to that ecological living space, take up the newfound opportunity to grow, establish themselves, and flourish. Species especially good at exploiting these new opportunities tend to be creatures biologists call "r-selected"—that is, species that are highly opportunistic. They can rush in; they are highly mobile; they are adaptable, and they can very rapidly reproduce their numbers. They can take over a situation and more or less control it unless they have natural enemies in sufficient abundance to keep their own numbers down. Some examples of these r-selected species are with us in the world right now. One is the common rat, another the cockroach, the house sparrow, and, finally, the plants we choose to call weeds, which tend to proliferate and dominate their local environments. It is possible—even probable—that within 50 years, when many current species disappear and their places begin to be taken by others, we will have a disproportionate number of species we would characterize as "pest" or "weed" species. That is the kind of biological world our children are going to have to contend with. We might want to wish them luck.

What can we do about this entire situation? The current extinction spasm is to some extent an already existing problem, but it has not yet become an almighty problem. We can still think of it as a kind of challenge. What can we do to try to counteract the situation? Let me suggest a shopping list of initiatives that we should think about. One is that we need many more parks and reserves around the earth. The total number of protected areas now amounts to about 2% of the earth's land surface. Two percent is a pretty good average when you consider that in the U.S., the figure is 1.6%, a figure that includes all the big parks in Alaska. Some countries, such as Kenya, have as much as 6% of their land surface set aside as parks and reserves. Tanzania, one of the most impoverished countries on Earth, with a total national budget that is less than New York spends on ice cream each year, has set aside 15% of its total land area for parks and reserves. In Zambia, farther south, the figure is about 25%. Worldwide, however, the average figure is only about 2%. Scientists seem to believe, estimating as best they can in an uncertain situation, that we would need 10% of the Earth's land surface before we could do even a basic job of safeguarding sufficient natural environments to keep species alive.

What are the costs? Roughly, the bill to set up these parks and reserves would be about $1 million. Another $20 million would be needed annually to maintain them. That might sound like a lot, but consider that $100 million is the amount by which the total armaments bill increases worldwide from one day to another!

How should we safeguard the tropical forests, the areas that need the most urgent attention? If we want to safeguard a sufficient area of tropical forest, it might have to be as much as 20% or even 25% and not the 10% global fraction mentioned above. We might need to think in terms of 1 billion dollars a year.

Dr. Ira Rubinoff, director of the Smithsonian Tropical Research Institute in Panama, has just written a very interesting and visionary paper suggesting that, according to his arithmetic, we may need 3 billion dollars a year to sufficiently safeguard tropical forests, a preliminary but informed reckoning. Is 3 billion dollars a year such a big sum? If we were to divide that figure up among the citizens of the developed countries (never mind the developing ones), it would amount to less than one martini per month per adult.

Obviously, such financial support is not available right now. The cause of conservation is a very long way from having that kind of money at its disposal. In the meantime, all these species are under threat. I mentioned that 1/10th of all plants are under threat; let us say that 1/10th of all species are under threat, or a half million species, disap-

In the past, when an outburst of extinction has occurred, the Earth has generally retained some concentrations of biological diversity, or "pools of species," from which the rest of the planet could be colonized after the geologic catastrophe had passed. Right now, when evolution has to try to pick up the bits and restore the situation, it will very likely not have that reservoir of species with which to do the job.

pearing at a rate of one per day. Given the money we do have available, we cannot, by a long way, help all endangered species—regrettable as that may be. We have to allocate our scarce conservation dollars to the best effect possible. And that means choosing those species and ecosystems that would give us the best returns on our scarce conservation dollars. Whenever we choose to conserve a bunch of species "over here," an implicit decision is made that those species "over there," which are not getting our conservation dollar, are somehow not so "deserving" as the species we have chosen. We are assigning priorities and saying that certain species are in some way more important than others. We may not be quite sure why we are making that choice, but we are making it anyway. It is an awfully tough act of life to face up to.

Such decision-making is called "triage." The word is derived from the French verb meaning "to sort out." In conservation, we find this term used in the sense of choosing. The question is not whether we should consider triage for the future, because we are already practicing triage right now. When any of us decides, for example, to give money on behalf of a particular species, be it a tiger, a turtle, the California condor, or whatever, we are ruling out alternative choices of giving. The case of the California condor illustrates the impact of such choices. I have seen a lot of cost-benefit analysis that has gone into the program for the condor; a great many people have made a fine effort to work out the best way to assist that bird. The amount of money to be spent is $25 million over a period of 30 years, and the chances of success are rated at only 50-50. We should question whether we should consider spending that same amount of money on behalf of perhaps 100 species in the middle of the Amazon, for which there is a 95% chance of success in a conservation program and an equally good chance they will disappear if we do nothing. That is the essence of triage. Part of the question is understanding what can be done and determining through what organizations our donations can be put to use. These topics urgently need as much informed public discussion as possible.

Sometimes I am advised by my conservationist colleagues not to talk about triage to public audiences; they fear it will give the wrong impression, that someone will say, "OK, if you want to choose in favor of the tiger or the Californian condor, which species are you deciding are not worthwhile and can be put over the side of the boat?" That is not the way it is at all. When I suggest that we need to choose consciously, as methodically as possible and with as much information as possible, I am not making bets about which creature would win a beauty contest or should appear at the top of the conservationists' lists. Various magazines have asked me to write articles about this; they say, "Come up with a nice little list, Norman Myers, of species that you think we can do without." I am not going to do that. My own personal philosophy is that every species, as a manifestation of creation's life force on earth,

Species especially good at exploiting these new opportunities tend to be creatures biologists call "r-selected"—species that are highly opportunistic. They can rush in; they are highly mobile; they are adaptable, and they can very rapidly reproduce. Some examples of these r-selected species are the common rat, the cockroach, the house sparrow, and, finally, the plants we choose to call weeds.

deserves to have its own chance to live out its life span—if we can possibly manage it. That gets us into the realm of aesthetics and ethics. There are other issues as well. Consider the smallpox virus, which has now been backed into a corner in a flask, so to speak, in one or two laboratories. It is being maintained at a cost of only a few thousand dollars a year, but some people would say that the smallpox virus has caused so much harm, so much misery and suffering, that we should pull

The North American opossum *(Didelphis virginiana)* has increased its range thanks to the spread of suburbia, which means an increased food supply and the elimination of predators and competition.

Photo: Bob Braine

the plug on the thing and eliminate it by deliberate choice. Yet it turns out that medical people are now surmising that we may, one day quite soon, establish that the smallpox virus can assist us with some of our medical research. So there is no species that on scientific, economic, ethical, or aesthetic grounds should be put over the side of the boat.

Unfortunately, that is not the way the world works. The amount of conservation money we have to assist threatened species is only a small fraction of what we would need to do a sufficient job. We can and must get on with the job and make the best of it. We need an open and ongoing discussion as to how we should go about making choices. And we had better start trying to assemble the necessary information to do a better job with the funds we have. I can see no greater challenge, agonizing though it will be for the conservationist community, than to start deciding right now where to put our priorities. Because with every day that goes by, with every bit of conservation planning that we do, we are, in effect, already making choices; we are already embarked on a course of triage. We are not doing it deliberately or with systematic thought, but we are doing it. Let us start doing it as consciously and methodically as we can. ∎

This article was originally presented at the National Zoological Park Symposium for the Public. Norman Myers is a pioneering wildlife conservation consultant who spends his time shuttling between Kenya and Oxford. He authored The Primary Source: Tropical Forests and Our Future, The Sinking Ark *and numerous other accounts of the global ecological crisis.*

Don't Cough on Me, Armadillo

by
Drake
Zimmerman

Armadillos are funny looking critters that hop like bunnies and don't look up too often. That makes them a great source of road kill along highways. My friends from Oklahoma say: "Yum, just like possum." Yum?! Forget sushi, guys. Armadillos are a massive animal repository of the leprosy bacillus.

One graduate student wrote his doctoral thesis in Public Health on the incidence of leprosy in road kill on Texas highways. With the number of armadillos running all over the south, why we don't have more active cases of leprosy is a marvel of modern luck.

Contagious still? Yes. Like TB, leprosy is usually transmitted by coughing. Don't cough on me, armadillo. People typically catch it from others they come into close contact with. Like relatives, people in crowded streets. Inhale the wrong droplet from a cough and some time in the next 50 years, you may develop a little spot or lesion—maybe like an age spot. After a certain age, how would you even notice? Then a little numbness....

Think about telling someone that you have leprosy. Assuming that someone can competently identify what you have, you have to admit to having the disease before you can get treatment. The guys at work will be happy to hear that you noticed your leprosy before you could expose them for a second decade. Do you imagine that the boss will be happy to send the rest of the crew down for tests? Rural places like the Amazon in Brazil aren't quite over-doctored to begin with. Some areas the size of Illinois have only one doctor. Health-care is not exactly state of the art everywhere. If the proper medicines have been donated and delivered in, they are lucky. Reading to a fifth grade level is considered providing skilled labor.

Imagine the dialogue: "Hey, Doc, I noticed that I have so little feeling here that the end of my finger rubbed off. Just a little leprosy, you say? I'll tell Mom and the kids after I stop by the clinic for the multidrug therapy (MDT) and some Band-Aids. Thanks for letting me know that I've only been contagious for a few years. No problem."

Photo: Bob Braine

Nine-banded armadillo family (*Dasypus novemcinctus*) grubbing for insects.

Guilt, anyone? "Sorry, sis. Did I cough on you, too, little brother? It won't happen again." Tragedy continues as carriers often run away out of shame, and slip into anonymity in the cities or jungles, to fend for themselves, rather than confront this perfectly curable disease. Education could stop it. The carriers stay contagious, while the totally stoppable disease progressively rots their bodies into utter misery. When, or if, they return to civilization, it is often too late to do anything but beg.

The tragedies of contracting leprosy continue

The courtship of the nine-banded armadillo.

Photo: Bob Braine

because people who get it hide it for as long as they can. "It's just a cut on my finger, Uncle, just a cut. It'll heal soon." Imagine the terror of slowly realizing that you have leprosy. Let it go and you will just be left with stumps. While fewer than before, beggars with leprosy are in Kampala, Nairobi, São Paolo and Medellín, not just Delhi and Jakarta. Not to mention small towns.

After visiting a village off the end of the road in western Kenya, the aid group's Land Rover gave the local woman a ride to the market. "Any leprosy here?" I asked "No, not for years," replied the aid group's employee, an experienced African hand in the seat beside me.

"Oh, yes, we do have leprosy," came from the back seat. "We've always had leprosy. We have a few cases in the village right now. Many villages have it. It hasn't gone away. But we don't have as much as before," our passenger offered brightly. A dermatologist had visited a village a few years back and had trained community volunteers about what to look for. While most cases were identified, some kept turning up. The locals referred the patients to the District Hospital in Kisunu, some 25 miles away. There were several cases active in addition to those in treatment. Slowing, but not stopped. Such is progress.

Leprosy is targeted for elimination by the year 2000. Already the world is down to only 550,000 new cases a year. MDT is widely known and the drugs are available free in most areas.

MDT means taking several drugs, with the idea that if one drug doesn't kill the leprosy, the others will. Treatment arrests leprosy, stop-

To stop the disease of leprosy, active cases have to take the medicine every day for six months. If the patient misses one day, the treatment must be recommenced. What have you ever done consistently for six months, not missing a day?

Photo: Patrick McMullan

Armadillo sex.

ping the progressive deterioration, but treatment takes a while. Once finished, the carrier is no longer contagious. MDT requires consistency to work. To stop the disease, active cases have to take the medicine every day for six months. If the patient misses one day, the treatment must be recommenced. What have you done consistently for six months, not missing a day?

The problem is that the bacilli that survive on missed days are the ones most resistant to the drugs. If the people taking the drugs aren't consistent, the bacilli that survive could be incurable strains. That's natural. And that's another reason why stopping leprosy now is more important than ever.

Eliminating leprosy by the year 2000 means shooting for the goal of fewer than one case per 10,000 people. For example, in India, the goal is to get cases under 80,000 per year; that would be an 80-90% reduction.

Like tuberculosis, leprosy is usually transmitted by coughing.

Fortunately, leprosy is curable. With education, we can identify the skin lesions early. Education helps get people to treatment early. Concentrating on the year 2000 focuses the mind and heart on reducing the rate of leprosy to zero. One case in 10,000 is way too many. One case in a million is still too many. One in a billion will take some doing. Then we just have to keep people away from armadillos.

Know anyone who has been to India recently? Kenya? Bangladesh? That nice couple from church who helped at a clinic in the Amazon? Who coughed on them? Do they cough on you? Don't cough on me, armadillo. ∎

Drake Zimmerman, J.D., C.F.A., is an investment advisor and money manager and past president of the Rotary Club of Normal, Illinois. He is the U.S. Coordinator of Rotary Against Malaria (RAM) working to help build malaria control and basic health care infrastructure in over 90 countries affected by malaria.

Boubous: Two Stork Stories

Marabou stork (Leptoptilus crumeniferus): a resident in tropical Africa from Senegal to Somalia, south to Botswana; rare in South Africa. It breeds in Botswana, north to Ethiopia and Somalia, west to Senegal. Frequent to common in most of range, locally abundant or very abundant near large colonies and in towns. Probably increasing through association with humans, and scavenging on rubbish dumps.—*Brown, Urban & Newman,* The Birds of Africa, Vol. 1, *Academic Press, 1982.*

by
Andy
Dobson

Bronx, New York, October 1992: In 1992, Jake, the Bronx zoo's oldest denizen, died. He had been captured in the wild as an adult bird in 1938 and had never managed to breed successfully in captivity. However, he had been very helpful in controlling the zoo's feral population of peacocks; whenever a female and her young brood wandered inadvertently past Jake, one of the brood would inevitably disappear and Jake's throat pouch would appear to twitch for a while. A postmortem revealed that Jake was really Jacqueline. She was replaced by a mixed group of six young birds who it was hoped would form a small breeding colony.

The young birds needed their wings clipped. The six birds watched the four keepers coming into the exhibit. This was more than normally came to feed them. Why were they spreading out across the exhibit like that? Suddenly two of the keepers rushed forward and tried to grab a bird. It hopped away and, spreading its wings, realized it could fly again. Several others attempted to join it in the air and three of them straggled up high enough for the wind to catch them and blow them up over the fence and into the south Bronx.

"Shit," muttered the keepers, "best get some help and get after them."

The junkie rubbed his eyes, cleared his throat and spat into the street. He needed the next hit bad, but if he took it now, he'd need to spend the rest of the day raising coin to get him through till dark. "Fug it, need a hit," he mumbled, as he staggered across to the park. The large grey and white bird with the naked skin neck appeared before him as he entered the park.

He pitched forward onto the grass as the bird advanced towards him; it clacked its long beak against the ground around his head. He ran screaming from the park, scattering a short trail of tiny glass tubes behind him.

All of the birds were re-captured and returned to the zoo. Their new exhibit is covered with an invisible fence. They have yet to breed in captivity, but they regularly raise their beaks while courting and clack them together as they lower them to the ground.

It is puzzling that the marabou stork seems to be increasing in Africa, whereas the apparently ecologically similar greater adjutant is decreasing in Asia.
—Hancock, Kushlan and Kahl, *Storks, Ibises, Spoonbills of the World*

Photo courtesy of Andy Dobson

Maribou storks.

Greater Adjutant Stork (*Leptoptilus dubius*): the most massive and ugliest of the Asian storks, standing 120-150 cm to the top of the head when erect. It often appears shorter, owing to its hunched stance. Its general color is slate-black, gray and white, with a feather-less head and neck, a massive wedge-shaped bill and a naked ruddy pink gular pouch, hanging from the front of the neck. It was named "adjutant" because it walks with the deliberate, measured gait of a military adjutant.

This is, perhaps, the most endangered of all the Asian storks. In the early years of the 20th century, the greater adjutant was a very common bird in Indian cities during the non-breeding season, and they gathered in great numbers to breed in southern Burma. Today, the bird is uncommon to rare in many of its former haunts and the Burmese breeding grounds are said to be deserted. If the decrease of the past 50 years continues at the same rate, the species might cease to exist in another few years.

Whenever a female and her young brood wandered inadvertently past Jake, one of the brood would inevitably disappear and Jake's throat pouch would appear to twitch for a while. A postmortem revealed that Jake was really Jacqueline. She was replaced by a mixed group of six young birds who it was hoped would form a small breeding colony.

Guwahati, Assam November, 1993: We'd come to Kaziranga Lodge to search for breeding greater adjutant storks. Two Indian biologists had reported finding nesting birds in a number of villages along the edge of the Bramaputra river. If we could confirm their reports, it might be possible to get them funding to further their survey of the birds. It had proved hard to get into Assam, as parts of the west and north of the district were subject to guerrilla activity. We'd been driven out to see our first nest early on the first morning. We'd crossed the Bramaputra by a long bridge that linked islands in the river just to the south of Guwahati, the capital of Assam. The stork nest was high in a tree behind a small village, several miles from the river. The Himalayas appeared 70 or 80 miles away as we drove into the village. It's probably the largest altitude change on the planet, the river is only a couple of hundred feet above sea-level, the Himalayas rise to nearly 30,000 feet. The stork looked down from the nest 80 feet up in the tallest tree around. After 10 minutes, another bird appeared and circled around as I tried to take photographs. Eventually it settled by the nest and the birds greeted each other by raising their beaks and lowering them while clattering the bills together.

A crowd had gathered around us and an elderly woman from the village asked us if we'd like some tea. We were told by one of the crowd that she was a guerrilla; we returned to her house where a poster in one of the two rooms explained that the adjutant storks were part of Assam's culture and should be protected. The women explained to us that the pair of birds we'd seen were safe for now, but eventually the daughter of the family who owned the piece of land on which their nest stood would be old enough to marry. They would then probably cut down the tree to pay her dowry. "Couldn't we set up a fund to pay the dowry?" I asked. "There are many such girls in Assam," the women replied.

We drove back into town after visiting several other villages and locating a small colony of 14 birds on the edge of one village. "It would be nice to see if I can get some pictures of the birds at the local garbage dump," I said as we drove towards the city. "I remember there were always many there when I was a child," said Professor Bhattacharjee. We got to the dump half an hour before sunset. It covered a large area to the east of the town, smoke rose from several small fires around the edge of piles of garbage, lean-to tents were built into the sides of several piles of garbage. I climbed onto the roof of the car to look for storks. The inevitable black kites wheeled around the dump, constantly alert for any food source. Each time I located a stork-sized object in the falling evening light, I'd realize it was a human child combing the garbage for dinner. Eventually, I located a lesser adjutant lurking on the edge of the dump. Some children also noticed it and threw stones in its direction. I realized there were no greater adjutant storks here, and there probably had not been any for some time. Humans seemed to have out-competed them in their quest for garbage. ∎

Andy Dobson is Professor of Ecology and Evolutionary Biology at Princeton University. His main interests are population dynamics of animals, parasites and their hosts.

A marabou stork.

Photo courtesy of Andy Dobson

chapter 2

Alien Invaders

Concrete Jungle II, Alexis Rockman (1991)

Alien Invaders—They Came from Planet Earth

Release of wildlife into territory foreign to it involves, not a calculated risk, but a risk too great to calculate. The animal moving game, however, proceeds through the land.
— George Laycock, The Alien Animals

by
Michael
Crewdson
and
Mark Dion

By definition, an exotic or alien species is a plant or animal taken from its native ecosystem and transported to a completely new environment. Such biological invasions are almost always due to human activity—whether we are bringing tiny organisms back on our clothes from a trip to the Bahamas, importing tropical birds as pets, or even letting loose fish native to one stream into another.

In the U.S. alone, there are more than 4,500 "alien invaders" that have established populations in the wild. These range from the common daisy and Kentucky bluegrass, both Eurasian in origin, to serious threats like Eurasian gypsy moths and "killer" bees from Africa. In the World, the number is countless.

The alien introduction can be accidental. When humans move, whether it's in ships, trains or 747s, spores and seeds cling to clothing, rats hide out in the hulls of ships, microscopic larvae in the ballast of ocean liners. Creatures get a free ride—hundreds if not thousands of miles away from where they evolved over thousands of years. Sometimes they arrive in a new world where they face no enemies, predators or diseases to stop them from proliferating. Like a human going back to the Stone Age equipped with automatic weapons, life is easy for the alien. They run rampant in their new environment, perversely succeeding. Forty pairs of starlings turn into 10 million.

In the 1800s, "acclimatization societies" were formed to deliberately introduce European birds into the United States. Their two successes, starlings and house sparrows, are now among the most common of all birds in North America, crowding out native species like bluebirds and woodpeckers.

The introduction can be purposeful. English colonists, not feeling at home in their new lands like New Zealand and Australia, turned loose creatures that went out of control in their new environments. In 1859, Thomas Austin brought 24 European rabbits to his estate in Victoria. The rabbits flourished and Austin was hailed at the time for his unparalleled success with breeding. By the 1870s, Australia

A selection of species introduced to the Americas since 1492.

Illustration: Mark Dion

was awash with rabbits. They slurped up water at scarce watering holes and nibbled rich grazing lands bare. When they ran out of food in one area, they began mass migrations, with thousands of rabbits springing across the outback. Mass hunts were organized. Thousands of bunnies were clubbed, trapped, shot, and gassed in day-long operations. In 1887, more than 15 million rabbits were killed in New South Wales. But the rabbits were undeterred, and they continued to turn large sections of Australia into desert. The rabbit problem continues to this day.

The introductions continue. The *New York Times* recently reported that golden snails native to South America were released by a commercial concern into Vietnam during the late 1980s. These snails, which were intended to be sold as gourmet treats, spread from their release site, and began to reproduce dramatically. Now there are billions of snails devouring Vietnam's rice paddies. As in the case of most introductions, catastrophe followed good intentions.

While some may argue that natural invasions have always occurred on earth—seeds being carried by the wind, continents colliding and new land bridges forming, the incredible mobility of humans has drastically accelerated these processes. During the era of airplane travel, there is a tremendous interchange of flora and fauna—and the chances of "hits"—or an alien species surviving and thriving—are increased.

When there is a "hit" and an exotic species survives in the wild, its effect on the environment is unpredictable. Entering an evolved habitat, a forest or stream with an existing predator-prey balance, the new species can become a form of biological pollution, changing the pattern of life and sometimes threatening the natural order. Zebra mussels were a hit. African bees were another hit. Who knows what the next hit is?

Photo: AP/Wide World Photos

Nutria (*Myocastor coypus*)
Length: Over 20 inches
Weight: As much as 17 pounds
AKA: The swamp rat

The American South has an alien monstrosity lurking in its wilds. Imagine an unchecked population of giant rats running amok in the swamps and bayous of Louisiana. It's actually happening. Millions of nutria, a native of South America and the second largest rodent in the world, are eating their way through the fragile swamp lands of the American south, causing untold ecological damage in their new home.

The nutria is a semi-aquatic rodent native to wetlands in South America. Like the beaver, the nutria has webbed hind feet and is an excellent swimmer. And like the rat, the nutria is active in the breeding department. The male nutria lives with harems of up to three females, each capable of producing two litters of five young a year. Nutrias sometimes wind up being eaten by the alligators that share the swamp with them, but the swamp rat's only real enemy is man, who has all but given up hunting them.

The plague of swamp rats is historically blamed on E.A. McIlhenny, the man who brought Tabasco sauce to millions of Americans. In 1938, McIllhenny imported six pairs of the nutria from Argentina to start a farm, where he would raise nutrias for their pelts. His farm of giant rodents quickly reproduced and escaped captivity when a hurricane hit in 1940. From that original population and perhaps some other introductions, the population of wild nutrias exploded into the millions.

For years, Louisianans culled the wild colony for their golden brown pelts which were sold in the fur trade, but soon, the market collapsed and the swamp rat pelt became valueless. Without being hunted by trappers, the population of nutria experienced an even greater growth spurt, creating a full-scale ecological disaster which continues to this day. Nutrias are now being blamed for destroying huge tracts of marsh land ecosystem by their voracious appetites.

Death Cap Mushroom
(Amanita phalloides)
Area of Contamination: Continental U.S.
Home Territory: Europe

Negative #239113, Courtesy Dept. of Library Services, American Museum of Natural History

This is one example of an introduced fungus that is spreading rapidly across North America, leaving dead humans in its wake. The death cap mushroom, an extremely deadly member of the Amanita family, is said to have been accidentally introduced into North America in the roots of nursery plants brought over from Europe.

Mushroom experts say that this greenish-hued mushroom probably first arrived in the northeast section of the U.S. sometime during the 1920s. And they have flourished in their new environment, having successfully made the trip to the West Coast. And they are spreading.

The damage this alien fungus has wreaked is not well documented. But at least every year, someone dies from eating the death cap. Children are likely victims, because they typically grow on suburban lawns in groups of well over a hundred. The other most common victims are recent immigrants from Asian countries who have been picking and eating these deadly mushrooms possibly because they mistake them for an edible type which grows in their homeland. Mushroom societies around the country have been translating warnings into Chinese and Korean to warn of this fatal mistaken identity.

The effects of eating a death cap are truly gruesome. After eating the mushroom, raw, dried or cooked, the victim feels no effects for 10 hours. Then intense and painful stomach cramps, diarrhea and vomiting set in. After this, the symptoms disappear, and the victim thinks he/she is in the clear. The next day, the eater's liver and kidneys fail. Coma, convulsions and usually death follow if no treatment is given. If the victim survives the death cap poisoning, they often need liver transplants.

Photo: AP/Wide World Photos

Kudzu Vine (*Pueraria lobata*)

Some alien invaders are plants. Drive anywhere in the American Southeast, such as Georgia, Alabama, or Kentucky, and you will see what look like giant, misshapen topiaries on the sides of the road. These green giants are trees, houses and utility poles, covered with the Japanese invader vine, kudzu.

Kudzu had its premiere in 1876 at the Japanese pavilion of a Philadelphia Centennial Exposition where it was touted as an ornamental vine. The plant seemed like an ideal candidate for introduction into American gardens and as an ornamental vine on houses. It had beautiful purple flowers with a pleasant grape-like scent. And it grew extremely fast. What wasn't known then was that kudzu, once released into the ideally humid growing conditions of the Southeast, would one day cover a large part of the American South like a shroud.

Although kudzu was sometimes used as an ornamental plant by gardeners, ultimately, it was the U.S. Government that turned the vine loose on the South. In the 1930s and 40s, the U.S. Soil Conservation Service, like a deranged "Johnny Appleseed," scattered hundreds of thousands of Kudzu seedlings along highways and farms to fight soil erosion. The idea was that the extensive mats of roots put out by the kudzu would prevent overworked soils from blowing or washing away. The kudzu plan worked—only too well.

The wide-ranging effects did not become apparent until the 50s, when Southerners noticed that land, trees, telephone poles, abandoned cars—and, in fact, anything that stood still—were disappearing under acres of kudzu's all-embracing, bright-green leaves and tendrils. Cutting its hosts off from the light of the sun and weighing them down under hundreds of pounds of vegetable mass, kudzu began killing trees, pulling down power lines, and cutting off phone service.

Kudzu's virility and invasive power are insidious and creepy. During the hot months when Southern temperatures regularly top 90°F, a kudzu vine can grow at a rate of one foot per day and 60 to 80 feet in a year, making it one of the fastest growing—and most aggressive—plants in the world. A kudzu vine gets a foothold on a host by using native vines like poison ivy as a ladder. Once it climbs to the top of its victim, the original kudzu vine sends down multiple shoots which are, in turn, used as ladders by other kudzu shoots and colonizing vines until the entire victim is covered in a grotesque green veil.

Zebra Mussel (*Dreissena polymorph*)
Size: Fingernail size
Origin: Western Russia Near Caspian Sea
Habitat: Any firm surface in fresh water

Photo: AP/Wide World Photos

A worker sprays zebra mussels off the walls of the town pumphouse in Monroe, Michigan where the mussels clogged Monroe's only water intake from Lake Erie.

The monstrous success of the zebra mussel rivals any paranoid science fiction story. Within a single year of their discovery in the waters of Lake Erie in 1988, they had encrusted any and every hard surface in the lake, as well as having spread through the entire Great Lake Chain. Sometime in the mid-1980s, a transoceanic ship must have discharged Dreissena larvae in its ballast water. The North American plankton-filled lakes proved an ideal habitat for the mussels, which have now infested all lakes in close proximity to the Great Lakes and all connecting river systems. Inevitably, zebra mussels will colonize most rivers and lakes of the continent.

Zebra mussels generate fibers which attach them to any firm surface, be it wood, stone, metal, plastic, rubber, glass, other mussels—anything firm. They form vast colonies; some beds in Lake Erie contain as many as 70,000 individuals per square meter. By attaching themselves to each other, they may produce large mats which extend over soft mud lake bottoms. Feeding on phyto and zoo plankton in immense quantities, the mussels doubtlessly have a significant effect on the aquatic food chain. The remarkable clarity of Lake Erie is attributed to the mussels' filter feeding activities. Colony encrustment has caused serious industrial problems as intake pipes and engines have become fouled. Most rocky areas of the Great Lakes are completely covered with several inches of mussels. So many in fact as to change the oxygen level and pH of the surrounding waters. Larval mussels continue to spread from lake to lake across waterways and as stowaways in recreational boats.

Gray Squirrel (*Sciurus carolinensis*)
Length: 14–23 inches head to tail
Weight: Up to 1.5 pounds
Origin: Eastern North America
Habitat: Woodlands, city parks

In the late 1950s *The Last Red Squirrel* was published in England. It was a thinly-veiled racist fable lamenting the decay of British purity caused by an invasion of rough foreigners. To do this, the book employed the story of the introduction of the American gray squirrel and its consequent spread across England. Unfortunately, this would not be the last time that social values would be grafted onto natural phenomenon, or that animals would be clothed to represent human obsessions.

In 1890, G.S. Page of New Jersey made a gift of ten gray squirrels to the Duke of Bedford at his Woburn Estate. The squirrels charmed many, who imported them to decorate their land. Predictably enough, while the gray squirrel increased its range, the only native tree squirrel —the little red squirrel *(Sciurus vulgaris)*—began to disappear. Whether the gray squirrel imported a disease or simply over-stressed or out-competed the reds remains uncertain: both are possible. Folk mythology sprang up claiming that the large vicious grays used their formidable claws to castrate the more genteel reds. Regardless of the reason, the European red squirrel persists. To make matters worse, the introduced gray squirrels have changed their diets from seeds and nuts to an exclusive taste for tree bark. They can completely girdle and kill a wide variety of trees.

European Carp (*Cyprinus carpio*)
Length: 48 inches
Weight: Up to 80 pounds
Origin: Eurasia
Range: Worldwide

In May 1877, Rudolph Hessel, the government fish culturist, was certain that the 345 live carp he had brought back from Europe and released into Druid Hill Park

Pond in Boston, were to find a special place in the hearts of American anglers. Little did he know that he had just set free the most destructive exotic fish ever introduced to the U.S. For some years, Hessel's enthusiasm was shared by farmers and aquaculturists who shared in the carps' off-spring. Spring floods washed the fish far beyond their ponds and into the extended watershed. By 1895, Game Commissioner of Nevada George Mills was less than hospitable regarding the fish: "Several years ago, during the carp furor, the general government was *particep criminis* in foisting upon this state, and in polluting our waters with that undesirable fish, the carp. Time has now established their worthlessness, and our waters are suffering from their presence." The carp had greatly affected the aquatic ecosystem by uprooting aquatic vegetation while feeding. The young carp ate the insects the other game fish needed. They muddied the waters, interfering with photosynthesis, thus impeding the plants' return, which not only destroyed the spawning grounds of other fish, but also destroyed the resources for migratory aquatic birds. The carp is extraordinarily prolific. One third of the female carp's body weight consists of just the ovaries; she can produce 400,000 to 500,000 eggs per pound. Their adaptive skills have assured their persistence and reputation as the most hated game fish in America.

Giant African Snail
(*Achatina fulica*)
Size: Almost football size
Origin: African mainland, Madagascar, Mauritius
Habitat: Subtropical and tropical vegetation zones

Numerous species of snails have been intentionally and accidentally transplanted around the globe. U.S. Fish and Wildlife Service Inspectors classify snails as one of the most potentially dangerous of all smuggled animals. Many gastropods are not only agricultural pests, but are also vectors for various human and livestock parasites and diseases.

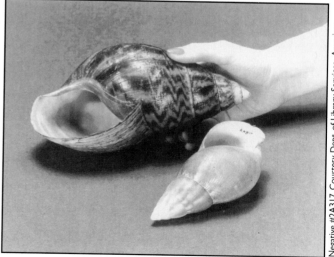

Negative #2A317, Courtesy Dept. of Library Services, American Museum of Natural History

The giant African snail is a cosmopolitan agricultural pest with a diet diverse enough to include most fruits, cotton and rubber plants, legumes, flowers and carrion. A true titan among snails, it weighs over a pound. The snail is amazingly prolific, producing over 300 eggs every few weeks. An English tourist named W.H. Benson was so taken with the impressive snail that he packed a few in his bags while traveling from Mauritius to India in 1847. By the time he reached Calcutta, he had tired of the traveling companions and deposited them in the botanical gardens. Without their native predators or pathogens, the snails prospered and spread through Southern Asia. Achatina received a boost during the World War II when the island-hopping Japanese army spread them throughout the Pacific Islands as a potential food source. The ensuing American forces reported that snails on some roadways were so numerous that their crushed bodies became a slippery hazard. To complete the folly, the carnivorous snail *Euglandina rosea* was introduced to control the African snail. It prodigiously multiplied consuming not only the other introduced snail, but also every native snail. Every wild tree snail on Moorea is now extinct and on nearby Tahiti, the pattern is being repeated. In Hawaii, 22 snails are extinct and 19 are endangered.

Photo: AP/Wide World Photos

Mongoose
(Herpestes nyula)
Length: 14–26 inches
Weight: 3–5.5 pounds
Origin: India and Nepal
Diseases: Weil's Disease (infectious jaundice), trichinosis, rabies

By the year 1660, the first sugar cane fields began to spread across Jamaica. For the black rat (*Rattus rattus*), which had long before arrived on the earliest European sailing vessels, it was boom time. Over the next century, the plantations would change the face of the island, and the rats would have an endless resource, which allowed them to multiply to such a degree as to diminish the annual harvest by one fifth. Not that the rats eat all the cane, but rather they nibble the stalks and thus allow fungi to invade and ferment, ruining the entire plant.

Colonial planters searched for a biological control for rats and after disappointing performances of introduced voracious ants and marine toads a desperate plantation owner, W.B. Espeut, turned to India's efficient pint-sized predator: the mongoose. After an impressive start in the fields, more mongoose were introduced and spread throughout the Caribbean (and in Hawaii in 1883). Soon an error in judgment became clear: while rats are nocturnal, the mongoose is a diurnal species. They are also not selective eaters and after taking a heavy toll on local birds, reptiles, insects and even land crabs, they turned to domestic livestock from poultry to piglets.

The mongoose has proved to be a dazzlingly prolific and successful predator, virtually exterminating numerous birds and lizards wherever it has gotten a foothold. Meanwhile, in Jamaica the rats have become more numerous than ever and on many West Indian Islands, they ruin 25% of the sugar crop. Today, six islands offer mongoose bounties.

Sea Lamprey
(Petromyzon marinus)
Length: Sea-run adults measure one yard; land-locked adults are smaller
Range: South of Greenland to North Florida (Great Lakes)
Habitat: Coastal; spawns in rivers and streams; some freshwater populations exist

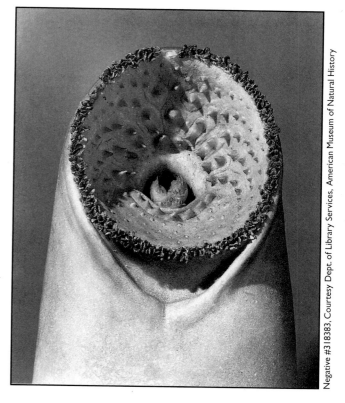

Negative #318383, Courtesy Dept. of Library Services, American Museum of Natural History

In 1921, the Welland Ship Canal completed the long desired by-pass to Niagara Falls. Ships were not the only things to take advantage of this historic new passage to the Great Lakes: the sea lamprey also negotiated the pathway. A parasitic, jawless fish with a slender, eel-like body, the sea lamprey feeds by attaching itself to other fish with its muscular, funnel-like oral disk which is armed with numerous rasping teeth. Once clinging to a host, they gorge themselves on its blood and body fluids. Later, the vampire-like lamprey drops off the host, which often dies from the attack directly or later succumbs to secondary bacterial or fungal parasites that exploit the open wound.

Once able to invade Lake Erie and spread through the remainder of the Great Lakes chain, the sea lamprey caused a drastic population reduction of lake whitefish, suckers and especially lake trout. Confronted with this biological catastrophe, which had serious economic repercussions, the U.S. Fish and Wildlife Service developed a powerful selective poison (3,4,6,-trichloro-2-nitrophenol) known as Dowlap, which showed no adverse effect on other wildlife, but destroyed sea lamprey larvae. By 1962, the lamprey has been reduced to 20% of its peak population. The tenacious lamprey continues to be a problem, but no longer threatens the total collapse of the Great Lakes fishery.

Climbers destroying nests and larvae of gypsy moths.

Gypsy Moth (*Lymantria dispar*)

Length: Larva measure one inch and adults 1.5 inches
Life Cycle: In winter, egg stage; eggs hatch in April; pupae form in midsummer; adult moths emerge in July or August

One of the most destructive introduced species in North America, the gypsy moth continues to expand its range. During periodic population eruptions, in which it appears to rain caterpillars and the sound of their eating is audible, forested areas can become so defoliated as to appear to be experiencing a second winter. Tree mortality may result if moth populations remain high for several successive summers. Vegetarian composition in the forests of the Ozark and Appalachian mountains have changed to reflect a dominance of trees with gypsy moth resistance. While oaks and aspen trees are the most common hosts for the pests, they are known to feed on the foliage of hundreds of species.

The gypsy moth came to North America from Europe because it was mistakenly believed to have some potential for silk production. In the late 1860s, it was actually introduced by E. Leopold Trouvelot near Boston. The moth spread so quickly that by 1890, state and federal agencies had already tried and failed several times to eradicate the pest. Biologists remain baffled by the timing and location of the Lymantria population explosions, despite over 100 years of careful observation and records. In recent years, viral and fungal plagues have managed to keep the gypsy moth in check.

Giant Toad (*Bufo marinus*)

AKA: Cane toad, marine toad, bufo toad
Home Territory: American Southwest to Amazon Basin
Area of Contamination: Australia, New Zealand, the Caribbean, Florida

This giant, warty species of toad has been purposely introduced throughout the world with similar bad results, but none as bad as in Australia. In 1935, the toads were brought "down under" and disaster followed. They were shipped in to fight insect pests that were devouring sugar cane crops. Now, the toads live throughout Australia. The pest insects were not affected by the presence of these noxious toads. However, everything from cats and dogs to small children have been adversely affected. When eaten or touched, the cane toads release a toxic secretion that can kill dogs, cats and the native population of reptiles that attempt to eat the toad. Human babies who come into contact with the toads on lawns have been hospitalized after merely touching the beastly amphibians.

In Australia, squads of toad eradicators roam the suburbs and cities at night with flashlights and clubs to try to put a dent into the poison toad population. But all in vain. Female giant toads can lay 30,000 eggs compared to Australian toads whose yearly egg count is in the hundreds. And cane toads live long lives—sometimes 20 years. Residents of Florida, Jamaica, and a host of other unfortunate sites, if they have not already seen the giant toad, will recognize its springtime mating call, the noise of a faraway tractor.

Starling (*Sturnus vulgaris*)

Negative #286757, Courtesy Dept. of Library Services, American Museum of Natural History

Prosperous New York drug manufacturer Eugene Scheifflin had two great passions: ornithology and the study of the works of William Shakespeare. As the leader of the American Acclimatization Society, Scheifflin spent a small fortune synthesizing his interests. He compiled a precise list of the names of every bird mentioned in the plays and sonnets of Shakespeare. His intention was to import and naturalize populations of each listed bird species. Unfortunately for the farmers and indigenous North American birds, the play *Henry IV, Part I* contains the line:

> *Nay, I'll have a starling shall be taught*
> *to speak nothing but 'Mortimer.'*

On March 6, 1890, Scheifflin released 40 pairs of European starlings into Central Park. He repeated this act the next year. One year later, the birds had already colonized Staten Island. By 1896, they had become a common sight in Brooklyn; New Jersey, Delaware, and Pennsylvania all hosted starling populations by the turn of the century. From New York, it took the birds 55 years to establish themselves from coast to coast all the way north to Alaska.

The starling immediately became an agricultural pest. These aggressive birds exerted sharp selective pressures on native species. Their superior strength and ferocity gave them the competitive edge in both next site selection and in limited food situations. Soon, many North American bird populations, such as the Eastern bluebird, were in serious decline. ∎

The Language of Pests

by
Shireen R.K.
Patell

*the pest, in a sense, is a very superior being to us: he knows where
to find us and how—usually in the bath, in sexual intercourse or asleep.*
—Charles Bukowski, "notes on the pest"

What exactly does the word *pest* mean? Conceived of in scientific terms, the word refers to "r-selected" species, characterized by high reproductive rates and short life-spans; in these terms, cockroaches, rats, pigeons and weeds are all pests. The "r" in r-selected stands for "rate of increase," which is determined by subtracting the death rate of a species from its birthrate. R-selected populations increase with no intrinsic environmental feedback, limited only by food availability. Because only "r" determines their population growth rate, they are said to be "r-selected." These species are extremely adaptable and able to live, indeed, thrive under the most degraded conditions. When ecosytems are disturbed, r-selected species are able to rush in and occupy any biological vacuum left in the wake of some disaster, be it man-made or natural. The biological success of these highly opportunisitc species presents a serious threat to the planet's biodiversity—the complex, highly diversified web of life that constitutes and sustains the Earth's array of ecosystems.

The word *pest* derives from the Latin *pestis* meaning "plague, pestilence, contagious disease." The pest is often a vector for disease; that is, the carrier of a pathogenic agent, which can then be transmitted to another species. The ubiquity of r-selected species makes them excellent vectors for a variety of diseases. Thus, it might be said that humans' fear and loathing of pests have legitimate scientific reasons: the threat they pose to our health as a species, and the threat they pose to the health of the planet as they undermine the biodiversity of nature. And yet, the notion of the pest is not as simple as all that. Pests cannot merely be regarded as a threat to humans and nature, as they are not conveniently located outside of us or nature. In fact, the success of the r-selected species testifies to the very persistence and adaptability of life. Their proliferation may be thought of as a kind of ecological scar tissue, marking both a past trauma and a healing.

In some ways, human beings may be the most pernicious pests of all. We invade, colonize and occupy, exploiting resources, both natural and human, for our own benefit; when an area becomes too degraded, we move on, often without picking up behind ourselves. Ironically, these behaviors may have actually contributed to the proliferation of various pests. Furthermore, our pest-control practices may eradicate one pest problem, only to bring about another, thus underscoring our ultimate inability to control nature, even as we try to dominate it. For example, *The New York Times* recently reported that Charles De Gaulle International Airport outside of Paris is overrun with rabbits, some 50,000 according

> **What is a pest for one culture, may be a delicacy for another. Whether a pest is described as a filthy free-loader or a rapacious colonizer and exploiter, the rhetoric of the pest carries with it a valuation, a moral undertone.**

to the estimate of one of the two full-time gamekeepers employed to keep the problem in check. The burrowing habits of rabbits can jeopardize the structural integrity of runways and taxiways.

Interestingly enough, the rabbits proliferated as a result of the airport's attempt to ward off two other pests: humans and birds. The airport first became a 5,000-acre rabbit field, when the pastures and farmland it had taken over were fenced in to keep out humans—humans, who are perhaps the biggest threat to rabbits: less humans, more rabbits. As for the birds, airplane collisions with birds can pose a serious problem; the airport employs 11 people whose sole job is to keep birds away from runways. In addition, electronic scarecrows are used to frighten off the birds. However, some birds are natural predators of rabbits: fewer predatory birds, more rabbits.

While in the scientific world, there may be certain criteria for determining whether a particular organism is an r-selected species or pest, in everyday parlance, the term denotes first of all an annoying person or thing—a nuisance; and only secondly, an injurious plant or animal, especially one ultimately harmful to human beings. Our ideas about what constitutes a pest are inextricably linked, even if only unconsciously, to our ideas of what constitutes us as human beings; the

PEST PROBLEM: Seven rats were caught in a single day near a playground in Indiana.

definition of a pest also becomes a way for us to define ourselves. The very language and metaphors we use to define and describe pests reveal our cultural values and anxieties. In fact, what is a pest for one culture, may be a delicacy for another.

Whether a pest is described as a filthy free-loader or a rapacious colonizer and exploiter, the rhetoric of the pest carries with it a valuation, a moral undertone. In fact, the adjectival form of the word—*pestilent*—has as one of its meanings: "morally, socially, or politically harmful." Indeed, throughout history there has been a certain racialization of vermin. The outcast group is often described in the very same language used to describe biological pests: unclean, exploitative, opportunistic, etc. One need only think of the anti-semitic discourse of World War II Germany, or the current rants against immigrants here in the U.S. to see how the rhetoric of the pest and that of racism are intertwined. That this confluence exists does not mean that biological pests do not pose real threats to biodiversity, health or the quality of human life, nor that the scientific definition of pests causes racism. Rather, racist appropriations of the figure of the pest reveal how social beliefs try to ground and legitimate themselves through identification with the natural world.

Yet, true to their adaptable, prolific nature, pests also appear in positive guises. Just as pest-control efforts have sometimes had unintended harmful consequences, pests have sometimes provided ironic benefits or have perversely been signs of life. Take, for example, the case of the shipworm: 600 million years old, this sightless creature, which can grow up to 12 feet long, feasts on wood. The shipworm bores into the wood pilings of piers, literally eating away their stability. Due to the extreme pollution in New York's harbor, the shipworm had largely disappeared from the Hudson by the end of the 1940s (as did most of the other marine life). But in the wake of the Clean Water Act of 1972, the shipworm resurged, one of the first indications of the renewed health of the Hudson (but bad news for the piers). Incidentally, the shipworm is a culinary treat in New Guinea.

In a more extreme example of the perversely beneficial side-effects of pests, in 1919, the citizens of Enterprise, Alabama actually erected a monument to the boll weevil, the scourge of their cotton-fields. The devastation wrought by the pest had demonstrated the precariousness of economic dependence on one crop, thereby leading to the diversification of agriculture, and the improvement of the state's fiscal health.

In the figurative realm, too, the image of the pest can take on positive connotations as a figure for the call of conscience. In the precincts of injustice, when there is a sense that something is just not right...there is something bugging you, plaguing you, eating at you. In Plato's *Apology*, standing before his accusers, Socrates presents himself as a gadfly given by the gods to the large, lumbering ox that is Athens in order to prick it into action, to stir it to life.

The mutability of the pest, both in its biological adaptability and its linguistic elasticity, reveals how the meaning of the pest is relational and dynamic. Much as we might like to banish pests, they are a part of nature; they are not zoned safely outside of us. In fact, the language we use to describe the pest may produce it in an image of ourselves which we would rather disavow. ∎

> **Human beings may be the most pernicious pests of all. We invade, colonize and occupy, exploiting resources for our own benefit; when an area becomes too degraded, we move on, often without picking up behind ourselves.**

> **Throughout history there has been a certain racialization of vermin. The outcast group is often described in the very same language used to describe biological pests: unclean, exploitative, opportunistic, etc. One need only think of the anti-semitic discourse of World War II Germany, or the current rants against immigrants here in the U.S.**

Shireen R.K. Patell is finishing her Ph.D. dissertation on the ethics of interpretation for the Department of Comparative Literature at the University of California, Berkeley. She lives in New York City.

The Mania for Native Plants in Nazi Germany

by
Joachim
Wolschke-
Bulmahn

"Native" plants are in vogue in the 1990s. To make reference to the words *nature* and *native* often means to claim authority, or as has been stated recently in the *Landscape Journal*: "The most blatant search for authority in landscape architecture now seems to be the native plant mystique." The doctrinaire plea for "native" plants is often accompanied by the condemnation of "foreign" or "exotic plants" as alien invaders or aggressive intruders, thus suggesting that native plants would be peaceful and non-invasive. Hundreds of publications give evidence of this biased viewpoint. In the article "Wildflowers: The Case for Native Plants," for example, it is stated that some non-native naturalized wildflower species in the U.S. exhibit "aggressive, weedy behavior." Characterizations such as "invasive exotic weeds," "non-indigenous invasive weeds," "exotic species invasions" and "foreign invaders" are common in relevant publications.

Many are concerned about our natural environment, but the certainty and missionary zeal with which so-called foreign plants are condemned as aggressive is significant. Such characterizations do not contribute to a rational discussion about the future development of our natural and cultural environment, but possibly promote xenophobia.

First, to elaborate on the vagueness of the term "native plants," it is remarkable that many who refer to "native" plants do not offer an unequivocal definition. When definitions are offered, they range from local to continental dimensions. In the article "Wildflowers: The Case for Native Plants," it is conceded that there "is some disagreement on the definition of native plants among botanists and ecologists. Most plants are native to a certain region, usually encompassing many states."

In Rodale's 1992 *All-New Encyclopedia of Organic Gardening*, under the heading "Natural Landscaping Styles," one can read that "most people use their state boundaries as cut-off points for plant selection. Others consider any plant native to North America to be acceptable." A wildflower garden is defined as "a place where plants native to the United States are arranged in pleasing design and grown under conditions to support their natural state." The idea of using only plants representative of a particular state or county, and the definition of *native* as belonging to a politically-defined space, may be an interesting garden motif, but it has nothing to do with nature and nativeness. From local to regional, from state to national and continental, one can find a variety of totally different categories to which the term "native plants" has been related. Considering the confusion among native plant advocates about the definition of the term, the ignorance with which they often criticize the millions of gardeners who are not willing to follow their vague and unclear use of the term "native plants" is remarkable.

Another major problem with the definition of what constitutes a

The native plants ideology is highly political; its advocates sometimes connect nationalistic and racist ideas about society with the call for "native" plants.

Photo: J.Wolschke-Bulmahn

Hitler with Alwin Seifert, the landscape architect in Germany who argued "nothing foreign should be added to the plant life."

native plant is the unclear dimension of time and history. In the U.S., for example, do we define a plant as native that is assumed to have been in a region before European settlement or, in some cases, even exploration? Or do we ask if Native Americans brought plants with them when they crossed the land bridge from Siberia? Some argue a "native" plant in the U.S. would be one that had been in a region before the arrival of European immigrants.

There is also the problem of time as a determining factor. Are we dealing with the past 100, 500, or 1,000 years? Since the 16th century, more than 2,500 species of tree and shrubs have been introduced to Central Europe. There was a much broader variety of plants in Germany before the last glacial period. Because of the Ice Age, many of these plant forms were extinguished and later, when the climate changed again, they could not make their way back because of the Alps. Many of those plants are considered today to be natives of North America or Asia, and they are cultivated as so-called exotics in German gardens. Yet, originally, they were natives. If one accepts an interpretation of nativeness that is not limited to recent history, then the answer to the question of whether we shall restore native plant communities in our landscapes could, with regard to Germany, also be the systematic reintroduction of species that were displaced by nature thousands of years ago.

The native plants ideology is highly political; its advocates sometimes connect nationalistic and racist ideas about society with the call for native plants. Alwin Seifert, a leading landscape architect in Germany during the Nazi period, was the most radical promoter of native plants. He claimed that German landscape architects had to respect the poverty of species of the German landscapes as destiny. In the landscape, Seifert argued, nothing foreign should be added and "nothing native must be left out."

In early 20th century Germany an increasing nationalism found its expression in garden and landscape design. The natural garden was seen by many landscape architects as the truly German garden; exotic plants were rejected. During the Nazi era, the exclusive use of native plants in the landscape became the landscape architecture swastika. Alwin Seifert introduced the criterion of nativeness—of being rooted in the soil—into garden and landscape design. In 1930, he stated his ideas about natural garden and landscape design as follows: "I wanted to bring garden art into the struggle of all living spaces which has broken out in our days between 'rootedness in the soil' and 'supra-nationality.'" According to Seifert, this struggle was "a fight between two opposing world views: on one side the striving for supranationality, for equalization of huge areas, and on the other the elaboration of peculiarities of small living spaces, the emphasis which is rooted in the soil." In 1933, immediately after the takeover by the Nazi regime, Seifert wanted to "ban all that until now has pleased the heart of a gardener: everything high-bred, overfed, conspicuous, foreign, everything that just is unable to establish intimate bounds with the flora of our garden, which has been apportioned by nature."

In 1941, German landscape architects started work on a so-called Reich Landscape Law that would forbid the use of foreign plants in German landscapes. This law could not be passed because of the fall of the Nazi regime. In 1942, a team of German botanists called for a war of extermination against *Impatiens parviflora*, a small forest plant that was seen as a stranger, competing with *Impatiens noli tangere*, considered a native. Regarding the extermination of *Impatiens parviflora*, the botanists applied an analogy from society to nature: "As with the fight against Bolshevism, our entire occidental culture is at stake, so with the fight against this Mongolian invader, an essential element of this culture, namely, the beauty of our home forest is at stake."

It has seldom been noted that similar tendencies toward racist argumentation for the exclusive use of native plants can be found in America. A prime example is the writing of the American landscape architect Jens Jensen, a contemporary of Alwin Seifert. The following quote from Jensen's 1937 article "The Clearing" is illustrative of how racism was

Do we ask if Native Americans brought plants with them when they crossed the land bridge from Siberia? Some argue a "native" plant in the U.S. would be one that had been in a region years ago, before the arrival of European immigrants.

Photo: J. Wolschke-Bulmahn

American landscaping architect Jens Jensen, who had close ties to the Nazis, was an advocate of ridding American gardens of "foreign plants," particularly of "Latin" or "Oriental" origin (1937).

an important motif in his plea for native plants: "The gardens that I create myself shall...be in harmony with their landscape environment and the racial characteristics of its inhabitants. They shall express the spirit of America and therefore shall be free of foreign character as far as possible. The Latin and the Oriental crept and creeps more and more over our land, coming from the South, which is settled by Latin people, and also from other centers of mixed masses of immigrants. The Germanic character of our race, of our cities and settlements was overgrown by foreign character. Latin spirit has spoiled a lot and still spoils things every day." Such ideas about the alleged negative influence of so-called "Latin people" were more than welcome in Nazi Germany.

Jensen had close connections to Nazi landscape architects. During the Nazi period, he published articles in the German magazine *Gartenkunst (Garden Art)*. The above quotation is taken from this magazine. His publications confirm racism as an underlying motive for his plea for the exclusive use of native plants. In a personal letter to Jensen in 1936, Michael Mappes, the editor of *Gartenkunst*, commented on Jensen's garden design for his home in Wisconsin. Mappes stated that he and a number of German garden designers would strive for similar ideals as a "result of the spiritual change with the take-over of Adolf Hitler." In another letter, Mappes congratulated Jensen on his lecture presented at a horticultural congress in Berlin in 1938. According to Mappes, the lecture reflected Jensen's "truly Nordic fundamental attitude, appropriate also to our park and garden design based on German character." In this lecture, Jensen stated: "The Nordic, or if you please, Germanic, mind is not imbued with formalism of any kind. To him it is an affected thing. It does not speak the truth and the truth should be told by an intellectual people. To him it is foreign." Jensen's nationalism, racism and close connections to Nazi landscape architects have been ignored among garden historians in the U.S.

Today, there are good reasons for using so-called native plants in gardens, including low maintenance, adaptation to place, preservation of plants and wildlife from extinction, and aesthetics. Advocacy of the use of "native" plants may be a moral response to some of the many environmental problems we have all over the earth. However, there is no reason for a native plant doctrine, nor for the assumption that so-called native plants would serve environmental goals. The segregation into good and bad plants, natives and non-natives, and the condemnation of the latter as aggressive invaders is too simplistic and helps to mask problems rather than engage them.

Sometimes one finds frightening evidence that ideas about the alleged relationship between a people, plants and the soil as found in the Nazi-Blood-and-Soil ideology, seem to flourish in today's discussion of so-called native plants. Thus, it is stated in the book *Landscaping with Native Plants of Texas and the Southwest*: "Plants are a part of our great national heritage. The plants that have sunk their roots in Southwest soil since the last Ice Age can help us understand that our psyches and society are equally rooted to the earth."

The Jewish writer Rudolf Borchardt, who was persecuted by the Nazis, offered an important criticism of doctrinaire advocates of native plant use that is still relevant today. He wrote in 1938: "If this kind of garden-owning barbarian became the rule, then neither a gillyflower nor a rosemary, neither a peach-tree nor a myrtle sapling nor a tea-rose would ever have crossed the Alps. Gardens connect people, time and latitudes. If these barbarians ruled, the great historic process of acclimatization would never have begun and today we would horticulturally still subsist on acorns....The garden of humanity is a huge democracy. It is not the only democracy which such clumsy advocates threaten to dehumanize." ∎

Joachim Wolschke-Bulmahn is Director of Studies in Landscape Architecture at Dunbarton Oaks/Trustees for Harvard University in Washington, D.C.

The missionary zeal with which so-called foreign plants are condemned as aggressive is significant. Such characterizations do not contribute to a rational discussion about the future development of our natural and cultural environment, but possibly promote xenophobia.

Tree of Heaven

by
Mark
Dion

Growing through the cracks in the pavement, rising up through subway grates, and even sprouting from rooftops, the *Ailanthus altissima*, or "tree of heaven," is the most conspicuous example of urban flora. The tree thrives in waste zones: vacant lots, highway medians, alleyways, industrial fringes and other disturbed sites. Ailanthus seedlings develop thick, ropy roots, which can thrive in concrete and rubble, growing as much as 5 feet per season. In a few years, the tree can reach a height of 20 feet. A mature ailanthus can obtain a height of over 90 feet. Toxic soil, noxious air, insects and dust, which constrain the growth and spread of many plants, seem to have little effect on the ailanthus.

The tenacity of the ailanthus is so well-esteemed that author Betty Smith made it her chief symbol of inner-city survival in the 1943 novel *A Tree Grows in Brooklyn*: "No matter where its seed fell, it made a tree which struggled to reach the sky. It grew in boarded-up lots and out of neglected rubbish heaps and it was the only tree that grew out of cement."

The ailanthus is a native of China and was imported to England as both an ornamental plant and as a food source for silkworms as early as the 1750s. It first made its appearance in the new world in 1784. Perhaps its modern naturalization to American soil could be considered a reintroduction, since the fossil record clearly demonstrates that the ailanthus flourished in western North America before the last ice age (from 70 to 100 million years ago). Its predominance in New York's urban core is most likely attributed to its introduction into Central Park by Frederick Law Olmsted. He was greatly impressed by its exotic, tropical appearance and vitality.

In many parts of various cities, particularly in low-income neighborhoods, the ailanthus may be the sole provider of natural shade and green. However,

ALIEN FLORA

species: Tree of Heaven
(Ailanthus altissima)

location: West Canal street,
New York City

date: 7/28/96

Mark Dion

Specimen collected by Mark Dion

the tree of heaven has many drawbacks. The male plant produces such a disagreeable odor that a law was passed in 1875 making it illegal to harbor the tree in the District of Columbia. The tree's smell has earned it the name "stink ash" over much of its range. Its pollen may produce hayfever-like symptoms in those who suffer from allergies. The thick, yellow roots of the ailanthus are poisonous and have fouled springs and wells.

Perhaps the most pernicious aspect of the ailanthus is that as an invasive species, with superior dispersal and a high reproduction rate, the plant flourishes at the expense of other plant species. The ailanthus has the ability to rush in and colonize disrupted spaces, out-competing slower shrubs and trees. Thus, the ailanthus is responsible for the impoverishment of biological diversity.

The resilient ailanthus makes the most of a crack in the sidewalk.

Photo: Bob Braine

While many consider the ailanthus a noxious, vermin weed, in some areas of the world it is a commonly planted decorative tree, aiding in erosion control, watershed protection and temperature regulation.

In the city of New York, the ailanthus has recently become the victim of a mysterious species-specific epidemic. Hundreds of trees have fallen to a withering disease which peels away the bark and allows for opportunistic insect and fungi invasions. The deaths may be the result of a fungi or could be related to the last decade's decreased rainfall. An emergency investigation into the cause of the tree of heaven's plague has been initiated by the State Department of Environmental Conservation.

For some, the ailanthus blight represents an opportunity to reestablish native oaks, white pine, and other tree species considered more desirable. However, in many waste zones and urban fringes with vastly reduced city budgets, the native plants will not be replanted, nor would they be likely to withstand the harsh, urban conditions. In some untended areas, the tree has all but eliminated other plants and now that it is on the decline, there are no wild plant stocks to fill the gaps left by dead ailanthus. Now that it faces a significant threat, the ailanthus, so long considered a scourge, may have at last gained some appreciation. ∎

This article is largely indebted to Reiko Goto's and Tim Collins's installation along the Brooklyn Waterfront produced for Creative Time *in 1985.*

The male plant produces such a disagreeable odor that a law was passed in 1875 making it illegal to harbor the tree in the District of Columbia. The tree's smell has earned it the name "stink ash" over much of its range.

Lake Victoria Cichlids

by
Dr. Melanie L.J.
Stiassny

Not long ago, I was asked to give a talk in a public education series on the biodiversity crisis. The series was entitled "The Decline of Life on Earth," and my paper was to address the question from the perspective of a tropical freshwater biologist. As I prepared my talk, it occurred to me that the title of the series "The Decline of Life on Earth," although powerful, reinforced a common misconception. Are we really witnessing a decline of life on earth?

My guess would be that in terms of the mass living material (technically the planet's biomass), the last 150 years has actually seen a net increase. Our species entered the industrial age with a population of one billion, and today has exploded to over 5 billion and rising. Also increasing is the biomass of the crops we sow to support our population, and the animals we have selected for domestication and consumption. It is a sobering thought that throughout human history a total of only 7,000 kinds of plants have been grown and collected for food. Of these, 20 species supply 90% of the world's food, and today just three—wheat, maize, and rice—supply more than half. In other words, life (biomass) is burgeoning. What is in precipitous decline is diversity and it is the effects of this cascading loss of biodiversity that are the real crises we face.

As terrestrial animals, we often overlook the situation in non-terrestrial habitats, yet the world's waterways, which are critically important, are highly threatened. More than 75% of the earth's surface is covered with water, and 97% of that is ocean. Only a tiny percentage, less than 0.01%, is freshwater (the remainder is ice and groundwater). Yet this tiny percentage holds a tremendous diversity of life. Of the 20,000+ species of fishes described so far by scientists, (and many more remain to be discovered), 40% live in freshwater. In other words, almost half of the fish biodiversity is contained within a very vulnerable 0.01% of the earth's water. The freshwater rivers and lakes of the planet are like inverted islands, isolated and surrounded by land and, just like other islands, these aquatic refuges are among the most fragile of habitats.

My specialty is tropical freshwater ichthyology and, in particular, one very important family, the Cichlidae. I have the dubious distinction of being an expert on a group of vertebrates that has undergone one of the most dramatic human-induced extinctions in recorded history. Before I document the devastation, let me give you a very brief background of these extraordinary fish. The Cichlidae is a large family of tropical spiny-rayed fish that occur naturally in fresh waters throughout the Neotropics, Africa, Madagascar, southern India and Sri Lanka. Most species are rather small, growing to only about 20 cm, but a significant number are considerably larger and some reach almost a meter in length. Their importance as a source of protein in the tropical world cannot be overemphasized, and they are a crucial resource, both as natural populations

As recently as 1970, Lake Victoria was home to a flock of over 300 cichlid species. These cichlids comprised more than 99% of the lake's fish species and were a food resource upon which 8 million human lives in Kenya, Uganda and Tanzania depended. Today that species flock is devastated, and cichlids now compromise less than 1% of the biomass.

and as subjects of fish aquaculture. Cichlids are also the subject of intensive study by evolutionary biologists, partly because of the situation found in the Great Lakes of Africa. These lakes are real "hot spots" of aquatic biodiversity. Each of the three largest lakes, Victoria, Malawi and Tanganyika, harbors its own huge flock of cichlid species, a staggering number to have evolved, and now coexist, in one lake basin. The cichlid species flocks of Africa are one of the biological wonders of the world and are natural laboratories of evolution.

The youngest of the lakes, and the one with the youngest cichlid flocks, is Lake Victoria. As recently as 1970, Lake Victoria was home to a flock of over 300 cichlid species. These cichlids comprised more than 99% of the lake's fish species and were a food resource upon which 8 million human lives in Kenya, Uganda and Tanzania depended. Today, that species flock is devastated, and cichlids now comprise less than 1% of the biomass. More than half of the described species are extinct or have population sizes so small that the chances of recovery are minimal. This is truly a mass extinction, and its causes are complex, but I will try to summarize what has happened.

The first major impact on the Victoria ecosystem occurred in the early 1920s with the introduction of a modern gill-net fishery. Overfishing soon reduced the volume of cichlids caught and other species were introduced into the lake to supplement catches. Among those introduced was the Nile perch *(Lates niloticus)*, a voracious predator that in its native Nile waters can reach nearly 2 meters and 300 kilograms. At first, the Nile perch constituted less than 2% of fish landings and was actually disliked by the local fisherman as it destroyed their nets. Also, unlike the cichlid, which readily dry in the sun, the Nile perch has an oily flesh requiring precious firewood for its preparation.

Throughout the 1970s, Nile perch populations grew and at the same time a trawl fishery was introduced into the lake to harvest the smaller cichlids. The 1980s saw an explosion of Nile perch populations, a 10,000-fold decrease in the abundance of cichlids, and an abrupt disappearance of about half of the cichlid species. Local fisherman could no longer afford to spurn the perch and a massive, new fishery was born. Today, the Nile perch is heavily exploited in Lake Victoria and the fishermen's landings are the starting points for caravans of refrigerator trucks that lumber each day over newly-paved roads to inland fish markets

Coulter et al. 1986, Environmental Biology of Fishes Vol. 17(3):161-183, Fig. 7.

THE EFFECT OF NILE PERCH INTRODUCTIONS INTO LAKE VICTORIA: Cichlids are abundant initially, but become scarce after exponential growth of Nile perch populations (top). The changes in fishing methods from the capture and sun drying of small fish to the more cumbersome handling of Nile perch and the need in some areas to smoke-cure these large fishes (middle and bottom).

bearing tons of Nile perch. In terms of increased biomass, the introduction of the Nile perch into Lake Victoria is a success. Certainly, for the time being more Nile perch are being harvested than was ever the case for native cichlids. But at what price and for how long?

Until very recently, Lake Victoria had oxygenated waters throughout the water column. During the long rainy season, oxygen levels dropped off steeply below 50 meters, but enough oxygen remained to support a thriving deep-water cichlid community. By 1990, this was no longer true and now the lake appears to be permanently stratified, with oxygenated waters at only the 25-meter level for most the year. Much of the lake is no longer able to support aerobic life. The causes of this profound change are complex and the jury is still out on a final answer, but one thing is clear: by disrupting the balanced biotic ecosystem of Lake Victoria, a complex series of changes in the physical properties of the lake have been triggered.

At the moment, the Nile perch populations are burgeoning, but this is only possible because of a sequence of unexpected events. One other Lake Victoria fish has also flourished in the new lake regime; this is a small sardine-like species *Rastrinobola*. These lake sardines live in huge shoals just above the deoxygenated water, but they frequently get trapped and suffocate. Their bodies become a new food source for a small lake shrimp *Caridina*. By chance, the lake shrimp is able to tolerate very low oxygen levels and appears to be thriving in the now deoxygenated waters of the lake while feeding on dead lake sardines. The Nile perch, after depleting the cichlids as its food source, has now turned to feeding on the lake shrimp. Whether *Caridina* will be able to support the Nile perch populations is an open question. But at least for the time being, the lake has seen an increase in biomass, but at a terrible cost to biodiversity—a microcosm of the global trend I outlined earlier.

The need to maintain maximum biodiversity is surely greatest as rates of environmental change increase—diversity in genes and species provides the raw material for systems to adapt to change. The loss of each additional species reduces the options for nature to respond to changing conditions. If *Caridina* cannot carry the perch populations, very soon there will be no alternatives left and Lake Victoria itself may "die." I hope it is not too late to do much about Victoria, but at the very least there is an opportunity here to extend our understanding of the extinction dynamics of tropical freshwater systems. It is imperative that the lessons drawn from this biodiversity disaster be carried to other freshwater systems throughout the globe. ∎

> **Throughout human history a total of only 7,000 kinds of plants have been grown and collected for food. Of these, 20 species supply 90% of the world's food, and today just three—wheat, maize, and rice—supply more than half. In other words, what is in precipitous decline is diversity and it is the effects of this cascading loss of biodiversity that are the real crises we face.**

Originally presented at the Friends' Third Annual Environmental Lecture and Luncheon. Melanie L. J. Stiassny, Ph.D. is Associate Curator of Ichthyology at the American Museum of Natural History, specializing in cichlid species distribution.

The Himalayan Blackberry (*Rubus armenioncus*)

by
Holly
Reinhorn

It is difficult to imagine the Pacific Northwest landscape without the Himalayan blackberry. It grows along freeways, creeps up the sides of abandoned barns, traverses creeks with a mass of thick, thorny canes. In spring, its dense, white flowers are in bloom throughout the country-side and in summer, its famous wild berries are sold at countless roadside stands.

Yet despite its rustic appearance and gastronomic benefits, the Himalayan blackberry poses a serious environmental threat. Classified by local botanists and plant pathologists as the most "aggressive biological success story in the region," the Himalayan blackberry is thought to have choked out more native vegetation and subsumed more acreage in the last century than any introduced plant west of the Cascades.

Roots: While both the origin of the Himalayan blackberry genus and the history of its cultivation are somewhat confused, the most common accounts trace its discovery to an anonymous group of German explorers on expedition in Armenia and Iran in the mid-1800s. These explorers found the plant growing wild in the Caucasus Mountains and, presumably after eating the berries, decided to bring it back home for scientific study.

Other theories hypothesize that the plant may have reached Europe by accidental cross-pollination, its seeds and flowerheads trapped in the wool of Eastern European sheep, herded across the continent and sold by migrant livestock traders along the Rhine River. The next historical mention of the Himalayan is in 1899, when it was formally introduced to German gardening society by well-known European horticulturist Theodor Reimers of Hamburg. Reimers, who eventually named the plant after himself is said to have cultivated many hybrids in his famous walled garden, where the plant adapted exceedingly well to the mild climate and heavy rainfall of the region and within a short time had escaped the confines of the garden and spread throughout the Rhine River valley into Western Europe and Scandinavia.

The next leg of the journey was at the turn of the century when the Himalayan is reported to have arrived in America, roughly 20 years after the introduction of its cousin, the evergreen blackberry or *Rubus lacineatus*. The evergreen blackberry, which some believe followed a similar introduction pattern to the Himalayan in Europe, is thought to have arrived in the Pacific Northwest trapped in packing materials or in the hair and hooves of animals on early 19th-century trading ships. Bolstered by the warm, wet climate and an environment that was virtually competitor-free, the evergreen had already established itself throughout Oregon and Washington by 1901 when the Himalayan blackberry was officially introduced in Northern California and christened "The Himalaya Giant" by horticulturist Luther Burbank. Burbank, who

The proliferation of the Himalayan blackberry compromises all native plant conservation efforts. It is impossible to kill or control due to tips or canes which take root and spread at lightning speed. It sprouts wherever there is disturbed ground and survives equally well in urban, rural and natural environments.

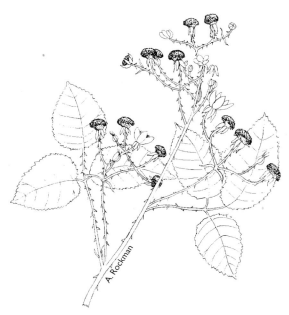

The Himalayan blackberry.

claimed that the Giant was descended from "original seed obtained in the Himalaya Mountains," planted it in *his* garden as well, where it made another nefarious escape up the Columbia River into Oregon, Washington and British Columbia and where, without any native pathogens to stand in its way, it has currently outcompeted its cousin the evergreen blackberry by 10 to 1.

Profile of a Killer: The proliferation of the Himalayan blackberry compromises all native plant conservation efforts. Impossible to kill or control due to tips or canes which take root and spread at lightning speed, it sprouts wherever there is disturbed ground and survives equally well in urban, rural and natural environments. Over time, its spiraling, thorny canes, which can cover up to 20 square feet per year, create impenetrable walls of bramble, subsuming gardens, fence rows, hillsides, commercial crops, agricultural machinery, and vacant lots resulting in a steady increase of unusable land. The plant's spread is also aided by a variety of different birds, among them the starling (another introduced species), which consumes the berries and excrete the seeds, dispersing them over hundreds of miles. At the edges of streams and lakes, the Himalayan remains a constant threat to regional biodiversity, choking out riparium vegetation near the water's edge and competing with and limiting the growth of trees and other woody species which provide large-scale sedimentation, shading and proper spawning environments for fish. It is also a hazard in urban zones where its thick, uneven growth near the edge of roads creates extreme visibility problems for residential drivers and where harvested berries can retain high levels of toxicity from the days of leaded gasolines. Injuries and fatalities also occur along the shoulders of freeways where people who have pulled over to pick berries can get hit by cars and/or fall over hillside guardrails into deep, thorn-filled thickets.

The Two Faces of Eve: Unlike other bio-invaders in the Pacific Northwest that have necessitated state-funded removal programs (such as the purple loostrife which destroys wetlands or European dune grass compromising both sand distribution and several bird species on the Oregon Coast), the Himalayan blackberry is difficult to classify because its environmental impact has not been entirely negative. It provides habitat and food to wildlife and humans have depended on its berry yields for nearly a century. The Himalayan is also closely related to other commercial cane crops, making herbicidal assaults impossible without also compromising raspberry, marionberry and boysenberry harvests.

Several popular methods of removal which have had limited private success over the long term include Cross-Bow and Round-Up herbicides, industrial power mowers and, in several cases, domestic goats, but in most situations where the Himalayan blackberry has a foothold, little can be done to remove it short of clearcutting an infested area and unearthing the extensive root systems by bulldozer.

Brave New World: Because the Himalayan blackberry has entrenched itself beyond what could ever be brought under control, the Oregon Department of Agriculture has not placed it on the state's newly established Noxious Weed Registry or adopted any official biocontrol initiative. The region has become a world-renowned infestation study-site which provides plant ecologists from such diverse points as Chile and Australia the opportunity to institute preliminary controls in their home countries against the aggressive assault of the Himalayan blackberry which continues its spread on five continents. ∎

Unlike other bio-invaders in the Pacific Northwest that have necessitated state-funded removal programs, the Himalayan Blackberry is difficult to classify because its environmental impact has not been entirely negative. It provides habitat and food to wildlife and humans have depended on its berry yields for nearly a century.

Holly Reinhorn writes fiction and currently attends the Iowa Writers Workshop. She is a recipient of the 1996 Tobias Wolff Award for Fiction.

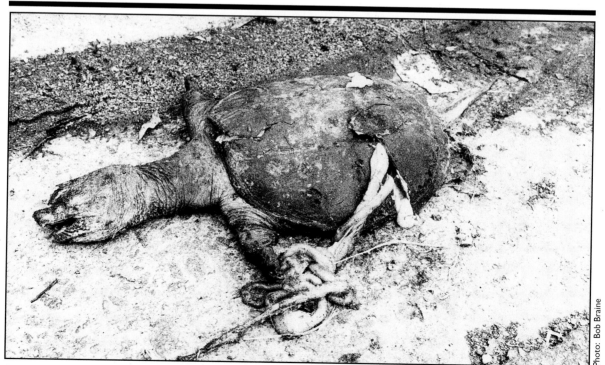

SNAPPING TURTLE, SNAPPED: With exceedingly long life spans, the predatory snapping turtle can accumulate poison chemicals such as pesticides in its fatty tissues. In some areas, when the turtle dies it must be treated with toxic waste protocols.

Photo: Bob Braine

chapter 3
Cats and Dogs

Dog Jobs

Pick up any encyclopedia of dogs and read the various breed descriptions, especially the "uses." You may notice that the majority of pure-bred dogs have been, so to speak, reassigned to desk jobs. They are living museum pieces.

For instance, no breed formerly employed to hunt other large predators is relevant today. Nearly all large predators except man have become rare or extinct. These anachronistic dog breeds survive in a sort of zoo-at-large in which they are trotted out by lumbering handlers so a kennel club judge can determine their cosmetic fitness for an ersatz job.

The Irish wolfhound is a classic example. Having aided the successful human campaign to exterminate the European wolf, it became virtually extinct itself. Later it was artificially "reconstructed" using outcrosses to other breeds, but the resulting large mutt was a wolfhound look-alike that had never hunted the wolf and never would. Now, like other coursing hounds that once pursued wolves, elk, and gazelles, it chases captive-like released jackrabbits and mechanical lures.

Or take the Rhodesian ridgeback. Bred to hunt African lions, it is more likely seen today stretched out next to the Barcalounger. The closest it comes to a lion is the electronic glow of a TV nature show about the Serengeti plain.

Dog breeding has become nothing more than an animal antique business in which the antiques are copies. Herding dogs (replaced by barbed-wire and jeeps), hunting dogs (replaced by the scope and rifle), sled dogs (replaced by the snowmobile) and even terriers (replaced by rat poisons) are all out of work and should probably be, as the dog people say, "extinct" (a misuse of the term since a dog breed is not a species or even a subspecies).

Somehow, a few breeds did become "extinct" when they became obsolete. The dog called a turnspit once ran a treadmill that turned a roasting-spit, but the cruel practice and the breed both disappeared in the 19th century.

Other breeds that should have disappeared have not. Pit bulls and other fighting dogs constantly reproduce more of themselves to mutilate, their success probably owing to the fact that they mirror the worst in humans. These fighting dogs along with the shivering toy companion dogs are the only modern breeds that are successful in their original purpose. Otherwise, the purebred dog contributes little to human society other than job growth in the pet food and accessories industries.

What follows, then, is a brief survey of directions the breeding of useful, specialized dogs should take.

by
Gerald
Heffernon

The purebred dog contributes little to human society other than job growth in the pet food and accessories industries. In 50 years, vegetarianism will be essentially mandatory. When meat-eating inevitably becomes taboo, what will dogs eat?

Photo: Gerald Heffernon

Upright dog: a hindleg walking breed with "toddler" qualities.

Flying dog: an insectivorous gliding dog.

First of all we must face reality: in 50 years, vegetarianism will be essentially mandatory. A moral society, not to mention the Earth, simply cannot support beef ranches, hog barns and chicken farms that waste grain and cropland, destroy rainforests, erode topsoil, and consume and pollute water.

Therefore, when meat-eating inevitably becomes taboo, what will dogs eat? Do dogs actually need meat? Foxes, which can interbreed with dogs, are largely fruit and insect eaters. Bears, close relatives of the dog, are mainly vegetarian and some are entirely insectivorous.

Keeping in mind the above, as well as other social and medical needs, here are some breeds of the future:

1. Bat-like insectivorous dogs. Ideally, they would glide from tree to tree (in the manner of flying squirrels and gliding marsupials), or actually fly (like a bat). These tiny, large-eared dogs would help control flies and mosquitoes.

2. Bear-like insectivorous dogs. These large-clawed, digging dogs bred for immunity to stings and bites would help control ants, termites, cockroaches, and Africanized (killer) bees by destroying their nests.

3. Epidemic-Control dogs. Genetically engineered for antiseptic saliva, these keen-nosed, hound-like dogs would be employed at international airport checkpoints to prophylactically lick the hands and faces of disembarking passengers who exhibit telltale smells or disease-carrying characteristics humans cannot detect. The dogs would

Green dingo: a vegetarian, photosynthetic dog that excretes oxygen.

also be deployed at crowded sports or cultural events. They would be vegetarian.

4. Babysitting dogs. The answer to the prayers of two-income families, these protective, nurturing dogs would be fine-tuned to babysit young humans. They would be spot-monitored by remote camera and be capable of using communication systems to contact parents in an emergency. Young babies would be suckled; the feeding of weaned children would be via the usual post-hunt regurgitation method used by wild canids. This breed would be vegetarian.

5. Population-control dogs. Although small, child-substitute breeds with flat muzzles, big eyes and even naked skin already exist, the addition of hind-walking "toddler" breeds would further replace human children in this over-populated world. Vegetarian, of course.

6. Mental health dogs. With its particularly well-tuned empathic powers, this dog would provide ESP therapy to the mentally ill. It would have soft, clawless feet, with which to walk on the backs of human patients, providing a therapeutic massage. Another vegetarian breed.

7. Photosynthetic dogs. A further refinement of the vegetarian dog, they would convert light into energy through photosynthesis, a process associated with plants, but also observed in certain crabs and worms. The ultimate goal would be urban and space station dogs that excrete oxygen.

It is obvious that meat-eating dogs cannot persist in conjunction with huge populations without becoming a food drain or even a last resort source of food. We can avoid that unattractive scenario if we restore the human/dog symbiosis and create environmentally friendly, innovative and useful breeds of dog. Luckily, *Canis familiaris* has the broad, flexible gene pool to provide the above-mentioned services.

Dog breeders will simply have to push the canine genetic envelope. But it's been done before: a Great Dane, after all, is just a huge Chihuahua—which is why the new breeds suggested in this essay are not so unlikely. ■

Gerald Heffernon is an artist and urban naturalist who resides in Davis, California.

> It is obvious that meat-eating dogs cannot persist in conjunction with huge populations without becoming a food drain or even a last resort source of food. We can avoid that unattractive scenario if we restore the human/dog symbiosis and create environmentally friendly, innovative breeds of dog. Dog breeders will simply have to push the canine genetic envelope.

Photo: Gerald Heffernon

Frog spaniel: an insectivorous dog for ponds and other aquatic habitats.

Urban Animal Adaptation: Killing with Kindness

by
Alan M.
Beck

The urban environment is the natural climax community of developed humans. It most resembles a "detritus community" with little primary production and most of the indigenous animals surviving on dead or decaying life. The dominant primates, humans, and even their domestic, carnivorous house companions, dogs, live almost exclusively on proteins brought in dead from other communities. Dogs now depend on humans for their survival and not on the predatory adeptness inherited from their wolf ancestors. Indeed, their most crucial adaptation has been their sociality. The selection of all our domesticated species was not based on the skills of their adult ancestral species, but rather on the retention of the ancestor's *juvenile* qualities, particularly tameness, small stature and social tolerance of others. Even the retention of juvenile features has served our domestic species particularly well by increasing human nurturing behaviors.

Domestic species have been selected not to compete with their own kind, but to better serve human needs and desires, including the preference for calm temperament and smaller size. All plants and animals, including dogs, produce more offspring than is required to replace those that die. In this way, there is a larger population of individuals from which the best can be selected, while all those with a variety of genetic traits less adapted for the present situation die before adding to the gene pool. In an apparent perversity, dogs are now being punished for their ecological success. People are so dedicated to lowering the dog population, that animal shelters frequently collect healthy animals from the streets, only to be killed in shelters as strays. Interestingly, the same cultural belief system that captures and kills stray dogs and cats protects wildlife, such as deer, although they may indeed be starving. Many humane shelters will not even give an animal up for adoption to a person unless there is a person home all day and the situation is perfect; if a perfect situation is not found, the animal is put to death. Apparently dogs and cats have to be killed, lest they die—what can only be called "preventive death!"

Our all-too human trait to see the value of the individual, instead of the whole population, has given people little sympathy for the apparent cruelties of natural selection. Therefore, there is a war against the apparent over-population of dogs and for 40 years, certain groups have condemned animal breeding and made animal sterilization (spay/neuter) almost a "battle-cry" to action.

Indeed, humane shelters have made spay/neuter the "poster child" for all the evils humans can do to dogs. Humane society efforts have been so successful that there has been a decrease in the dog population for many years and now some animal shelters have to get animals from shelters in larger cities that still have at least some animals for adoption.

People are so dedicated to lowering the dog population, that animal shelters frequently collect healthy animals from the streets, only to be killed in shelters as strays.

Adding to the problem, many of the larger pet shops and their chain stores do not even buy their dogs from breeders, but instead display shelter animals, which are "for adoption," that is, sold at no profit. At first this may appear to be humane, but is it in the best interest of the dog population?

Humane society animals are often in shelters because they were not behaviorally sound and they were given to the shelters as an alternative to being put to death. This means that an increasing number of dogs getting into people's homes are coming directly from shelters or from pet shops brokering for the shelters. It is almost a certainty that this will increase the proportion of dogs that have what people consider to be behavioral problems. It appears that people have not yet noticed the ever-increasing population of behaviorists to help owners of these recycled animals.

Just as modern society has created a new niche for people who would not be otherwise able to compete, we are now doing the same to our companion animals. Selection for misfits, which now become more fit in this new morass of human values, is superimposed onto natural selection. Indeed, killing with kindness is the new selection for animals who can no longer survive in nature and will only be tolerated in urban centers, where neurotic behaviors are perceived as natural. If the dog population becomes too intolerable for people, there will be a shift to other pets, perhaps even to wildlife. That will be a sad day for dogs, wild animals, and people. ■

An embarrassing example of anthropomorphism. Alan Beck is editor of Skeptic *magazine.*

Dogs now depend on humans for their survival and not on their predatory adeptness inherited from their wolf ancestors.

Alan M. Beck is Professor of Animal Ecology and Director of the Center for Applied Ethology and Human Animal Interface at Purdue University.

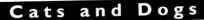

What the Cat Dragged In

Source:
Vanished Species
David Day,
London Editions,
1981

Alexis Rockman

The following story details the events responsible for the extinction of the Stephen Island wren, a bird which was simultaneously discovered and made extinct in 1894. The wren's tale appeared in the *Canterbury Press* in 1895.

"At a recent meeting of the Club in London, the Honorable Walter, the well-known collector, described this veritable *rara avis*, specimens of which he had obtained from Mr. Henry Travers of Wellington, who, we understand, got them from the light-house keeper at Stephen Island (a one-square mile island off the northern tip of New Zealand's South Island), who in his turn is reported to have been indebted to his cat for this remarkable ornithological "find." As to how many specimens Mr. Travers, the lighthouse-keeper and the cat managed to secure between them, we have no information, but there is very good reason to believe that the bird is no longer to be found on the island, and as it is not known to exist anywhere else, it has apparently become quite extinct. This is probably a record performance in the way of extermination. The English scientific world will hear almost simultaneously of its discovery and of its disappearance, before anything is known of its life-history or its habits...It was not a flightless bird, but from its structure, it was evidently very weak-winged and thus fell an easy prey to the lighthouse-keeper's cat...all New Zealanders who take an interest in the preservation of whatever is specifically characteristic of the colony will deplore the extermination of such a creature. It is, indeed, saddening to reflect how one by one the rare and wonderful birds which have made New Zealand an object of supreme interest among scientists all over the world are gradually becoming extinct...And certainly we think it would be as well if the Marine Department, in sending lighthouse-keeps to isolated islands...were to see that they are not allowed to take any cats with them, even if mouse-traps have to be furnished at the cost of the state." ∎

Trapping Feral Cats

by
Don
McKinnon

"Queensland, thou art the land of pests." That's the first line of an old bush ballad that was written before the turn of the century. The author of the ballad didn't know how profound a statement he'd made. We've got them all in that state—camels, donkeys, rabbits, horses, cats, the works, I could keep going. He should have changed the wording "Queensland" to "Australia" and he would have had it down pat.

I worked in the bush from 1944 to 1970; it was only ill health that pushed me out of the bush. I was always appalled by the destructiveness of the cat. One instance: the top knot pigeons, on those Gulf Rivers where I worked, they'd come in and they'd roost in the low, scrubby bushes and they were murdered, they were slaughtered by the cat. They were "sitting ducks." But again, man was up there and he used to shoot them too. That was just one instance.

The cat wasn't regarded as a pest, simply because it did no apparent damage to livestock. Whereas old dingo, they'd spend good money on him and keep you working 12 to 14 hours a day with massive strychnine baiting programs. Strychnine was the poison in vogue at the time. The casualty rate used to go in this order: hundreds of the predatory birds, (the wedge-tail, kite hawk, crow); poor old goanna used to gorge on them; and the long-haired bush rats; and hopefully they'd get a few dingoes. If they got six or seven dingoes, they'd reckon the program was successful.

I noticed with this baiting they used to turn up a few cats. I'd always had an interest in them as I knew they were getting into the birds and I thought that I'd specifically try to get a cat with the bait. If I left it on the ground, a bird would pick it up so I started planting it. I started to get the odd cat with this hidden bait. The device I developed is the end result of that.

I found that the cat would take these baits if I concealed them; I'd cover them with bark, a tuft of grass, put them in the mouth of a fallen log and put a little bit of grass over them and he'd smell them out and root them out. I'm sure of that, because I have killed cats with them. I'd also shoot a few and I used to use the rabbit trap with a bit of fish oil decoy. If I trapped one in a rabbit trap, he'd be dead in two to five minutes because I used to put strychnine pads on the jaw of the trap and when the trap got the cat he'd tear the strychnine pad and he'd poison himself. It was better than leaving him there until whenever you picked him up.

I've killed over 500 cats over 40 years in the bush. I've kept diaries of all this information.

I used to get the pocket knife and open them up (as long as they weren't too smelly when I got to them). I found that the whole bush presented a giant smorgasbord for this pest—from the humble bush cock-

Everybody used to say it's bad luck to kill a cat—but what about the birds and other animals?

Photo: Bob Braine

ANOTHER CAT BITES THE DUST: Domestic and feral cats can take an enormous toll on local wildlife populations.

roach and the grasshopper, to skinks and geckoes, larger lizards and, strangely enough, last were birds. I think they ate more lizards and grasshoppers than birds. Also, they used to carry a fair bit of red meat. I strongly suspected that this meat came from bandicoots, possums or bushrats, and perhaps some of the larger birds. They will eat carrion if the need arises. I remember once I was riding a young horse and he was pretty toey. I found a dead cow; she'd been dead for a while. I got off and led the horse up and the hawks and the crows had been at it and they'd cleaned out the flank, eaten the guts out of it. A bush cat came out of a hole in the cow, right between my legs!

I've been asked about their breeding habits in the bush. I wasn't studying them or killing them all the time, but I did find that most years the semi-ferals would have two litters of two to six kittens. I've never seen any white ones; they'd be easy targets in the bush.

If I did find a litter, if I had poison with me (strychnine), the cat would clear off to the nearest bit of cover and these kittens would go for me. I'd get one out with my foot, and put a bit of strychnine on the back of his neck. I'd knock the other kittens on the head. As soon as I left she'd come and shift that kitten, so I'd get the females that way.

Folks have often asked me about the location of them and how many there were. Well it's pretty hard for a layman like me to judge, but I think every river and creek up in the north—nearly every man-made water—has got a resident cat population. When I first went north, the stations were huge. When the blokes came back after the war they cut the stations up into smaller properties—that meant more watering points, more homesteads and as the people came out and took their places they'd bring cats for "ratters." They also had working dogs and the dog used to win—the cat would go bush. But there were often cats on newly established waters, I don't know where they came from. I used to try and get rid of them if I could. I think I was the only bloke doing anything about them up there then. Everybody used to say it's bad luck to kill a cat—but what about the birds and other animals?

Random baiting methods for dingoes, both with strychnine and later 1080 (another poison), always harvested a few cats (not too many, but here and there) along with large numbers of the non-target species. One of the saddest sights I saw in the bush was a wedged-tailed eagle in convulsions after taking a gut full of strychnine. The kite hawks too (the whistling kites), they'd gorge on it. The blokes would throw tons of the stuff off the back of the truck—kill two bullocks and dice them up, load them with strychnine and spread it for 20 or 30 miles. Our wildlife is getting a bashing between the cats and man. I've also seen the echidna dead after those baits. I think he was eating ants off those strychnine baits.

Being over 60 now and having spent most of my life in the bush, I've learnt to love this country, warts and all, and I'd hate to see some of the more exotic diseases brought in. The one I'm referring to is rabies. Can you imagine the scenario if a rabid cat or dog got off a wrecked boat in Queensland? I don't know what we'd do. I don't know how we'd get rid of the cats unless we had a massive program of shooting and baiting.

Should it happen in North Queensland, that a rabid animal comes ashore and infects the cat, because of the topography of the country—it's a vast area with flat country as well as rough mountain country—and the fact that it's all got cats in it, where we would be I do not know. I'd hate to see it happen. And by doing my bit to keep the cats down, I get people aware of them and at least I'm doing something.

And there's market potential in feral cat control. When we do establish a business, we are confident there will be a ready market with national parks; when I can convince them that quolls can't get into the device. They can't get into it and experiment, but parks are still a bit worried about it. They are looking for maximum impact on the cat and minimum impact on non-target species.

I've got a subject cat at home. They don't grow into much at my place—you know what I mean? I observe them a lot. I think they are fascinating creatures. But the subject cat I've got at home, when I started to produce bait here—sundried fish—I said to my wife (she's always asking me if she can feed the cat, feeling sorry for him, cause I starve him

I've killed over 500 cats over 40 years in the bush. I used to get the pocket knife and open them up (as long as they weren't too smelly when I got to them). I found that the whole bush presented a giant smorgasbord for this pest; from the humble bush cockroach and the grasshopper, to skinks and geckoes, larger lizards and, strangely enough, last were birds.

Cat and rats from cabin of S.S. Ethelhilda: an illustration of the inefficiency of the cat as rat-catcher.

sometimes to see how he goes on the baits) "yeah you can feed him," so she gave him a big feed. She gave him custard and all that stuff and after he had a big feed I threw him that and he took it! I threw him a bit of smoked fish which he wouldn't eat, then I threw this back and he wolfed it. That's not the only trial I've done. I took it up to the rubbish dumps north of Townsville in the little hamlets up there and it was accepted straight away by the cats.

From 1946 to the early 60s there was a market for cat skins for the fur trade. The kangaroo shooters used to get ten bob for the hide of a big red 'roo; they'd shoot a bush cat with his winter coat on the skin and they'd get six or seven bob. They were worth harvesting and the 'roo shooters would have to come to town with the hides probably once a month; they might have 150-200 'roo skins, but they also had a little bundle of cat skins. If 10 to 20 shooters were operating, it would make a hell of an impact on the cat.

I soon realized that they were making an impression on them and there was a marked decrease in the cat problem. I only surmise that from the tracks I'd keep an eye out for. Whole areas were shot out. With the demise of the fur trade, within two years cats were moving back into that country. I had thought they were gone forever. Then I started to pick up cat tracks in areas that had been clear as feral cats moved back into the area where they were previously shot out.

I worked along the lines of the hidden bait theory, looking for ways to conceal the bait while excluding other animals. I'd done enough poisoning, killed enough birds in my time. I didn't want to kill anymore. After much trial and error, I developed this device, then the baits. I have done this work quietly and at my own expense with some financial help from my two sons. I use the word quietly as I am aware there is a cat lobby out there and, though misguided, they can be quite vocal. They've got to be educated, those people; they pat their cat on the head when he brings in a bird from the back yard. One woman said to me, "Look, isn't he clever, he's brought in a bird!" I said, "Yeah, give him an aspirin, it'll make him catch more birds." She never gave him an aspirin: she woke up to it!

The bait storage system holds about a dozen baits; you load them up.

I'll get into the baits now. I've been married for 40 years and when I started to make these baits in the kitchen at home, my wife started threatening to divorce me and she's still doing it!

There is a paw-entry for the cat. I don't think it's the whole answer for the feral cat, but I have killed cats with this device, with fish baits and strychnine. I've done about five field trips and the first three or four, I used to just watch the tracks and I had blank baits in it. Sometimes the cats showed a bit of interest and they'd prowl around it and they'd put out a bait. Sometimes they'd show no interest at all.

The last field trip I did, I took some strychnine. We went up to the Gulf; last September it was. That area up there, I'd worked there 40 years previously, close to the coast. In September through October, the finches used to be there in the thousands; the little bull-finch, red beak, black throat. There wasn't a finch to be seen last year. Maybe something had gone wrong with their tucker. I had a look and there was plenty of the seed that they used to go for, the dry button-grass, kerosene grass. But there were no finches. I had a look around and from the beach back there were cat tracks everywhere. Now, I'm not saying that there was a mass of cats there, but just from the tracks I think there were 20 cats working the Eight Mile Creek, that's a salt-water creek there, for about 12 miles up along the coast. We put the device up and put strychnine in it, in fresh fish that we caught, and we got about six cats with that device—simply by them clawing out the baits.

I've heard some people say cats are hard to poison—and I agree: they are. I've set a lot of baits in my time and got nothing. I make no false claims with the device. But I have killed the feral, the real bush cat, especially up in the Gulf, with that device. Not a great deal of them, but it has been done.

I used to make the device out of PVC, but during the oil war (the Gulf War) the PVC went 'through the roof' in price and it became very hard to get in the right sizes, so I went for the fiber glass. It's sturdy. You can pick it up and take it anywhere. You could take it to an area where you know there's a cat hanging out and with a suitable bait, you could pick that cat up and then you could move it on. That was my idea in the first place—it had to be mobile.

I'll get into the baits now. I've been married for 40 years and when I started to make these baits in the kitchen at home, my wife started threatening to divorce me and she's still doing it!

This is smoked liver—I've tried that up on the beaches north of Townsville. Those little hamlets there, they've got cats in every rubbish dump. What I'm after is a bait that will keep, that you can take out with you and it won't go rotten like fresh fish or fresh meat. Cats will accept that: the smoked liver. It's odoriferous, I've got it in two bags. It's not rotten, but you can smell the liver. That liver is boiled, then you put it in the smoke-house. Cats don't mind it. ■

Don McKinnon is a wildlife conservation professional who lives and works in Australia.

ANIMAL BITE REPORTS

1993

Dog: 10,739
Cat: 1,476
Human: 1,401

1994

Dog: 10,554
Cat: 1,502
Human: 1,349

(Department of Health, City of New York)

Brochure from the Australian Nature Conservation Agency

Cats have been in Australia since European settlement, although there is speculation that they may have arrived with Dutch shipwrecks in the 17th century. By the 1850s, colonies of feral cats were established in the wild. Intentional introductions of cats to the wild happened in the late 1800s in the hope that they would control rabbits, rats and mice. Feral cats have since spread to cover all of Australia.

Feral cats are found in most habitats across mainland Australia, Tasmania and on many offshore islands. They are very adaptable animals and there seem to be few environmental factors that limit their distribution. Feral cats can survive in dry conditions because they are predominantly nocturnal and can utilize the moisture from their prey and so do not require drinking water.

Cats can have two litters a year which average four kittens per litter. Few young survive to be weaned at about eight weeks of age with females becoming sexually mature when they are approximately one year old.

Feral cats generally eat small mammals although they also eat birds, reptiles and insects. In pastoral regions in Australia, young rabbits make up the majority of their diet. However, in areas where rabbits are scarce, feral cats will prey largely on native animals.

Feral cats have impacted heavily on the island fauna. They have caused the extinction of a subspecies of red-fronted parakeet on Macquarie Island. Because islands are usually small and isolated, the presence and impact of feral cats is more obvious than it is on the mainland, particularly if other predators such as foxes and dingoes are absent. However, there are no foxes or dingoes in Tasmania and currently there is no evidence to suggest that feral cats have had an impact on native wildlife.

Determining the impact of feral cats on native wildlife on the Australian mainland is more difficult. It is complicated by other factors such as introduced herbivores like rabbits competing with native animals for food and shelter, and habitat loss caused by clearing, grazing animals and urban development. However, there are instances where feral cats have directly threatened the successful recovery of endangered species. For example, feral cats have killed many of the captive bred malas (or Rufous hare-wallabies) that were released in the Tanami Desert of the Northern Territory during 1990 and 1991. A single feral cat was found reducing the numbers of rock wallabies in an isolated colony in tropical Queensland.

Feral cats also carry infective diseases such as toxoplasmosis and sarcosporidiosis. These diseases can be transmitted to native animals, domestic livestock and animals. Toxoplasmosis can cause damage to the

> **I was always appalled by the destructiveness of the cat. The top knot pigeons would come in and they'd roost in the low, scrubby bushes and they were murdered, they were slaughtered by the cat.**

central nervous system, can cause blindness, respiratory problems and general debilitation in wildlife. In humans, toxoplasmosis can also cause debilitation, miscarriage in pregnant women and congenital birth defects. Feral cats are also potential carriers of rabies, should the disease be accidentally released in Australia.

Current methods used to control feral cats include shooting, trapping, baiting and fencing. Trapping feral cats is difficult and labor intensive as feral cats can be quite trap shy. They will also not take baits as readily as other introduced animals such as foxes. However, feral cats have been eradicated from a number of offshore islands using these conventional control techniques. Eradication of feral cats from the mainland is impossible. Once an area is treated, it is quickly recolonized by either the offspring of feral populations, or by recruits from urban areas.

Barrier fencing has proved to be the most effective current control technique for feral cats. Unfortunately, the high cost of fencing makes this technique useful for only small areas of land. The fences also need regular maintenance to stop cats from getting through the enclosure.

Research is being undertaken to improve the effectiveness of baits and traps to control feral cats. The use of visual lures (such as feathers and cotton wool) and attractants (such as tuna oil) are being tested in an effort to attract greater numbers of feral cats to traps and baits.

The impact of feral cats on native wildlife is being studied in various parts of Australia in order to quantify it. It is important to determine the extent of the impact on native animals, so that appropriate control measures can be implemented or developed.

The potential to use biological control agents, as well as toxins and pesticides, to control feral cats is being investigated. If fertility control methods for foxes and rabbits are successful, their applicability to feral cats may be considered. ■

Tarred and Feathered, Mark Dion (1995)

There are instances where feral cats have directly threatened the successful recovery of endangered species. A single feral cat was found reducing the numbers of rock wallabies in an isolated colony in tropical Queensland. Feral cats also carry infective diseases that can be transmitted to native animals, domestic livestock, animals and humans.

People for the Ethical Treatment of Animals (PETA) Factsheet

Between 11 million and 19 million feral cats live in the United States. Each of these cats is at risk of being killed by a car, tortured by a sadist, or dying of starvation or disease. Despite their seemingly overwhelming numbers, it is possible to help these cats by humanely trap-

Photo: Bob Braine

Feral cat in landfill.

ping them. Once caught, the cats should be transferred to a humane animal shelter or to a veterinarian to be spayed or neutered, treated for worm and flea infestation, and then adopted. Because of the shortage of homes, the difficulty of resocialization, and the perils of our concrete jungle, it may be necessary to euthanize most unwanted cats who are trapped. You can ask your veterinarian to do this or, if your local shelter uses a painless method, take the cats there.

The cardinal rule of humane trapping is this: The animal comes first. All trapping procedures are practical applications of this one, most important consideration.

Always know the safe whereabouts of your trap. When not being used, a trap should be kept indoors or in a locked storage area. People can use a trap—even a humane trap—to harm animals. Take appropriate precautions to ensure that the trap will never be accessible to anyone who does not have your permission to use it.

Be extremely cautious about lending out your trap. A trap carries with it an enormous responsibility. Be sure that anyone using it understands this. If you do not know your borrower, ask questions. Do not be afraid to be abundantly inquisitive. Find out the exact location of the animal(s) trapped and how much is known about them. (For instance, is it known for certain that an adult cat is not a nursing mother whose babies are tucked away somewhere?) Do not lend your trap to anyone who is the least bit reluctant to satisfy your inquiries. Always verify the borrower's address and telephone number. Deliver the trap yourself and, if you have any doubts, don't take a chance. Politely refuse to lend your trap—the awkwardness you feel is a small price to pay to prevent an animal from being mistreated.

LABORATORY CONFIRMED CASES OF RABIES IN NEW YORK CITY (as of 12/14/95)

Bronx: 42
Queens: 3
Manhattan: 7
Staten Island: 62
Brooklyn: 1

TOTAL: 115

(102 by raccoon, 5 by skunk, 2 by opossum and 6 by bats; none reported by cats or dogs)

(Department of Health, City of New York)

Before you trap, it is prudent to obtain written permission from the owner of the property on which the cats roam. Also, wear thick gloves, as handling feral cats can be dangerous for both the cat and the handler.

Know ahead of time what you are going to do with the animal. If someone has agreed to take the animal from you, or if you are going to a local shelter, alert the person or facility before you begin. Never assume that the animal will be accepted unannounced.

If you are taking the animal home, prepare a soft, quiet place protected from other animals before you leave. It may take months (or years) of patience and kindness before the animal begins to trust you. If you are not ready to make a significant commitment, you should have other plans for the animal.

Line the bottom of the trap. Consider how uncomfortable you would feel if forced to sit on metal grating for any length of time. Lay a piece of cloth, a folded newspaper, or an old towel on the trap floor. It will not interfere with the spring mechanism, and the animal will be afforded a small measure of comfort. Do not use the same towel/cloth again for the same purpose unless you have washed it well—animals are very sensitive to smells. (Also, avoid putting bowls in a trap. When animals go in, they may thrash around trying to escape, and a bowl could cause injury.)

Be gentle: even humane traps (box traps) can terrify animals who have never been confined and at the mercy of others. When you are trapping, always use a vehicle. Even if the animal you want to trap is just a few blocks away, drive or have a friend drive you. Walking any distance with a terrified animal in a trap invites disaster.

Never leave a trap unattended. Plan to do your trapping when you have enough time to spend on site. Avoid trapping in bad or extremely hot weather. Cats are most likely to be up and about during early morning or late evening hours.

Do not set a trap and leave it, even for a few minutes. Anything could happen while you're away. Set your trap, then back off, but stay within sight of it. Be patient.

Make sure the trap is secure on firm, flat ground and does not wobble when touched. Turn the trap so that when the animals enter they can keep an eye on your car, your door, you, or whatever danger they would not like to turn their backs to. Place a small trail of food leading to a large feeding clump at the center back of the trap.

Immediately after the animal goes in, cover the trap with a beach towel (if you are trapping in cold weather) or a thin sheet (in hot weather). A frightened, trapped animal calms far more quickly when covered.

Be considerate. Gently carry the trap to your vehicle. The animals will be frightened, so be aware that even small things can aggravate or ease their stress. Although you may feel anxious, act calm. Don't slam doors. Speak quietly to the animals while you are transporting them; your voice and tone can reassure. Do whatever you can to diminish the trauma of the animal you have trapped.

If your local animal shelter will not lend you a box trap, invest in a long-lasting trap from the Tomahawk Live Trapping Company in Tomahawk, WI (715-453-3550). A cat trap costs approximately $42.00. This company sells live traps for other mammals, such as rats and raccoons, as well. However, trapping wild animals who have inhabited your basement or garage is not always the best solution; animals who have made your home theirs will travel long distances to return. ■

The cardinal rule of humane trapping is this: the animal comes first. Line the bottom of the trap. Consider how uncomfortable you would feel if forced to sit on metal grating for any length of time.

Feral Dogs

interview by
Michael
Crewdson

Thomas Daniels studied and wrote about feral and stray dog communities in New Jersey, Mexico, and the Southwest. His last work with these canines took place in the 25,000-square mile Navaho Reservation located in parts of Utah, Arizona, and New Mexico. He is now studying Lyme disease in the Northeast.

MICHAEL CREWDSON: Where did your work with feral dogs begin?
THOMAS DANIELS: I did my master's thesis on free-ranging dogs in northern New Jersey. The idea grew out of work Alan Beck had done in the 1970s, research among a group of stray dogs living in Baltimore. I felt there were a lot of animal behavior issues that could be explored in the feral dogs of Newark. I then wanted to apply what I had learned to groups of non-urban wild dogs—the dog packs found in Navaho country in the southwest.

MC: What was going on with the dogs of Newark, New Jersey?
TD: I had three different sites in the city, about one-square mile each. We were looking at social organization: the sizes of groups; the sex composition of the packs; breeding behavior. What we found was that these dogs really were not "feral." Even though they were strays, without owners, they were not wild dogs. They had a whole human society that took care of them and watched out for them. The dogs formed groups around the individuals in the community who fed them.

MC: What is the day in the life of a Newark stray dog?
TD: There was a coherent dog society that existed, one that wasn't obvious if you just saw stray dogs on the street. The dogs would form groups in the morning, and go out "foraging" with each other. They would go from house to house. They had specific routes they tended to follow, and places they knew to go for food. Toward the afternoon, they would split up and go back to their respective home sites to rest.

MC: What were the resting sites like?
TD: They would sleep anywhere: under a porch, under an abandoned car, in an abandoned car, even a basement of an abandoned house. There were a lot of abandoned buildings in the area. There was one pair of dogs in particular that I remember living in a building. They actually raised their pups there.

MC: Were most of these dogs successful?
TD: Most of them didn't do that well in the long-term. In the short-term, there was no trouble finding shelter or food.

MC: How did the dogs take to you following them around?
TD: They were fine. They were very well-socialized to the presence of people. They would be friendly. If they were hungry, you could go right up to one and give it food if you were so inclined. They had no problem with me following them. It was more the human residents in Newark

They seemed to have partitioned their time at the dumps. There would be a pack of dogs I would see at 8 p.m. At 10 p.m., you would hear some howling. The 8 p.m. dogs would leave. It was as though they set up a time-share. Even in what we think of as a chaotic environment, there is a social organization that exists.

who were concerned about my being there. A number of times, things got a little unpleasant. These were poor areas where drugs were pretty rampant. I was driving around constantly, and taking pictures of dogs. Invariably, you can't take pictures of dogs without taking pictures of people. That made a lot of people nervous. Some of the houses that the stray dogs were living in were also being used to sell drugs and also to shoot up in. They felt apprehensive about my being there.

Photo: Thomas Daniels

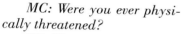
Feral pup emerging from his cave shelter.

MC: Were you ever physically threatened?

TD: There was one dog pack that lived in the old Newark Street jail. I was particularly interested in this group because they hunted squirrels together, and predatory activity was pretty rare. People were always going in and out of the jail, although it was no longer used as a jail. As it turns out, it was the headquarters of an undercover narcotics group. One day, I was taking pictures of these dogs. Two guys came out of the jail, pulled their guns on me and demanded I get out of my car. They went through my notebook. They took me inside and asked me what I was doing. They threatened to pull the film out of my camera. It was one of the hazards of doing work like that in the city.

MC: The dangers are different than those that arise while doing biological research out in the field.

TD: When I was out in Navaho country, I was more concerned about rattlesnakes and falling off sandstone cliffs—not unnatural threats to my well-being, as was the case in Newark.

MC: Why did you choose to work in Navaho country?

TD: For my doctoral thesis, I was interested in pursuing dog work in a wild area, perhaps out West, in the desert. There are a hundred small towns on the Navaho Reservation. Each one of them has its own dump site, about a mile outside the borders of the town. As it turns out, these sites were great meeting places for dogs. If one of the Navahos didn't want their dog anymore (some of them had dogs because they were herding sheep), they would take them to a dump site far away from their town. It wound up being a great place to watch dog interactions.

MC: Would just about every dump have a population of dogs?

TD: Certainly, the ones I looked at did. Every dump I visited in

If the mother survives long enough to get the pup up and running, and the pup becomes part of the pack, then it will have a decent chance. It may not be able to jump out of the way of bullets, but it should be able to find enough food to make it for at least a year or so. When a pup is abandoned, it invariably winds up getting killed.

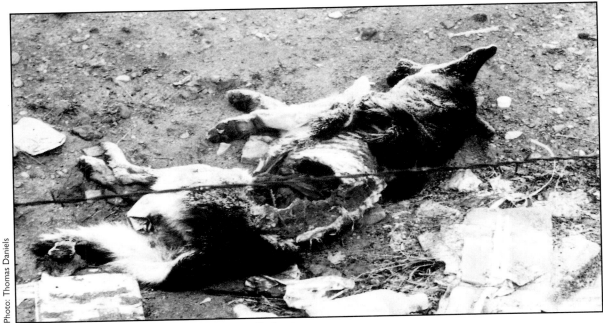

Photo: Thomas Daniels

A feral dog, probably shot and undoubtedly cannibalized.

Arizona and New Mexico had dogs living there. These dumps were also great places for "town" dogs to visit—dogs who just foraged in the dump at night. They were the most interesting because "feral" dogs lived there.

MC: What is a feral dog?

TD: An animal who was once socialized to people, but who, for some reason, has gone through a process where it loses this socialization. It's virtually unapproachable by humans. I call this "secondary feralization." The animal once knew people, but has been abandoned. It has made the break with humans, and it now fends for itself. This type of feralization is not generally successful.

MC: What is the other way animals can become feral?

TD: It's what I call "primary feralization." Pups who are born wild. They haven't lost contact with humans because they've never been in contact with humans.

MC: What are the wild pup's chances as compared to one who has been abandoned?

TD: If the mother survives long enough to get the pup up and running, and the pup becomes part of the pack, then it will have a decent chance. It may not be able to jump out of the way of bullets, but it should be able to find enough food to make it for at least a year or so. When a pup is abandoned, it invariably winds up getting killed. Most abandoned dogs don't do well. A dump provides them with resources to live for a few weeks, possibly a couple of months. Then, they have to either make the

> It was surreal to see 12 dead pups scattered in a dump, or to see a dog eating pieces of a couch, probably because that couch had some odor attached to it and the dog was starving.

break from the dump, or else something has to happen in terms of good luck, such as getting adopted or getting continually fed.

MC: What would kill them in the dump?

TD: It wasn't unusual to see coyotes feeding on a dog carcass, though I never saw a coyote kill a dog. People would come into the dump and use the dogs for target practice.

MC: Could you tell me about one example?

TD: I knew of two abandoned female dogs, both of which had litters. The pups were about eight weeks old. I watched them for several weeks, and then I went back one morning and discovered dog bodies littered all over the dump. Most of the pups had been shot. Getting shot was a major hazard for the dogs.

MC: What is a feral dog pack like?

TD: Typically it was several females with their pups, and maybe two males associated with them. The pack themselves were dynamic; they were constantly changing size. As the pups were born, the pack suddenly gets bigger. They tend to travel less. They're more stationary—centered around the den.

MC: Where were the dens?

TD: They were usually small holes dug into hillsides, underground burrows.

MC: Within the dump?

TD: Usually, they were just outside the dump. I spent a lot of time watching a dump outside of a town called Navaho, New Mexico. It was located right next to a canyon. In the walls of the canyon, there was a sandstone cave, three feet by four feet, where the dogs lived. During the evenings, the animals would come out of the caves in the canyon. They would wander down into the dump where they would forage for food.

MC: Did you name this pack?

TD: I called it the "Canyon Pack."

MC: And how did the Canyon Pack respond to your being there?

TD: They were fine as long as I didn't get too close. They would see me fairly often. But one day I was walking up the center of the canyon when all of a sudden five heads popped up from this grassy rise and there were five dogs barking at me about 20 feet away. It was a little peculiar because I had scared them so I was concerned they would get aggressive. They were all sorts of German shepherd mixes—not huge, about medium-sized. They barked for about 10 seconds and then took off up the canyon. A lot of times, they would be on the canyon floor, and I would be on the rim looking down, trying to stay unobtrusive.

MC: What did they look like? Were they thin and scraggly?

TD: They didn't look that bad. In Newark, I saw thin dogs that had mange, but here they looked O.K. They seemed to be in good health.

MC: What did the feral pups look like?

TD: They all tended to look like shepherd mixes, depending on the

Somebody asked me once if we have a greater responsibility to take care of endangered species or dogs? We need to focus our attention on the fact that this is an animal we put here, one that has to exist, and one we're constantly abusing. When we abandon an animal at a dump, we are not setting it free. We're giving it a death sentence. We have an obligation to these animals as much as we have an obligation to endangered rhinos. Animal rights activists scream about laboratory animals being abused, but we've abused dogs for over 10,000 years.

parents, of course. Many of them tended to be brown and black, or brown and white. Over time, you would see a generic kind of dog, but initially it had to do with who the parents were. We didn't see any huge dogs, and we didn't see any little dogs. Usually, you have a constant gene flow into the area, which produces a motley bunch of dogs.

MC: Were your dog subjects often shot?

TD: I just saw that one pack who were massacred. I often saw dead dogs show up at the dumps. But you never knew whether they were shot and then dumped, or abandoned and then shot. One time I saw a man driving to the dump with a dog hanging from his rear view mirror—it was still alive, dangling from its leash.

MC: Was there a problem with the feral dogs biting people in the area?

TD: No. These dogs left everybody alone. The key to being a successful feral dog is not getting in the way of people. The same is true of a stray dog in Newark. When a dog is able to remain part of the background, we tend to ignore it. If a dog is minding its own business—that's a good survival strategy. If an animal was a biter, chances are it wouldn't survive too long. If they bit somebody at the dump, they would get shot.

MC: Which dogs would bite people?

TD: I did a study for the local public health service on dog bites: a survey of dog bite reports on the Navaho reservation. Those dogs were not feral. They tended to be owned animals who lived in the town, but had access to public areas. Technically, they were non-feral, free-ranging dogs. If a person came too close to somebody's property line, or went by too fast, or were afraid of the dog, they might get chased. Potentially, they could be bitten. Generally, it was youngsters that got bitten.

MC: So, it was the human-owned dogs who bit?

TD: Yes. There were about 600 bites per 10,000 residents on the Navaho Reservation. Which is what you expect to see in a major city.

MC: Set the scene of feral dog life "down in the dumps."

TD: I would spend many nights at the dumps, because night is the time when the dogs would come in. Occasionally, you would have these fires started in the trenches where people dumped their garbage. At nighttime, you would see this eerie glow, and you would see these heat-waves rising out of these pits. Dogs would be silhouetted against the dump fires—while they ambled around foraging in the trash. They would get very close to the fires depending on how hungry they were. When I was working in Juarez, Mexico, people would throw garbage into the street and light it on fire. You would have dogs in the middle of the street literally eating, or attempting to eat, morsels of charcoal. You see a lot of strange things you wouldn't typically see, and you see them in an environment most of us are not generally exposed to.

MC: Surreal?

TOP 10 DOG NAMES IN THE U.S. (1991)

1. Lady
2. King
3. Duke
4. Peppy
5. Prince
6. Pepper
7. Snoopy
8. Princess
9. Heidi
10. Sam/Coco

(National Canine Defense League)

TOP 10 CAT NAMES IN THE U.S. (1991)

FEMALE:	MALE:
1. Samantha	Tiger/Tigger
2. Misty	Smokey
3. Patches	Pepper
4. Cali/Calico	Max/Maxwell
5. Muffin	Simon
6. Angela	Snoopy
7. Ginger	Morris
8. Princess	Rusty/Rusti
9. Punkin/	Boots/
Pumpkin	Bootsie

(American Veterinary Medical Association)

TD: To see 12 dead pups scattered in a dump. To see a dog eating pieces of a couch, probably because that couch had some odor attached to it and the dog was starving. To see dogs coming out from under busted-up couches during the middle of winter after a snowstorm. These are bizarre sights. I guess it was a surreal environment. Also, the dogs did surprising things. They seemed to have partitioned their time at the dumps. There would be a pack of dogs I would see at 8 p.m. At 10 p.m., you would hear some howling. The 8 p.m. dogs would leave, and the howling dogs would come in. It was as though they set up a time-share. Even in what we think of as a chaotic environment, there is a social organization that exists.

The number one rule of feral dog survival is to keep clear of people.

Photo: Bob Braine

MC: *Were pack-to-pack confrontations usually avoided?*

TD: I never saw any dog fights. In towns, you might see two dogs from the same group fighting each other for a scrap of food. Out in the dumps, there seemed to be more civility. Animals have been out there for a while. They don't want to risk getting injured. That's true of a wolf pack too. I believe, among dogs, there is some of that wolf ability to maintain a coherent social organization and to figure out how to respond appropriately to possible conflicts.

MC: *What is the biggest threat to a feral dog?*

TD: Not finding enough food and being injured by people.

MC: *Is there enough food being thrown out?*

TD: There really isn't, especially if you consider the large number of dogs who live in the dump, as well as those who come in at night from the towns. When a dog is first abandoned at a dump, it usually tends to hang around the dump—at least for a couple of weeks. I'm going to be anthropomorphic here, but my impression is that this is an animal that is separated not only from the human group, but also from the dog group they've known for their whole life. They've been thrown into an unfamiliar area. They don't know what to do next. The most attractive thing at the dump is the smell of food and the possibility of getting it. They'll stay for several weeks. And what's happening is that they're not getting enough food. They're eating pieces of tin foil with food scraps in it. They're getting progressively worse and worse. Their health declines. They have one of two options. They can get re-adopted, by walking to the nearest town. Or they can be incorporated into a pack. That's what happened to one of the abandoned pups. It was adopted by a pack, and it

People would come into the dump and use the dogs for target practice. Getting shot was a major hazard for the dogs.

was able to make it because of that adoption.

MC: Once a dog enters that pack, have they left humans behind?

TD: They're now with a group of animals who will not spend time with humans. So, in a sense, to become feral is to give up that interaction, and even the effort to have that interaction.

MC: Is there anything else you discovered or realized after spending time with these dogs?

TD: If you look at the history of domestic animals, the dog is probably the first domesticated animal we know of. It was probably the first animal we formed a relationship with. Charles Darwin actually listed several different kinds of artificial selection. He meant not what was happening in nature, but what man essentially was guiding. With the feral dog problem we have artificial selection. Dogs being loose in the environment is nothing new, but it seems to be getting worse. Most of the rabies in the world is spread by wild dogs.

MC: I hear that over 10,000 people die a year after getting bitten by rabid dogs.

TD: That's certainly the case in Asia and Africa. It's a problem that is not going away.

MC: What's the real root of the problem?

Photo: Bob Braine

Feral dog scavenges a Carribean beach.

TD: Somebody asked me once if we have a greater responsibility to take care of endangered species or dogs? On the surface, it seems like an easy answer. A dog is an organism that we've created. It's not an animal that is found in nature. Furthermore, we've got populations of dogs obliterating wildlife. In the Galapagos Islands, the single biggest threat to marine iguanas is feral dogs.

MC: Domestic dogs have also been blamed for spreading distemper and rabies to lions and other animals in Africa.

TD: As far as dogs go, we need to take a selfish or anthropomorphic view. We need to focus our attention on the fact that this is an animal *we* put here, one that has to exist, and one we're constantly abusing. When we abandon an animal at a dump, we are not setting it free. We're giving it a death sentence. We have an obligation to these animals as much as we have an obligation to endangered rhinos. While dogs are cheap animals to dispose of, the moral outlook we need to take will encompass these animals into our world view. We have a big responsibility to this *first* animal we've created. Animal rights activists scream about laboratory animals being abused, but we've abused dogs for over 10,000 years. What we do to other animals is what we do to ourselves. If we think about the implications for ourselves, then maybe we'll extend a little caring to other organisms as well. Endangered wildlife like lions and African wild dogs are dying from diseases that have been introduced by domestic animals. The domestic animals are vectors of diseases that are killing off its wild relatives. These problems occurring in nature are not going to decline. As more and more people move into animal habitats which used to be pristine, we're going to have more and more confrontations between us, our pets' diseases and the wildlife fauna that are already there.

MC: They might bring something back to us.

TD: Some people might argue that the Ebola virus is exactly that. This is a disease that kills between 70% and 80% of the people it infects, yet we still have no clue where it came from. Every time there is an outbreak, people die horrible deaths. The cause probably has something to do with the fact that these people are going into wild areas where they've never gone before. Not only are we going in and disrupting local fauna, but we're bringing diseases back. Lyme disease is a mild form of the same situation. We're going into a habitat where an organism lives, in this case, ticks. We now live in tick habitat, so we expose ourselves to their diseases. We have to learn to deal with the consequences.

MC: Now, we have a Lyme disease epidemic.

TD: Yes. We do.

One time I saw a man driving to the dump with a dog hanging from his rear view mirror—it was still alive, dangling from its leash.

■

Pet Bighorn, William Wegman, 1994. Black and white photograph, 11x14 inches. Courtesy of the artist.

chapter **4**

Rats

The Birth of the Super Rat

Randy "Butch" Dupree is Pest Control Director for New York City's Department of Health and popularizer of the term "Super Rat."

interview by Michael Crewdson

MICHAEL CREWDSON: *Is there an estimate of how many rats there are in New York City? We've heard that there's a rat for every person.*
RANDY DUPREE: Yes, but let me back up. That way of estimating the number of rats in a city came from London, England in the early 1900s. At that time, they were looking at a rat per acre, then somehow it become a rat per person. The United States Federal Government adopted "a rat per person" in 1972, as a way of estimating rat populations in cities. Now, having said that, it doesn't tell the real story. The truth is that there are maybe five rats per person in some areas of the city, and then one rat for every five people in other areas of the city. But, if you add it up together, it becomes a rat for every person.

MC: So, it's really an average.

RD: Certainly, if you're talking about Fifth Avenue and 60th Street, the rat population there may be a rat for every four or five people.

MC: Where are the rat problem areas?

RD: In the 1980s, the Federal Government identified what they considered were the rat problem areas in New York City. And they were areas that they deemed economically deprived. Those areas included: East Harlem, West Harlem, the South Bronx, Bed-Stuy and Brownsville in Brooklyn, and Jamaica in Queens. That's where our oldest housing stock is and that's where there are landlords who exploit the tenants by taking the rent out of the community instead of putting it back into the building. That's where there may be a higher population of people living in a smaller area, because of economic problems. There are more walk-up buildings where tenants have a difficult time walking down and

Illustration: Alexis Rockman

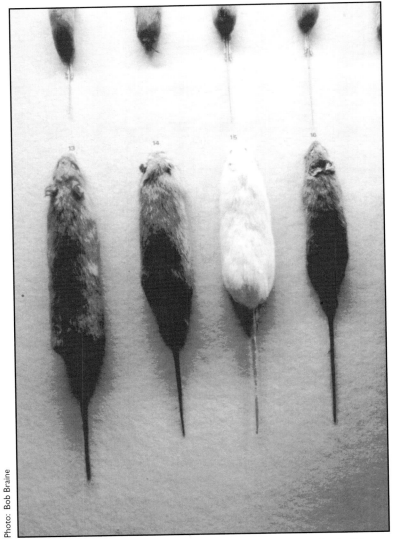

Photo: Bob Braine

Eastern wood rat (*Rattus magister*), Norway rat (*Rattus norvegicus*), albino Norway rat, black rat (*Rattus rattus*) (l. to r.).

bringing garbage to the basement because of crime. They have a tendency to do some other things with their garbage which causes problems with rats, like throw it into the alley. In these places, there may be four or five rats for one person.

MC: Where do rats live?

RD: The rats we have in the city are Norway rats. These rats are really burrowing rats—they stay underground. Unlike rats in Florida and California, which live in trees and on roofs, our rats live underground. That's where they build their nest; that's where they live. And they're nocturnal.

MC: What is the city rat lifestyle?

RD: Rats are social animals. They have territories. As long as there's enough food around, they won't travel any more than 100 feet away from where they were born. That's their range. Other rats, from different packs, can't come within that territory. And one thing we know about rats, is that they have two holes: one to come in and one to get out. There's an old saying that "every good rat has more than one hole."

MC: Are rat bites still a problem in the city?

RD: Oh yes. And there are two kinds of rat bites in the city. There are the reported rat bites. Those are the bites for which a person goes to a medical facility or doctor. The doctor has a responsibility to report it to the Department of Health. Last year [1995] we had about 250 reports of rat bites. That's one kind of rat bite. The other kind are those that are not reported. They're not reported because of a number of reasons: the people don't have health coverage; they think they can treat it themselves, and there's a certain stigma attached to being bitten by a rat. You wouldn't want anybody to know. These bites, we might not ever know about.

MC: How did the term "Super Rat" come about?

RD: In the 1970s, we had a lab where we tested the efficacy of our poisons. We trapped live rats in New York City and sent them to this lab, which was in Troy, New York. They would feed the rats the poison which we used in the city to make sure it was killing the rats in the time it was supposed to. We found that some of the rats were eating the poison and not dying. This was at a time when there was a fiscal crisis in the city, when all the agencies were being cut back. I was the director for the Bureau of Pest Control, where there was going to be a loss of personnel. I said that it was certainly a bad time to talk about cuts when we had rats—Super Rats—in the city. And that those Super Rats, when they mated, would create Super Rat offspring. It was difficult to talk about cutting the budget when we had a large population of rats in the city that were not dying. And that's how that came about.

MC: So Super Rat means…?

RD: A rat that no matter how much poison he eats, his body builds up an immunity to it, thereby actually causing him to *not* die. The more poison he eats, the more vitamin K his body produces, warding off the effects of the poison. Vitamin K is the antidote for the poison we use. The more poison the rats would eat, the more vitamin K their bodies would create. The Super Rat was a rat that wouldn't die.

MC: Are they still around?

RD: I'm quite sure they are. But, why do we have Super Rats? In fact, the city that had the most Super Rats was Chicago. Because people use the same poison over and over again, thereby allowing the rodents to build up a resistance to that poison. And that resistant strain of rat can be reproduced by mating. We used a chemical called Warfarin in most of the cities. For years and years and years, that's all we used. And we used it because it was a relatively safe product for non-target animals. Safe if your dog accidentally eats it; safe if your cat or your kid ingests it. Cities felt good using a product that was safe. Rats became accustomed to that. It doesn't happen now because we change our chemical on a monthly or quarterly basis. Now rats don't have an opportunity to build up that resistance.

MC: Is this cutting down the rat population?

RD: We do not have rats that we don't have the tools to kill. I think that the poisons we use now are new-generation chemicals...the rat eats it once and dies.

MC: How long have you been battling rats?

RD: For 25 years.

MC: Have you built up respect for the rat?

RD: I certainly have. I went to the Columbia School for Social Work where I was part of the model cities program. One day I met with someone from the health department and he asked me to be in charge of oper-

Parents sometimes send their kids to bed with crackers, cookies or bread and milk. If you live in an area where rats live in the building, you should not do that. They will climb into the child's bed or crib for the food.

In other countries, rats are not hated. In some parts of India, they are revered. In some parts of South America, they are eaten.

ations for the Bureau of Pest Control. He's talking to a social worker who first of all doesn't like rats and second, doesn't know anything about them. I said "no thank you." There was no way in the world that I wanted to be associated with rats. Then he told me what the salary was. And I said "maybe." He told me I didn't have to know anything about rats. He just wanted me to manage 150 people. When I got here, I went to meetings where people would ask me questions and I had to refer that question to someone else. It was ridiculous. So then I went to the Center for Disease Control in Atlanta to learn all I had to know about rats. And certainly after all the years I've been in battle with them, I developed a healthy respect for what they can do, how they live and their survival rate.

MC: Other than the fact that occasionally they will bite someone, why are rats so hated?

RD: In other countries, they are not hated. In some parts of India, they are revered. In some parts of South America, they are eaten. In the United States, they are looked upon with such distaste and disdain because they are associated with filth and unclean environments. And that's why people don't want to go to a doctor if they have been bitten by a rat. Because it's admitting that they have rats, that they live with them. James Cagney said it best, "you dirty rat." In the city, rats are associated with garbage, refuse, harborage, anything that you're trying to discard.

MC: What are the local rat-associated diseases?

RD: Understand that we have not had a disease associated with rats in New York City for about 25 years. However, one disease associated with rats is lepdospirosis, which is caused by the urine of a rat. If you have a cut and rat urine gets in—you could get it. One man died from it around 30 years ago. He was fishing under a bridge in the Bronx and dug for worms in rat-infested soil. That's how he got it. Then there's Rat Bite Fever, which is like a flu you get after getting bitten by a rat. It is caused by the organic matter around the rat teeth and gums getting into the cut.

MC: In New York City, people were talking about the Super Rats being giants, as big as cats. Is that true?

RD: That's incorrect. They're called Super Rats because of their ability to resist chemicals—not their size. The average rat is a pound, and that's a fact. But, when someone sees a rat when they don't expect to, it becomes larger than life. I remember that over by City Hall around eight or nine years ago, there were reports that rats were running down the street attacking people. I was at a conference in Albany, and they called me back here because some lady said she was attacked by a horde of rats. The lady got off work one night around 6:30 p.m. and she was walking to her car. There was a big vacant lot there, where a restaurant had blown up—and the rats had moved into the hole and they were living there. The next street over there were Chinese restaurants. And every night, the rats would migrate to the garbage cans, because they

In the United States, they are looked upon with such distaste and disdain because they are associated with filth and unclean environments. And that's why people don't want to go to a doctor if they have been bitten by a rat. Because it's admitting that they have rats, that they live with them. James Cagney said it best, "you dirty rat."

knew when the restaurant owners would put out their garbage. Now, they happened to be making their trip to the garbage cans at the same time as this lady is walking in the middle of the street. And when she saw these rats, she started running the same way the rats were running. The rats were even more afraid of her, than she was of them. She was screaming and the rats were running, scampering all around—and she thought they were coming after her.

MC: What is the typical "rat bites human" scenario?

RD: Parents sometimes send their kids to bed with crackers, cookies or bread and milk. And if you live in an area where rats live in the building, you should not do that. Rats have a keen sense of smell, and they'll track the source of that bread or milk. They will climb into the child's bed or crib for the food. If a rat walks across you while you're sleeping, you throw your hand up in a response reaction. Then, the rat responds with a bite. That's what usually happens in rat bite cases.

MC: I've heard that if you corner a rat, it will attack.

RD: Who corners a rat? People normally want to get out of the way of a rat.

MC: So the idea is not to corner a rat?

RD: Exterminators who have had long experience in the field, when they go into rat-infested basements, they make a lot of noise. They'll shout: "Hey rat! Here I come! Get out of the way! I don't want to surprise you! Go back into your hole or get back into whatever it is." No one wants to meet a rat face to face.

Illustration: Alexis Rockman

They Scurry Among Us

by
Cameron
McWhirter

For many hours the immediate vicinity of the low framework upon which I lay, had been literally swarming with rats. They were wild, bold, ravenous; their red eyes glaring upon me as if they waited but for motionlessness on my part to make me their prey.
—Edgar Allan Poe, "The Pit and the Pendulum"

Man and the rat will always be pitted against each other as implacable enemies.
—Hans Zinsser, *Rats, Lice and History*

In 1848, Karl Marx published his concise *Manifesto of the Communist Party*. It opens with the famous slogan: A spectre is haunting Europe—the spectre of Communism.

These days, that spectre is DOA, for better or for worse. But the recent death of interclass struggle has allowed humanity to return to more primal fears. I refer to the spectre of interspecies contention that has terrified humanity for at least ten centuries, the spectre of Rattism.

The rat is humanity's urban doppelgänger, a ghost shadowing civilization's troubled dream. Babylonian cuneiforms show rats bearing plague to humanity's earliest cities. Throughout the centuries, the rat has subsisted on the waste and garbage of our lives, an eternal speciestariat, struggling in a symbiotic battle against a hated ruling class: *Homo sapiens*. Rats have adapted so completely to urban ecosystems that today they thrive in every city in the world, from the sewers of Manhattan to the river banks of Khartoum. No mammalian species has spread so quickly throughout civilization's artificial environments—and adapted so well.

They also wreak havoc. They attack human babies; they chew power lines; they devour billions of dollars worth of food every year. They spread numerous diseases.

As a species, they hate us. We are the ruling species of our created environs. They are perpetual scavengers. They need our refuse for food and the dark recesses of our buildings for shelter. But we are their enemy; they know this fact by instinct. In this interspecies war, we have killed, and continue to kill, hundreds of millions of them. They have killed millions of humans through the spread of disease, including the Black Death which wiped out whole cities in Europe.

Our loathing of this worthy opponent is deeply embedded as an archetype. From ecclesiastical treatises against witches to the German fable *Der Rattenfänger* to Edgar Allan Poe to H.P. Lovecraft's "The Rats in the Wall" to Camus' *The Plague* to George Orwell's *1984* to the cinematic diptych *Willard* (1971) and *Ben* (1972), the rat has been presented as the archetype of wild Nature out to get us.

> **More than any other animal in the concrete jungle, this rodent reminds us that evolution, the interspecies battle for dominance, allows no safety zones.**

Neg. #34077, Courtesy Dept. of Library Services, American Museum of Natural History

Conditions that favor the breeding of rats and the spread of bubonic plague. This model represents a corner saved from an actual house in California.

The word comes from *ræt* in Old English and from *ratta* in Old High German. It is believed by etymologists to have been taken by invading Barbarians from the Latin verbs *rodere*, to gnaw, and *radere*, to scrape, to shave. And to this day, that is how we see the rat, a sinister force gnawing at the foundations of human control.

The genus Rattus contains between 137 and 570 species, depending on which scientific classification you employ. Only the two most populous species, however, have repeatedly shaped the course of human history: *Rattus norvegicus*, the Norwegian or brown rat, or *Rattus rattus*, the black rat or roof rat.

Since first scurrying out of the Asian steppes, the rat has become an unavoidable companion of urbanized *Homo sapiens*. Part of its unmitigated success among us has been due to the absence of natural predators. In the wild, otters, owls, snakes and other animals regulated rat populations. In cities, only humans kill rats—and, in general, we do a poor, unsystematic job. Rats, as a species, have never really been hindered by the mass slaughter of individual rodents during human campaigns to destroy them. Their reproductive cycles are too rapid and their survival tactics, too good. They can survive intense cold and heat variations. To enhance survival, they have developed into nocturnal animals in many cities, to avoid human hunters.

With the rat, Mother Nature declares smugly to *Homo sapiens:* "Don't worry, we'll make more."

Yes, billions more.

The rodent eats our food and lives in our homes. It has marched with our armies; scampered in our markets; spread diseases that have transformed human history and culture. Our subways, our sewers, our walls are its byways. At every step of history, rats have been in our shadows, waiting to take advantage when humanity stumbles.

More than any other animal in the concrete jungle, this rodent reminds us that evolution, the interspecies battle for dominance, allows no safety zones.

In the 1950s, the U.S. Department of the Interior's Fish and Wildlife Service put out a pamphlet entitled "Rats—Let's Get Rid of Them" as part of a national effort to eliminate the vermin. For decades, national, state and federal officials have spent untold millions of dollars to destroy the pest.

Yet today, conservative estimates put the rat population of the U.S. alone at 200 million. And beyond our borders, the rat also flourishes. In 1994, rats ate 7.7 million tons of rice in China, enough to feed 40 million people, according to the Chinese Ministry of Agriculture.

Every major urban center on the planet—with the exception of a few islands—is home to the adaptable, fertile, intelligent rat.

As a species, they hate us. We are the ruling species of our created environs. They are perpetual scavengers. In this interspecies war, we have killed, and continue to kill, hundreds of millions of them. They have killed millions of humans through the spread of disease, including the Black Death which wiped out whole cities in Europe.

THE MAIN SPECIES

Rattus norvegicus: The Norway rat first developed, according to most researchers, in the Caspian Sea and Tobolsk in what is today Russia. Some renegade scientists have speculated the species began in Northern China.

Wherever its origins, this species—probably the most populous rat on the planet—quickly spread across the Earth thanks to a simple vector: the sailing ship. Records show this species arriving in Europe about 1553. It is believed to have gotten its misnomer (the species is not believed to have appeared in Norway until 1762) because English sailors first noticed the ships while trading in Norwegian ports.

Its first arrival in North America occurred around 1775. Wherever Europeans sailed, the Norway rat hid in the cargo hold, then climbed off at port and set about surviving and reproducing.

Today, the Norway rat is the most common species in American cities. Comfortable with water, the Norway rat prefers dank sewers and basements.

According to the U.S. Public Health Service, the Norway, or house rat, ranges in weight from 10 to 17 ounces, making it much larger than its cousin, the roof rat, which usually doesn't reach more than 12 ounces. Its ears are small.

The Norway rat can get up to 18 inches long, and can live up to three years. The average life expectancy though, is about six months to a year because of predators and disease. It is identifiable by its blunt nose, thick middle and brownish fur. The Norway rat is an excellent swimmer and climber, skills that have proved essential for adapting to modern cities. The species is omnivorous, not only does it eat everything that humanity eats, but it has also been known to eat soap, plastic and paper. The female bears two to three litters a year, with each litter containing six to 12 pups. This species includes the white laboratory rat used in modern experiments.

From the earliest research into the realm of animal psychophysics and conditioned reflex, Norway rats by the thousands have spent their brief lives in mazes and laboratory cages. The scientific fetish for rat torture stems from a long-standing disregard for their innate intelligence.

Professor of Neurology C. Judson Herrick, in his opus *Brains of Rats and Men, A Survey of the Origin and Biological Significance of the Cerebral Cortex* (1926), argued that the rat's brain "stands near the bottom of the mammalian scale." Herrick, whatever his personal brain size, missed the point: perhaps survival instinct is more important than brain size.

These rats formed the basis for B.F. Skinner's ground-breaking experiments in behavior modification, the basis for his theories on the survival of the human race. "An organism which has received a painful shock will also, if possible, act to gain access to another organism toward which it can act aggressively," Skinner wrote in *Beyond Freedom and Dignity* (1971).

When and if the Norway rat ever gets its payback, those white-smocked scientists are going to look like animal control cops in *Conquest of the Planet of the Apes.*

Rattus rattus: The black rat is thought by biological archaeologists to have originated in southeastern Asia. Like the Norway rat, this species followed civilization's expansion by sneaking onto ships and caravan wagons. Its infamy comes with what it bore along with it across Europe: the Black Death—the bubonic plague that devastated Europe for centuries, killing as many as one third of the entire continent's human population, hundreds of millions of people. Hundreds of millions more have died in Asia, Africa and the Americas from lesser outbreaks of the virus.

EXPRESSIONS EMPLOYING THE RAT

a rat's head: a fool (Brit.).

desert rats: nickname of British soldiers in North African campaign, World War II, who were first so called by Mussolini.

fight like a cornered rat: to fight furiously.

look like a drowned rat: repulsive looking, disheveled.

rat: a despised, distrusted, selfish, unethical person, often "dirty rat."

rat: a new college student.

rat: an informer or squealer.

rat: a railroad train, short for "rattler."

rat-face: someone sly and underhanded.

ratpack: originally a teenage gang, then a gang of any kind.

rat race: a way of life or job, etc., in which action or activity is more important than goals, like a lab rat on a treadmill.

rats: a star (backwards spelling, Brit.).

ratshit: the worst.

ratso: derogatory nickname.

the Ratcatcher: a nickname of Winston Churchill in World War I because he said of the German fleet: "If they do not come out to fight, they will be dug out like rats from a hole."

This Elizabethan woodcut shows a ratcatcher advertising his services.

Through a series of biological interactions, the black rat became a vector into human civilization of a plague infinitely more destructive than any disease before or since. The source is a bacterium, *Yersinia pestis*, the larvae of which gestates in the belly of the female adult *Xenopsylla cheopis* (great name for a band), the rat flea. The flea, living in the fur of the black rat, infected rats living among the garbage of medieval European cities. As they died, the rats crawled out into the light of day, near to humans. Leaping off the dead host, the fleas landed on humans. In the unsanitary cities of the Middle Ages, the disease spread quickly among rats, then humans. The disease was quick. Within days, it caused a person's lymph nodes and groin to swell, revealing buboes, a purplish round growth. The pressure was released only with the bursting of blood vessels, causing usually fatal internal bleeding. The blood, as it seeped out of the body, had a blackish color. Hence the ghoulish moniker of this rat-borne disease, which—if left untreated—has a 75% mortality rate.

Black rats fared little better than the humans dying around them. Infected rats developed distended spleens and kidneys and discolored livers.

This disease, and thus the rodent that bore it to us, altered human history. Kingdoms were destroyed. The power of religion in Europe waned. Jews, blamed for the mysterious death, were persecuted throughout Europe. The psychological effects on human society, at seeing neighbors drop dead and rot in the streets, at seeing whole villages left barren, have yet to be fully catalogued.

Children still, to this day, sing this sinister rhyme:

Ring around the rose-y
A pocket full of posies

to give one green rats: to malign, slander, or backbite (Brit.).

to have rats: to be crazy, eccentric (Brit.).

to rat-hole: to hoard food.

to rat out: to withdraw dishonorably.

to smell a rat: to suspect something is bad.

Ashes, ashes
  We all fall down.

Ring around the rose-y, the scarlet mark on the skin, was the first sign of plague. A pocket full of posie petals was supposed to help ward off the disease. But no matter what humans did in the Middle Ages, they could not stop the rat-borne death.

"We all fall down."

And bubonic plague is not gone. Cases continue to pop up throughout the world. Human victims have been documented in the southern U.S. within the last five years. The cause: the black rat.

This species is also believed to be the vector for spreading typhus. Typhus was a key factor in the demise of Napoleon's invasion army of Russia. Later, the disease killed millions during the Russian civil war of 1917 to 1921. Rats, and typhus, were also present at the Nazi concentration camps. Part of the rat's development as a vector for disease in human populations is its ability to sneak into almost any city structure. It gnaws through most common construction materials, including steel. A grown rat can squeeze through a hole the size of a quarter. It can jump four feet, if need be, to reach safety or food.

Researchers place the black rat (also called the roof rat) in South America and southern North America in the 1500s. Today, it is widespread throughout much of the Americas, though it prefers warmer climates. The species fights often with the larger Norway rat, and has been displaced from many northern U.S. cities, though it thrives in Florida. It has disappeared from many parts of Europe, thanks to its competitive relatives, and has been declared an endangered species in Virginia.

According to the U.S. Public Health Service, this species ranges in weight from four to 12 ounces. The roof rat can get up to 17-1/2 inches long, and can live several years. Average life expectancy, like the Norway rat, is about six months to a year because of predators and disease. It is identifiable by its pointy nose, slender middle and black fur. Its ears are larger than the Norway rat. The roof rat does not like to swim, but it can to survive. Like most rodents, the species is omnivorous.

While not as prolific at the Norway rat, the roof rat female bears two to three litters a year, with each litter containing six to 12 pups. To this day, the roof rat is more common in cities in the southern United States than the Northeast or Midwest. The species got its common name because it favors nesting on the rooftops of buildings. In the wilds of Asia, they nested in trees.

Part of its unmitigated success among us has been due to the absence of natural predators. In the wild, otters, owls, snakes and other animals regulated rat populations. In cities, only humans kill rats—and, in general, we do a poor, unsystematic job.

DIET

The rat, whatever species, is voracious. Their primary objective from birth is to eat. As catalogued in the masterwork *More Cunning than Man: A Social History of Rats and Men* by Robert Hendrickson, rats have been known to slaughter pigs, chickens and any other domesticated animal. They have been observed hunting seafood including crabs and lobster. They have been known to chew the toes off of elephants at zoos.

They have caused the extinction of numerous species of birds on Pacific islands by eating their eggs. They have eaten leather boots, light bulbs, paint, glue, seeds.... Anything humanity stores or discards is a possible meal for the rats.

Humans themselves have not been immune to rat attack. The criterion is simple: they have to be weak. Enfeebled elderly and infants have been killed by rats. Hans Zinsser, in his 1934 work *Rats, Lice and History*, reported that babies have had their noses chewed off in their cribs, and starving rats once devoured a man who went into a disused coal mine.

INTELLIGENCE

Despite the almost universal hatred of the human race, despite poisons, traps, clubs and guns, rat colonies flourish in our cities. Rats thrive in any climate. They eat anything. They reproduce at a phenomenal rate. They are much more resistant to radiation than humans. They thrive on human waste and squalor.

But most terrifying of all, they think.

Prior to this century, scientists presupposed the higher intelligence of the human race. The human cerebral cortex was considered the exclusive master of mnemonic function.

But experiments by Watson as early as 1907 and later by Skinner showed that rats have the ability to learn. Beyond the tricks of maze-crawling and eating cheese, rats have been observed cautiously sending taste-testers to try suspicious food. They have been known to dig special airtight caves for emergencies in flood regions. They work in packs to steal eggs or other food too heavy for one to carry.

They learn to improve their chances for survival.

As reported in *More Cunning than Man*, one exterminator observed rats in a meat locker. About 200 rats formed into a writhing pyramid so one rat could leap to an unreachable side of beef. That rat then crawled up to the hook, and gnawed the beef loose so it dropped to the ground for all the rats to eat.

The real threat to humanity is not the rat's teeth or claws, but its brain.

"The rat is mankind's Number One four-legged enemy and probably the most astute," was the conclusion of a May 1993 report by the World Health Organization.

One exterminator observed rats in a meat locker. About 200 rats formed into a writhing pyramid so one rat could leap to an unreachable side of beef. That rat then crawled up to the hook, and gnawed the beef loose so it dropped to the ground for all the rats to eat.

SOCIAL ORGANIZATION

Rat social life is a dark mirror of our own. Like humans, they are communal. They live in colonies, hidden in the crevices of human structures. Conservative rodentologists estimate 500 rats for every mile of American sewer. Rat nests have been found under floorboards, in attics, in basements. Nests have been found made of clothes, trash, newspaper, even money.

The burrows contain several females, with males competing for the right to mate with them. High-ranking males set up territories around the burrows. Rats don't like to venture far from their homes, but will if they must. They have been known to travel miles in a single night in search of something to eat.

Rats communicate by squeaks and squeals, used as either warnings or as a sign of aggression. Like humans, rival groups will often attack each other. Rats have been known to attack and kill rats from other colonies when they enter their burrow. On other occasions, they have been known to adopt outsiders into the community.

The size of packs ranges from families of half-a-dozen to legions of several thousand rats. Every night, these hordes emerge in New York, Los Angeles, Atlanta, Dallas, Cleveland; every city in America, every city in the world. They forage among our waste, among our food, inside our buildings. While we sleep, rodent armies take over our world.

Professor of Neurology C. Judson Herrick argued that the rat's brain "stands near the bottom of the mammalian scale." Herrick, whatever his personal brain size, missed the point: perhaps survival instinct is more important than brain size.

DISEASES

Rodent swarms don't simply wreak havoc on our food supplies; they also spread disease.

We all know the plague drill. Diseased fleas and lice use the rat as a host until the rat dies. Once dead, the insect will jump to humans, spreading death. So long, medieval Europe.

But the plague, which is still around in India and other parts of Asia, is by no means the only disease borne by rats. Rattus and other Rodentia are vectors for numerous illnesses hitting humans and livestock. They can spread rabies, rat-bite fever and more than 30 other diseases.

Two examples: Tsutsuamushi fever, a typhus first identified by the Japanese. A type of lice, in the larval stages, lives in rat fur. It transmits this typhus by sucking the blood of rats and then jumping to humans. During World War II, it disabled thousands of soldiers.

And trichinosis is a common and dangerous stomach illness often transmitted by infected rats. Rats, or their fecal matter, are eaten by pigs rummaging in garbage. The pigs become infected. Humans, eating pork that has not been properly cooked, then become ill.

A grown rat can squeeze through a hole the size of a quarter. It can jump four feet, if need be, to reach safety or food.

Stephen W. Barthold, a veterinarian and Professor of Comparative Medicine at Yale, in a frighteningly clinical 1994 report "Infectious Diseases of Mice and Rats" details the potential illnesses carried by rats. Lice, fleas and mites in rat fur also carry disease.

These diseases, ranging from viral to bacterial, include cowpox virus, hemorrhagic fever with renal syndrome, Tyler's disease, *Salmonella enteritidis* and *Streptobacillus moniliformis*. Investigators even suspect that the mysterious and often fatal epidemic on an Arizona Navaho Indian range could have been caused by a rat-borne virus.

Terrorists? The Tri-Lateral Commission? The Man?

Try guerrilla interspecies warfare—rats spreading diarrhea, fevers, stomach pains and ringworm among their enemies in the urban ecosystem.

> To paraphrase Marx's manifesto: "Let the ruling humans tremble at the rat revolution. The rats have nothing to lose but their chains. They have a world to win." The rats are gnawing on those chains right now.

ENCOUNTERS WITH HUMANS

The urban human encounters the rat and the rat's work at every turn: work, home, restaurants, streets and subways. These run-ins with our evolutionary shadows are inevitable, always queasy and occasionally ghastly.

In New York City, with a population of roughly 9 million, experts estimate a one-to-one ratio of rat to person. Rat attacks have been reported in all neighborhoods—from the slums of Washington Heights to upscale Greenwich Village. The subway system even has its own rat patrol.

USA Today reported that New Yorkers reported 264 rat bites in 1993 compared to 154 in 1992, an increase of 70%. Complaints about rat infestations were also up by thousands to 22,245. A key reason for the increase: federal cutbacks of pest control programs.

Worse, direct human encounters with rats haven't been pretty. Some examples:

1983: Kendleton, TX—Police arrested a man for arson after he torched the one-bedroom house where his family had been living. The family had recently been evicted because the man's nephew had been attacked by rats. The rats gnawed the infant's nose, face and hands. Police reported numerous rats running from the home during the fire.

1986: Houston, TX—The Associated Press reported that a mother was arrested and charged with endangerment after rats gnawed her five-month old daughter's wrist to the bone and bit her two older sisters when they were left unattended. The rats were attracted to a milk bottle left next to the baby in bed. "They went after the milk and then after the baby," the assistant district attorney said.

1993: Fullerton, CA— A homeless couple was charged with child endangerment when their pet rat, Homer, attacked and killed their newborn son. The child had been bitten more than 110 times. And they are not the first humans, either foolish or simply species traitors, who have tried to befriend the rat.

1994: Cincinnati, OH— United Press International reported that a retired schoolteacher had her car seized by police when hordes of rats where found living inside. The woman had been living in the 16-year-old car with the rats when a passerby noticed the rodents writhing in garbage in the back seat. Police didn't charge the woman, but ordered an exterminator to lay down poison in the car.

Despite the barrage of such irrefutable and horrific evidence, evolutionary "fifth columnists" continue to spread propaganda that the rat is our "friend." They have developed strong Rattus clubs across the country. Particularly strong chapters in California hold annual conventions. Several now maintain websites, which carry charters pledging kindness toward rodents.

ADAPTIBILITY

In early attacks against the behaviorist movement in modern psychology, scientists asserted repeatedly that rats

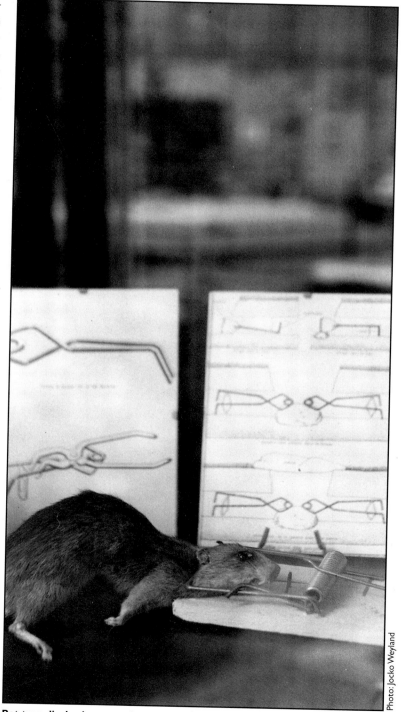

Rat trap display in exterminator's window in Paris.

EXPRESSIONS EMPLOYING THE MOUSE

as drunk as a mouse: very drunk (Brit. obs.).

as sure as a mouse tied with thread: very uncertain (Brit.).

as warm as a mouse in a churn: very snug (Brit.).

mouse: a bruise on or near the eye.

mouse: affectionate term for an attractive young woman, sweetheart or wife.

mouse, mouser: a mustache.

mouse: a small military rocket.

mouse: a timid informer, squealer.

mouse-piece: in beef or mutton, the part just above the knee joint (Brit. obs.).

mousetrap: a submarine (Brit.).

mousetrap: the female pubenda (Brit. obs.).

mousetrap: a cheap nightclub or theater.

mousetrap: a play to trap a would-be tackler by the offensive line in football.

to mouse: to fake an opponent out of position, to fool or mislead.

to mouse: to neck (obs.).

to mouse over: to sample, dip into.

to speak like a mouse in cheese: to speak faintly or indistinctly (Brit. obs.).

trouser mouse: the penis.

were not humans; therefore studies on their behavior had little relevance to understanding humanity.

They were partially right. Rats are, in fact, better than humans when compared by the only measuring stick important to evolution: survival. The key to species survival, as Darwin pointed out with his research on the Galapagos Islands, is adaptability.

Rats followed humanity to adapt in every possible environment, with the exception of Antarctica. They have thrived in the bowels of ships, the trenches of war and the sewers of cities. By Darwin's standards, rats could prove to be the fittest mammal on the planet and certainly the most indestructible creature in the concrete jungle.

If humanity ever destroys itself, Rattus is ready to step in and take over. Tens of thousands of people believe triangular-faced aliens with almond-shaped eyes fly around the Earth, waiting for the right moment to enslave the planet.

These people don't need to look any farther than their basement for the "aliens."

The rats are here and they are waiting.

Back to the Galapagos. Recently, nature groups set up a special turtle egg sanctuary in a desperate attempt to save the local species from extinction. Invading rats had been eating the eggs.

To return to Marx, and paraphrase his manifesto:

"Let the ruling humans tremble at the rat revolution. The rats have nothing to lose but their chains. They have a world to win."

The rats are gnawing on those chains right now.

USEFUL WEB SITES ABOUT RATS

The Mouse and Rat Research Home Page can be found at ww.cco.caltech.edu/~mercer/htmls/rodent_page.html.

This site, created by Professor Eric Mercer at Caltech, is *the* Web clearinghouse for rat information. Under headings such as "Genome Informatics" and "Veterinary Resources and Animal Husbandry," web surfers can learn about numerous rat diseases; view a "rat brain atlas;" contemplate "Controlling Rat and Mice in Swine Facilities;" and review the annals of the cryptic "International Rodent Numbering Commission." Points lead to other rat-related sites, including home pages for the Rat and Mouse Club of America, the American Fancy Rat and Mouse Association (AFRMA), and the Swedish Rat Society. ■

Cameron McWhirter, an investigative reporter, dreams of being a lightbulb: raw, flowing energy and singular of purpose. He can be contacted at lizard2@cinci.infi.net.

The Life of a New York City Rat

by
Edward
DeFreitas

You leave your warm, comfortable home that has running water in it and step outside. Within a few yards of your home is a food supply of an unimaginable amount, one that you and all your buddies could not possibly consume in a given day. You go home with your belly full, and the next night there's even more food out there. Would you have any trouble surviving? Or even prospering and multiplying? What I just described to you is a rat coming out of a sewer in any street in mid-town Manhattan.

They bring the food out—they call it garbage—and put it in plastic bags which wait all night on the street until they are picked up by the trash haulers. Before the sanitation gets there, the rats get to them and go right through the plastic. And believe me, the haulers are very care-ful before they pick up a bag. They know there might be a rat in one.

You'll always have rats in the city, because they eat what we eat. And we leave a lot around. Humans run the gamut from being fas-tidious to being slobs—like the Odd Couple. At one end is Oscar Madison and at the other end is Felix Unger. That's the length and breadth of the spectrum of the human race. And as long as you got Oscar Madisons, you'll have plenty of rats. There are rats in every sewer line, every storm drain in New York City. There's no question about that. ■

Edward DeFreitas works for Empire Pest Control in Manhattan, New York City.

Animals in the City

by
Dan
Dickerson

If you go out into the country and you walk through the woods, you're not going to see a rat or any animal. A country rat is going to take off before you get to see to it. Take that same rat or bird and put it in New York City next to the Long Island Expressway with trucks rumbling by all day. They become desensitized. Nothing affects them. It's a whole different animal. It's an urban species, whose sensitivity to people has been dulled. Or maybe its courage has been strengthened. They will walk outside in the daytime. They will put up with noise. If you brought an animal to the city from the country, it would have a nervous break-down in a couple of days. ■

Dan Dickerson works for the Board of Education Pest Control in New York City.

Rats: An Appreciation

by
Druscilla
Kehl

I have five pet rats and I just got two more yesterday. I have owned the small rodents for several years and cannot imagine my life without their companionship. But make no mistake, I am referring to the friendly, impish, docile animals bred by rat fanciers or available in some pet stores. Although, sadly, at most stores they are kept in less than ideal conditions. The owners don't care: most rats they sell are destined to be some snake's dinner.

Why did we first decide to get a pet rat? My husband thought that having one would enable him to better draw scary rats for his horror comics. (I myself had nothing against them, no pre-existing aversion to mice or rats.) Well, the first thing we learned was that there was nothing frightening about the plump little creature we took home that day. He had a boxy head, an avocado-shaped body, and bright, friendly-looking, black eyes. Like many domesticated rats, he had a white body and a black hood over his head and shoulders. There was little resemblance to the feral grey rodents that everyone imagines when you say the word *rat*. Our ratty quickly formed a bond with us, demonstrating intelligence and affection, and charming us with his antics. We began to realize that we were getting the level of response and interaction from this little animal that we might expect from one much larger, say, a dog or cat.

I think this is the key to the emotional relationships between rat-owner and their pets. These animals look at you with their bright eyes, grasp your fingers with their little hands, and you can sense them identifying you as an individual, their friend. Each rat has a special personality, some sociable, some shy, some willful and some docile. In almost every case, the pet owner can establish a close one-on-one relationship with an animal small enough to hold in his or her hands. There is something very gratifying in this.

Over the last few years

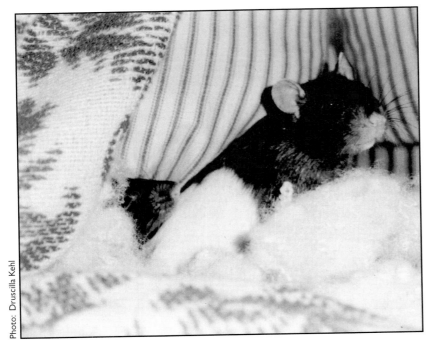

Photo: Druscilla Kehl

Pet rat Dewey on the couch.

we have owned a total of 15 pet rats. Their habitat has grown from a ten gallon tank to a large cage and tank complex that dominates our living room. While rats have a long way to go to being accepted as a popular pet, I am beginning to think that the ranks of rat-lovers are growing. There are several clubs in this country with growing memberships. There are web sites and on-line bulletin boards where rodent enthusiasts exchange advice, anecdotes and sympathies for lost loved ones. Organizations from England, Belgium, the Netherlands and Scandinavia are connecting with American ones; I have been pleased to discover a community of people out there who share the love and appreciation I feel for rats, those creatures who have long been the bane of humanity, but who, surprisingly, have turned out to be the ideal pet. ∎

Druscilla Kehl is a rat enthusiast and illustrator who lives in New York City.

> **While rats have a long way to go to being accepted as a popular pet, I am beginning to think that the ranks of rat-lovers are growing. There are several clubs in this country with growing memberships. There are web sites and on-line bulletin boards.**

Great blue herons have been known to "work" a network of houses rather than catch fish, their usual prey. A retiree who was unable to catch fish for his heron, resorted to a trip to the fish market. He later learned the heron preferred hot dogs and bologna.

Illustration: Alexis Rockman

Rat Newsletter

Pages from *The Potent Rodent* (summer 1996, issue 2) of the New York City Chapter of the Northeast Rat and Mouse Club International. The newsletter features advice on pet rat and mouse products, fiction and even a column on being a mouse addict.

For information, send e-mail to mikiodo@earthlink.net or write to: P.O. Box 1802, New York, NY 10009.

N.Y.C.C's Newsletter
NEW YORK CITY CHAPTER
of the
Northeast Rat and Mouse
Club International

Photos by Heidi Vickery

Book Reviews
by Cindee

Mice: A Complete Pet Owner's Manual
by Horst Bielfield. 80 pages. A Barrons Educational Series. ISBN 0-8120-2921-6. (About $7.00)

This book was first written in 1984 by a pair of German authors and then translated into English. Mice are very popular pets in Germany, so you can imagine the wealth of valuable information this book contains. It's a great guide for new mouse owners and people thinking about getting a pet mouse. In addition to important sections on the specific care of pet mice, it has a chapter on understanding the body language and communication of mice. There's also an introduction to genetics and a chapter on various species of mice. The photos and drawings are terrific . . . informative and plentiful!

Macmillan Illustrated Animal Encyclopedia
Edited by Dr. Phillip Whitfield. 1984. 600 pages. ISBN 0-02-627680-1 ($35.00)

The number of pages in this book devoted to the rodentia order is amazing . . . nearly 50 pages . . . AND it covers about 78 different kinds of rats, mice, and their relatives. There is even a color drawing of each one. Those intersted in exotics will especially enjoy this book. It describes the size, habitat, and range of the African Dormouse, Bamboo Rat, Northern 3-toed Jerboa, Four Striped Grass Mouse, Harvest Mouse, Forest Spring Pocket Mouse, and over 70 others! Even "the experts" will be impressed with the rodents featured in this encyclopedia.

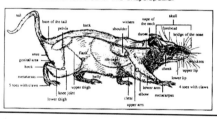

Hello. My name is Jonie Senese and I am 21 years old. I have two fawn rats. One male Pete and one female Clementine. My love for rats started a few years ago. I was introduced to a dumbo rat named Bud. I knew at that moment one of my own was in the future. My first experience in sharing my space with one Pandora was the best! Thanks to science teacher Cindee I am now blessed with my buddies Pete and Clementine. Thanks so much Cindee! (Note: Clementine has unfortunately passed away since this letter was written. Jonie now also has a male Siamese rat, Confuciss, adopted at the meeting from Cindee.)

Pandora
You were a gift to me that I hold very dear. You have a special place in my heart all to yourself.
Little girl of mine I love you so much. With all of my heart. Don't think for a second that I'll ever stop loving you, or forget you a second. For that will never happen. You are a part of me forever. I will love and cherish our time together forever. I love you sweetheart.

Petzie
My new tiny helpless baby boy. I hope that you know how much I love you. And I hope that with time you will love me too, because there is nothing in this world That I would not do for you.

Y U M! Raquel Cintron brought chocolate mousse mice to a meeting.

before / after

I told the hairless mouse that the sun wasn't good for her skin!

mice (a spontaneous effort by Mike and Philip)

mice stink
their babies are pink
they're very smart,
i think

they are no bigger
than castanets
they leave a trail
of raisinets
they dine on nuts and
other things
even cardboard and
cockroach wings

mice are curious
they seldom get furious –
i'm completely serious!

they have no spaces between
their teeth
but have no trouble saying
squeak squeak squeak
they make a better pet than
a worm
but hold mice tight for
they like to squirm

quite nice
these little mice
hey! who ate my rice?!

if you thinks you're cozy
and sleeping tight
and feel a gnawing in
the night
before you file proceedings
against your spouse
open your eyes –
might be a mouse!

BIG CHEESE!

Pages from the newsletter (clockwise from top left): book reviews of *Mice: A Complete Pet Owner's Manual* and *Macmillan Illustrated Animal Encyclopedia* with a rodentia section; 2 pieces of original artwork involving mice; a poem entitled "Mice" and a profile of a 21-year old rat owner.

chapter 5

Hosting Others

A Meter of Meadow, Mark Dion (1995)

Here's Worm in Your Eye

by
Bob
Braine

"Thar she blows!...Whoops!"

"Whoops?" I said to Dr. Ruth Weichsel, my chin resting on the cool metal of her ophthalmologic viewing device. "What do you mean, 'Whoops'?"

"It went back into its burrow."

Hmmmm. It went back into its burrow—in my eye. All along, I thought that it was only living in the surface slime. I had seen the worm that lived in my eye two days earlier. I had been editing slides on a light box for a travelogue slide show of my recent trip to Guyana, which is located on the northeast coast of South America.

My head had been aching beyond reasonable description, my eyes felt as if they were about to burst from their sockets and lie down upon my cheeks like some David-Caradine-induced Kung Fu extraction. I spoke to a friend of mine, who continually reminded me of the possibility of river blindness, a condition caused by parasitic worms that feast on spaghetti-like optic nerves.

You see, I already knew that I had a worm in my body, but it really didn't bother me. Aside from the crayon-like trails on my right foot and lower right leg and the unbearable itching ("it itch hot," they say in Guyana), I was happy with the worm in my leg. As soon as I got back from Guyana, I went to the dermatologist who had treated an earlier tropical-pathogen-induced leg condition, confident in her ability to help my infested organism reclaim the sovereignty of the body that is rightfully mine. She looked at the red squiggles and proclaimed that I had a hook-worm, which normally attacks the intestinal systems of cats and dogs. This one liked my leg better. I must have gotten it while standing calf-deep in a garbage dump in Georgetown, Guyana, snapping photographs of brilliant cattle egrets poking through the putrid rubbish amid mud-encrusted bulldozer tracks.

Anyway, it liked my leg and decided to move in. Little did I know that it had upward mobility in its real-estate portfolio.

I had no money when I returned from Guyana in April, 1994. The poison cream—thebendizol in a topical solution—cost $85, and I didn't have the bread. So I asked Dr. Weichsel if the worm had the capacity to migrate to other sites in my body. She assured me that it wouldn't, that my body would eventually fight this parasitic invader and break it down to its base molecular structure. Well, the raised, red, parasitic mole tunnels seemed to die down after a few weeks, the itching subsided and I was content...until, many weeks later when my head hurt more than a lot. My friend, the one so enthusiastically proposing the river blindness hypothesis, had given me the telephone number of one Dr. Kevin Cahill, tropical medicine specialist to the rich and famous, and the down and dirty alike. He is even the Pope's doctor on occasion.

"I just saw a worm swim across my eye, doc. Help," I said.

"There are tens of thousands of people in the world with worms in their eyes. Don't call me at 10:00 at night."

Photo: Paige Buonocore

Bob Braine examines his own eye for the hookworm, a minute roundworm parasite (one centimeter in length). Human infection occurs when individuals walk barefoot on contaminated ground. The larvae penetrate the skin and travel in the lymph and blood.

The moment I saw the worm undulate across my field of vision, I looked up at my girlfriend, who was sitting on the bed, and said: "Baby, something very bad just happened." At first, she didn't believe me. She just couldn't; so she relegated the vision to too much psychic stress. But to me, it was somehow gratifying to see this sinister nematode that had invaded my well-being. One can fight the enemy when it is visible. On the light box, I had been looking at slides of the stomach contents of a "double boom," a large, brown, armored catfish of the Amazon basin that grunts rhythmically when you haul it out of its aquatic world. The photos depicted thin, white, thread-like worms—I remember them well, undulating under my gaze, my glasses fogging from the heat as I wove forward and back to focus, kneeling in the oil-soaked Mazaruni river sand at the site of a former goldminer's camp. For years, I had been photographing evidence of pathology—microscopic worms, fish parasites, maggots on road kill, etc. Now I had unwittingly become my own subject matter. My camera ceased to be the vehicle of visual delivery.

I called Dr. Cahill that night and got hold of his answering service at 10:15 p.m. and left my name and number in a panic. A few minutes later, Dr. Cahill called me up and asked in an impatient voice, "What are you calling me at 10:00 p.m. for?!"

"I just saw a worm swim across my eye, doc. Help," I said.

"There are tens of thousands of people in the world with worms in their eyes. Don't call me at 10:00 at night. I won't be in tomorrow, but you can come in on Thursday morning. This thing has been in your head for weeks and it's not going to do anything within the next two days."

Meanwhile, I felt as if I were contemplating blindness. The prospect of blindness was unsettling. My eyes were filled with many floaters—strings of protein and things released from my retina becoming detached from its proper place. A common thing, I am told. These worms were not only in my eyes. They were everywhere in my body. For hours, I tilted my head on the light box, envisioning the fluids sloshing to the front of my cranium, causing the worms to coalesce on the very front of my eyeballs, where I could see them. I desperately wanted to see one again. I was only to be granted that one fleeting glimpse, like the proverbial white whale that Weichsel referred to. My parasite was loathe to show itself.

So, the fix: I went, very excited to have found "the man." He turned down the lights, took his little point light and looked into my left eye. "There it is!" he exclaimed.

This gratified me to no end. Someone else had seen it. He sent my blood to the Center for Disease Control down in Atlanta. I felt like I had the last word in parasite control. Dr. Cahill described the way in which he found out about some of these worms. They were sent to him by the emergency rooms of various hospitals after they had been extracted, along with the eyeball. The eye swells up because of the proteinaceous cysts which form around it. This leads doctors to fear the worst: a retinal contusion which could violate the sanctity of the eye socket and push into the brain where the pressure can kill you. When ER folks see this, out comes the melon-baller.

Well, I was lucky. If I had not actually seen the worm, perhaps this same fate would have been mine. I had the good fortune to be surrounded by people who steered me in the right direction.

Dr. Cahill then sent me back to Dr. Ruth Weichsel, a kind, fine-boned, 60-something woman, who had applied the New Bedford exclamation to my condition. She dilated my pupils and determined for sure my situation. The cure was the same poison cream, only this time in an oral solution under the brand name Mintozol. Yum.

Many people don't realize this, but insecticide is the main component of New York's beverage of choice. Caffeine is a plant alkaloid, a substance that is produced to prevent insects from eating its delicious green leaves. My diet that week consisted of anti-inflammatory steroids and

> My eyes were filled with many floaters—strings of protein and things released from my retina becoming detached from its proper place. A common thing, I am told. These worms were not only in my eyes. They were everywhere in my body.

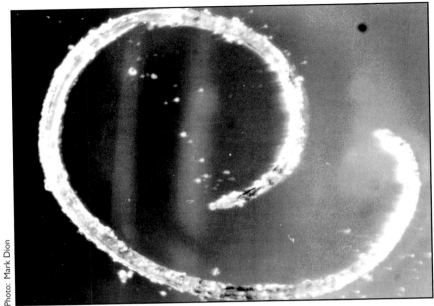

Photo: Mark Dion

Micro-photo of a roundworm.

Mintozol. Who could ask for more? I was drinking poison that was designed to kill bugs. It was like gargling with Raid. This lasted about one week. There was no sleep and nausea was with me every moment. All the while, my head ached. I'm sure that the steroids affected my mood significantly.

I took the required dosage for one week and then settled down waiting to feel normal again. My head throbbed with pain that was unstoppable. The cysts that had formed as a defense mechanism still had to break down. Until they did, I would still have a headache.

After another two weeks of peering constantly at the insides of my eyes against white paper, light, the sky—basically appearing to an unknown observer like someone looking vacuously around themselves for ghosts or angels—I decided they weren't dead. I went for another round of Minitozol. Delicious. Same things: a week of no sleep, nausea, etc.

I now have an understanding of all systems, both "natural" and "man-made." I never really felt anger at my parasites, as if their presence was somehow unfair. I recall a scene in a Gamera movie, the first one, I believe. A gang of Japanese scientists were watching a movie of another gang of Japanese scientists who had cut open the trunk of an elephant, revealing a seething ball of finger-thick, arm-long white worms. The viewing scientists coiled back in revulsion. I remember thinking how unfair for the elephant.

I have always thought of a bluefish I once caught. It had small, spherical, parasitic crustaceans attached to its gills. This sight had made my skin crawl. For some reason, when this was all brought right back home with my worms, I did not experience the same emotions.

So. Now, I am certifiably worm free. And I will wash my fucking feet next time I slosh around a third world garbage dump. Next. ∎

Bob Braine is an artist, boat builder, and photographer who lives in Brooklyn, New York.

What Scavenges on the Dead

Nunc putredo terrae et cibus verminorum.
(Now I reek of the earth and am food for worms.)

by
Diane Karluk, M.D.
and
John A.
Hayes, Jr., M.D.

In life, man is well defended, but not autonomous; he is the substrate on which hordes of microorganisms thrive. They, in turn, help digest food and maintain the protective barriers that are portals of entry to the internal environment. Their strategy is competitive: by utilizing nutrients introduced into or provided by the human body, a specific bacterial species may control, or colonize, a body-surface thereby excluding competitors. A state of health thus depends on colonization by benevolent organisms, those which will be sustained by ingested foods and the detritus of normal bodily functions without disrupting the integrity of the cells and viscera required by man.

In death, the rules of symbiosis no longer apply. There is a sudden exponential increase in available resources for microbes as the dying cells of the host dissolve following release of their own erosive molecules. As tissues break down and protective immune surveillance collapses, bacteria gain rapid access to the internal environment. They initially spread widely throughout the body within the fluid channels of the blood vessels. Because many of the body's bacteria reside in the colon, one of the earliest signs of decomposition is a green discoloration of the abdomen due to a proliferation of bacteria that produce sulfur-containing gases.

As the bacterial population mushrooms, large volumes of gas inflate the tissues, causing the body to become buoyant and to float in water. High tissue pressures created by the gases squeeze fetid, decompositional fluids from the body's orifices. Bloated corpses deflate and make hissing sounds when the malodorous gases are released by cutting the tissues in which they are entrapped. One

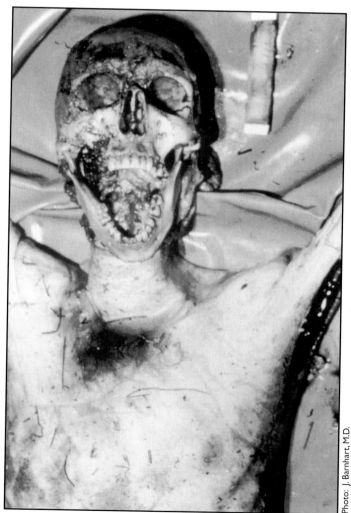

Photo: J. Barnhart, M.D.

Vulture feeding: the organs of the torso have been removed through the right armpit.

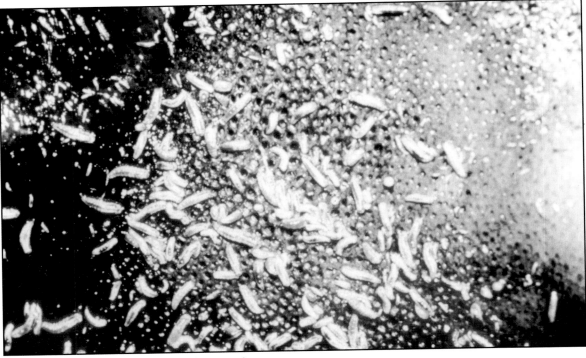

Maggots and flesh-eating beetles on a decomposing corpse.

18th-century English device, developed to confirm the death of an individual beyond a shadow of a doubt, used the emanation of sulfide gas from the decomposing body to precipitate the words "I am dead" in silver nitrate onto a pane of glass held over the corpse.

Competition for the newly available and temporary resource, the dead body, rapidly spreads beyond the microscopic world. The aromatic gases and pooling putrefactive fluids are irresistible to many flying insects, whose highly specialized scent-guided navigational systems help locate the body from up to two miles away. In areas where other carcasses have decomposed, flesh flies and blow flies can swarm to a body within seconds. If the body is indoors, within a sealed container, buried, or wrapped in a shroud, the arrival of flies may be significantly delayed or completely prevented.

Flies alight and feed on the moist, soft tissues in and about body orifices and open wounds as their soft mouth parts are unable to pierce skin. The semi-liquid environment of these sites is also an excellent medium for breeding. Thousands of eggs are rapidly deposited in the protein-rich liquors of decompositional fluid. Some flies lay single eggs while others deposit them in large clusters. Although blow fly eggs are each only 1–3 mm long, they are laid in vast quantities that have been described as having the appearance of grated cheese.

Maggots are believed to have prevented many Civil War deaths from gangrene and sepsis by infesting wounds and debriding the dead or rotting tissue.

Hordes of worm-like progeny, called maggots, emerge simultaneously from the eggs and burrow throughout the body as a group, rapidly consuming decaying soft tissues and viscera. The large numbers and frenzied feeding activities of the maggots can make the tissues of the body move conspicuously. Holes due to maggot burrowing may be erroneously interpreted as gunshot wounds or other injuries occurring prior to death. The amount of heat generated by the activity of masses of maggots can elevate carcass temperatures as much as 22°C above ambient temperature.

Maggots can only digest necrotic or putrefying tissue—occasionally, maggot infestations of live individuals are encountered, and maggots are believed to have prevented many Civil War deaths from gangrene and sepsis by infesting wounds and debriding the dead or rotting tissue.

When the maggots have matured, they migrate from the body in order to pupate. Depending on the fly species, the larvae may move directly beneath the corpse or far away. The speed of larval migration depends on the characteristics of the surfaces traversed. Hard surfaces, such as rocks or floors, greatly accelerate migration rates. Larvae have been observed to migrate up to 100 feet on a slaughterhouse floor in a single day.

Ants, wasps, and beetles prey upon the maggots, sometimes following migratory masses crawling from the body. They also consume the drier tissues of the corpse. Ants and cockroaches, common inhabitants in many households, leave numerous small superficial erosions as they feed upon exposed areas of skin. These marks may be mistaken for scratches and may give rise to suspicions of violent death, most frequently when Emergency Room staff examine victims of crib death who have been fed upon after death. In turn, predatorial insects, such as mites, approach the corpse to feed on other insects. Spiders, centipedes, and pill bugs may become inhabitants of the decaying body incidentally as an extension of their normal locale.

In this way, a corpse may be rapidly consumed and colonized by successions of invading insects. A body laying uncovered on the ground can be reduced by 90% of the original body weight in one week. A highly complex community can evolve over time to

The aromatic gases and pooling putrefactive fluids are irresistible to many flying insects, whose highly specialized scent-guided navigational systems help locate the body from up to two miles away.

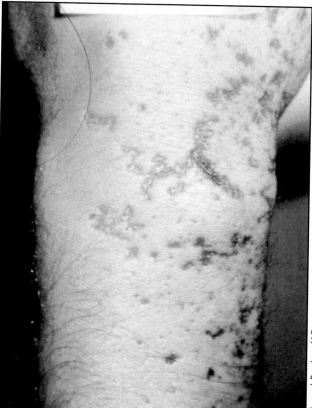

Photo: J. Barnhart, M.D.

Postmortem insect feeding: the erosions on the wrist are probably due to roaches.

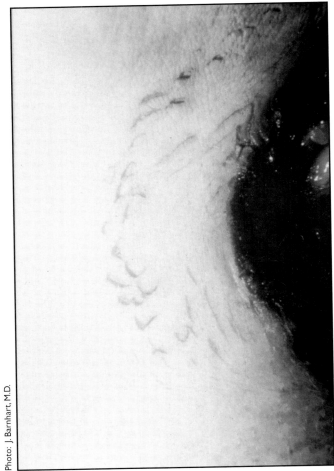

Photo: J. Barnhart, M.D.

Postmortem sharkbite: visible rows of V-shaped tooth marks.

include several hundred different insect species associated with a single decomposing body. In a given location during a particular season, the succession of insects invading a dead body is so predictable that an estimate of the time of death can be made based on the types and ages of the insects found in and around the body—the province of the forensic entomologist.

In aquatic settings, scavenging of a magnitude comparable to that of insects is the domain of crabs and other crustaceans. They will attack a body dumped in water, their bites leaving crater-like defects that may eventually denude large areas of uncovered tissue. All soft tissues and internal organs may eventually be consumed. Fishes also feed on soft tissues such as ears, nose, eyelids and lips, sometimes causing complete defleshing. The identity of such an individual can be extremely difficult to establish.

Larger aquatic creatures will also take advantage of the immersed body. In fresh water, turtles and alligators may feed on a body—one of the authors had a case in which the body of a woman, who had disappeared after a night of hard drinking by a pond, was found floating face up in the water a week later. When the body was spotted during an aerial search, the helicopter pilot described hundreds of turtles surrounding it, and it was discovered that the face and neck had been stripped bare of tissues. This was problematic, as it made it impossible to determine whether or not the woman had been strangled or had had her throat cut.

Both alligators and sharks are more likely to attack an already lifeless body. Generally, the limbs, dangling beneath the floating torso, are the target of shark attacks. Because of the structure of their jaws, sharks cannot chew their food well and much of the initial fragmenting of the food is done as the flesh is removed from the body. The shark attacks in an upwards direction, trapping the limb or pelvis in its mouth and tearing off the tissue (or entire limb) in a rolling motion. Shark jaws exert considerable pressure, and the teeth may score underlying bone, or may break off and become imbedded in the tissue around the wound.

A number of case reports of human remains recovered from the intestinal tract have been published, and stress the ability of the shark to interrupt its digestion at will, preserving swallowed food in the intestine in remarkably good condition for prolonged periods of time. Probably the most famous of these is the Australian "Shark Arm Murder" case, in which the arm of a man, severed by his assailants in an attempt to conceal his identity, was discovered in the gut of a tiger shark. Because of the unpredictability of the shark's digestive process, little information could be gained about the timing of the incident. However, the presence of a distinctive tattoo on the forearm identified the victim as a member of the organized crime community.

Holes due to maggot burrowing may be erroneously interpreted as gunshot wounds or other injuries occurring prior to death.

Carnivorous mammals and birds indigenous to a habitat, rural or urban, will devour the dead if given sufficient privacy to do so. Large animals such as dogs and wolves may widely disperse a corpse as they disarticulate and carry off parts to consume later in their dens. Some cultures have taken advantage of the appetites of local carnivores to neatly dispose of the dead. The ancient Egyptians cast the bodies of the poor and crippled into the desert to be eaten by jackals and hyenas. The Parsis of India place the dead in trees or *Dahkmas* (Towers of Silence) to be devoured by vultures so as to not defile the sacred elements, earth, fire, and water with decaying bodies. In modern Tibet, the dead are sometimes given "air burials." The body is dismembered and the flesh cut from the bones to speed up the consumption of the cadaver by flocks of birds. Birds have been reported to steal hair from decomposing bodies, using it to line their nests.

In modern cities in the U.S., potential carnivores larger than insects are generally limited to professional scavengers, such as rodents, and veritable dependents, house pets. Mice and rats commonly gnaw at any exposed soft tissues, particularly those of the face. A golden hamster was reported to extensively mutilate the face of its owner who had died at home from pneumonia. Her death was originally suspected to be due

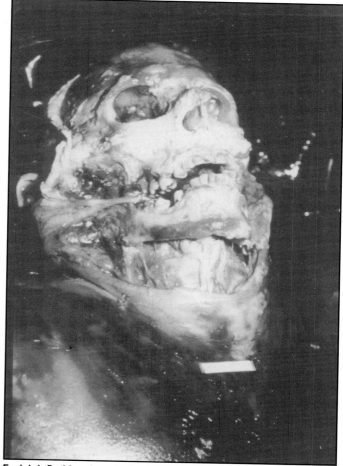
Facial defleshing done by freshwater turtles.

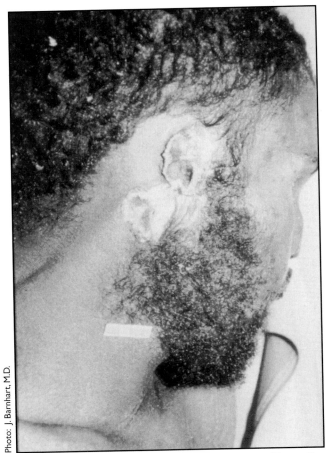

Photo: J. Barnhart, M.D.

Postmortem rat activity: the right ear, right eye and lower lip have been eaten away.

to homicidal violence based on the facial injuries. Further analysis revealed small paired bite marks on the face. Pea-sized fragments of tissue in the hamster's nest were identified as human soft tissues and confirmed by DNA analysis to be specifically those of the owner.

The voracious eating of the dead by household cats and dogs is well-known. The soft tissues of the face and head are preferred, sometimes to the degree that decapitation occurs. Dogs can drag the body from one area to another, or disarticulate limbs, thus confusing the interpretation of the death scene. Another frequent cadaveric target for rodents and pets is the genitalia, particularly the penis and scrotum. Postmortem castration and removal of the penis by animals almost invariably results in an initial suspicion of sexual assault.

In reports of feastings by such pets, it is often emphasized that no other food sources were available. To the contrary is the following story told to one of the authors by an emergency service technician: at a house to which he had been dispatched to check on a woman who had not been seen by neighbors for some time, the technician was greeted enthusiastically by a small white poodle. The woman was found dead on the kitchen floor, much of her face defleshed. A bowl filled with dog food sat only several feet from the owner's body.

In summary, then, it can be seen that death, while conclusive for the individual, represents a sudden expansion of physical resources whose beneficiaries are countless and diverse organisms. The ordered, functional array of anatomic parts in life is annulled by the centripetal forces of entropy in death. When we consider the forces that act to disperse a dead body, we better understand the elemental conservation of decay, the redistribution and recycling of the inanimate organic material to other vital organisms. Our lives are lived in flamboyant denial of our fundamental biologic equivalence to all other animals and it is only in death that we embrace our natural place in the global ecosystem. ∎

Diane Karluk, M.D. and John A. Hayes Jr., M.D. are forensic pathologists.

Parasites Who Know and Love Us

by
Guillermo
Metz

A sushi lover falls sick, diarrhea lasting weeks, the doctor diagnoses worms. Prescription in hand, he returns home and soon has a bowel movement that includes nine feet of what would turn out to be an 18-foot-long, ribbon-like, parasitic worm. A computer programmer complains of a periodic blur passing through his vision; by the time he gets it checked out, the worm has migrated to his brain and he can't even tie his own shoes.

Fortunately for the programmer, the worm was only causing pressure on his brain and had not yet begun eating it. The problem disappeared with medication. However, in the larger scheme, modern medicine has done little to eradicate parasites, which in one way or another still affect nearly every human on Earth. Improved sanitation and water filtration have gone a long way to limiting the spread of many parasites. Still, it is estimated that a billion people, 1/5 of the world's population, are infected by ascariasis or trichuriasis. Hookworm infects about a quarter of all people. Malaria still kills over 2 million people each year, just a small percentage of the estimated 500 million cases worldwide annually; and even in "first world" countries, diseases like Lyme disease are on the rise.

Nearly every organ, tissue, and fluid of the human body can be infected by parasites. Trypanosomes, protozoans that cause African sleeping sickness and Chagas' disease, live in the blood, lymph nodes, and cerebrospinal fluids. Various species of worms inhabit the intestine, lung tissues, and bile ducts. A variety of organisms invade the heart, brain, liver, spleen, and secretory glands. The effects vary from complete destruction of the tissues to almost complete harmlessness, and the same parasite can have either of these effects at different times. Parasites are simple, often just one cell. Even in their full complexity, they are just large tubes with tiny brains programmed to eat everything in their way and make lots of babies who will do the same. Yet, these simple parasites have evolved extraordinary adaptations to make full use of the human body—to lay eggs in it, raise their young in it, and feed on it—the host is home, snack bar, and womb, vital to their existence.

Roughly speaking, a parasite is any organism that has a harmful relationship with its host. Parasitism is so widespread in the animal kingdom that every known phylum is affected, acting either as host or parasite. There are many more parasites than free-living species, from bacteria to single-celled protozoans. There are immense worms 30 feet long (the record for the species our sushi lover was unfortunate enough to host), and beef tapeworms up to 60 feet long have been recorded. Often, the larvae of these huge worms are tiny. They enter the human body through the mouth, ears, nose, eyes—any opening they can find, or they simply drill their way through the skin before entering the blood-

Parasites are simple, often just one cell. Even in their full complexity, they are just large tubes with tiny brains programmed to eat everything in their way and make lots of babies who will do the same.

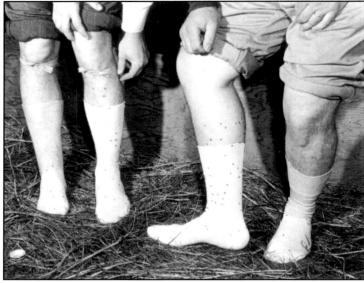

Photo: AP/Wide World News

Ticks.

stream and feeding on a Big Mac after we have taken the energy to break it down for them.

Protozoa: Nearly a quarter of the over 45,000 known species of protozoa are parasitic. The most significant protozoan genus among humans is *Plasmodium*. Four species of this are responsible for human malaria. As of the mid-60s, malaria was considered by the World Health Organization to be the most widely distributed and lethal human disease in the world, thus earning it the title of "the world's most murderous disease."

Other less-publicized protozoan diseases include Chagas' disease, caused by *Trypanosoma cruzi*, which infects as many as 18 million people worldwide, mostly in South and Central America. It is infective to over 100 species of wild and domesticated mammals. Infections begin when an infected long-snouted bug of the family Reduviidae bites a human, feeding on their blood and inadvertently transferring a few trypanosomes into the bloodstream. Within the human host, the flagellated parasites swim around, eventually entering various cells and multiplying. Each year in Brazil alone, one of the hardest-hit countries, several thousand people die of heart and digestive problems brought on by the disease—the parasites commonly cause irreversible destruction of muscle tissue and nerve ganglions during the acute stage. In Africa, tsetse flies spread a related organism, which causes sleeping sickness—symptoms include fever and painful swellings, headaches, tremors, and convulsions, leading to coma and death in many cases.

Closer to home in North America, *Cryptosporidium*, is an occasional scourge. They can't be killed by chlorine and, passing right through our best industrial filters, cause periodic contaminations in our drinking water. The infection, which causes gastrointestinal distress, and for which there is no effective drug, is not normally life-threatening, but can be fatal in immuno-compromised people, such as AIDS sufferers. The most recent serious outbreak in the U.S. occurred in Milwaukee in 1993, causing thousands of cases and 100 deaths.

Also common among AIDS patients are *Pneumocystis* infections. Long regarded a protozoan, but now placed closely to fungi, *P. carinii* occurs naturally in about 80% of humans as harmless amoebae. In the immuno-compromised, however, they increase in numbers until they fill the alveolar spaces in the lungs, causing pneumonia, which is often fatal.

Amoebiasis, which can be sexually transmitted, was once epidemic and is still a considerable health problem. Two particularly dangerous clinical presentations, primary amoebic meningoencephalitis (PAM) and granulomatous amoebic encephalitis (GAE), caused by *Naegleria fowleri* and other amoebae, attack the eyes and lungs, respectively, penetrating nasal passages, and entering the brain. In untreated cases of PAM, death occurs within one week of the onset of symptoms. GAE presents itself in immuno-compromised patients, causing death in several weeks to a year after the appearance of symptoms.

An unrelated protozoan, *Trichomonas vaginalis*, has the honor of causing the world's most common sexually transmitted disease, known as *T. vaginalis*, the prevalence of which has been increasing significantly. For some as yet unknown reason, this often strikes women while they are pregnant and is passed on to the infant at birth. Although such infections are limited to the genital tract and are not readily fatal, they can be extremely irritating and the strains are becoming increasingly resistant to existing drugs.

Tick-Borne Diseases: Lyme disease is becoming a buzz-word, with wealthy summer renters from Cape Cod and Nantucket to the Hamptons and as far south as the Carolinas checking each other for the dreaded deer tick. Carried by deer as well as mice, these ticks are no larger than a small freckle. They carry the protozoan parasite *Borrelia burgdorferi*, which commonly causes a rash and, if left untreated for even a short time, can land the infected person in the hospital with a high fever. Even if treated fairly early, infections can lead to a lifetime of arthritis; if not treated, coma and death can result. Tick-borne diseases on the rise include babesiosis. It produces malaria-like symptoms including fever, anemia, jaundice, and blood in the urine, and can be fatal. There is also a rickettsial infection, sometimes called "spotless fever" because of its similarity to Rocky Mountain spotted fever.

The Worms: Moving up the evolutionary ladder, the other major grouping of parasites can be broadly referred to as the worms. Helminth infections, like trichinosis, hookworm, heartworm, and even sushi worm, are not as common today as they once were, especially in countries like the U.S., where going barefoot is rare and the quality of our sanitary systems and drinking water has greatly improved in the last hundred years. Still, they continue to infect billions of humans and cause huge amounts of agricultural damage worldwide. In the U.S. alone, the cost of damages is estimated at $5 billion annually.

The helminths are extremely varied, not just in appearance, but also complexity and life cycle. The simplest worms, the cestodes, or tapeworms, are little more than long, gutless tubes modified to reproduce as much as possible, with several copies of sexual organs, capable of pro-

There are immense worms 30 feet long and beef tapeworms up to 60 feet long that have been recorded. Often, the larvae of these huge worms are tiny. They enter the human body through the mouth, ears, nose, eyes—any opening they can find, or they simply drill their way through the skin before entering the bloodstream and feeding on a Big Mac after we have taken the energy to break it down for them.

ducing millions of eggs a day. Sometimes, it is not the adult worms but the sheer quantities of eggs or larvae that cause problems in various organs or tissues of the host. For example, larvae of *Taenia solium*, or pork tapeworm, and *T. saginata*, or beef tapeworm, each measuring up to 10 mm in length, can become lodged in a variety of tissues. In large numbers, they can cause serious harm, including intestinal blockage, leading to death from starvation if not treated.

Slightly higher on the developmental and evolutionary ladder reside the digeneans, of which the schistosomes are the most significant human parasites, infecting over 200 million people worldwide. Schistosomes are bizarre, with unique and unorthodox morphology, physiology, and life-cycle adaptations, even among fellow digeneans. Adult worms are threadlike, from 10-30 mm in length but only 0.2-1.0 mm in width, and live in blood vessels, feeding directly on the cellular and plasma fractions of blood. Most schistosome eggs possess sharp spines which enable them to rupture blood vessels; some of the eggs become lodged in tissues throughout the body, and a proportion pass through the body. The latter hatch on contact with fresh water and infect a wide range of aquatic and amphibious snails, where they develop, then emerge, swimming in search of a final host. Able to penetrate bare human skin, the immature adults enter the blood system and are carried to the lungs. They migrate to the liver, where they pair up and mature before migrating to their final egg-producing sites. Pathologically, and on diagnostic tests,

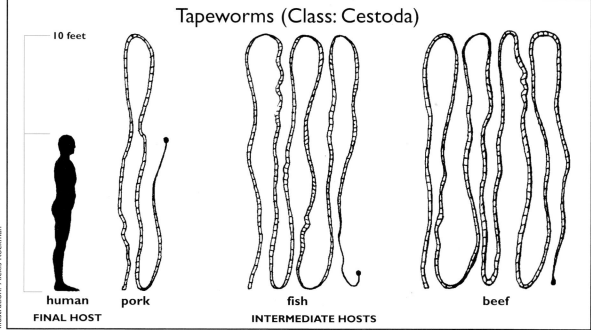

Tapeworms (Class: Cestoda)

10 feet

human
FINAL HOST

pork

fish

beef

INTERMEDIATE HOSTS

Illustration: Alexis Rockman

large numbers of calcified eggs mimic cancers, and there have been several cases of patients being operated on for lung cancer, only to find a large colony of eggs and squirming larvae instead. The increasing practice of building dams for hydroelectric power or irrigation in developing countries has been cited as a primary source of the spread of schistosomiasis, since new habitats are inadvertently created for snails.

Although the term nematode is sometimes used to describe all worms, they command their own phyla. Human intestinal nematodes are the most important human intestinal parasites, in terms of both their overall prevalence and their potential for causing serious harm. Because nearly all of the important parasitic species are soil-transmitted, in that either their eggs or larvae become infective after a period spent in soil, and they often reside together, most infected individuals fall prey to concurrent infections with two or more species, making their infections particularly harmful.

Ascaris lumbricoides, the largest human intestinal nematode, is also one of the most prevalent, infecting between 800 million and a billion people worldwide. Their eggs can survive up to seven years, and are transmitted via water contaminated with feces, usually becoming ingested on uncooked vegetables or in contaminated water. *Ascaris* larvae can cause bronchitis, while high densities of the adult worms can cause obstruction of the small intestine, and can also invade the bile duct, pancreas, esophagus, mouth, and liver. Children often ingest the eggs or larvae from infected soil or sandboxes.

Nearly as common, hookworm disease, is caused by two similar blood-feeding nematodes, *Ancylostoma duodenale* and *Necator americanus*. Although eggs and larvae can be harmful, the greatest damage is caused by the adults, which can drain a patient of up to 200 milliliters of blood a day in a heavy infection.

Another nematode group, the filarial parasites, require an intermediate blood-sucking insect host. Fortunately, some of the more common species cause relatively few serious infections, and those that are more harmful are not very common. However, two species, *Wuchereria bancrofti* and *Brugia malayi*, are widespread and extremely damaging, affecting some 250 million people at any given time. Clinically, the disease manifests as the host produces an inflammatory and immunological response to the adults; in their worst phase, they cause elephantiasis.

Other significant nematode infections include onchocerciasis, in which the larvae infest the eye, causing a variety of debilitating problems culminating in blindness. Loiasis, an infection caused by adult *loa loa* worms, creates swelling under the skin, and sometimes can be seen by the victim as it swims around in the eye. Guinea worms, which can reach up to a meter in length, crawl down the leg of a host, releasing about a million larvae into a blister. This blister eventually bursts,

Pathologically, and on diagnostic tests, large numbers of calcified eggs mimic cancers, and there have been several cases of patients being operated on for lung cancer, only to find a large colony of eggs and squirming larvae instead.

A common dog flea shows up transparent under x-ray microscope.
(Photo: AP/Wide World Photos)

releasing the offspring, *hopefully*, for the worm hops into water where the cycle begins anew. Trichinosis, which probably caused the biblical commandment for Jews to avoid pork, is relatively rare today, but persists among hunters who eat infected, undercooked, large game. Toxocara, a common roundworm disease of dogs and cats, infects 2–4% of children in the U.S. alone. Less common, but very dramatic, are the diseases of tapeworms and roundworms associated with the increasing popularity of sashimi.

It's Not Getting Any Better: According to Jerome Vanderberg, Ph.D., Professor of Medical and Molecular Parasitology at the New York University School of Medicine, "in the world at large, the problems are increasing enormously, the number of cases is increasing and resistance to the drugs is also increasing."

Even in a city like New York, he says, parasites remain a serious problem. "There are two main areas," he contends, "first, New York is a melting pot, immigrants coming in, students, diplomats, seamen—it sees more parasites and diseases than most cities." Secondly, there are the problems encountered by AIDS sufferers. Most significant are the parasites which have always been around, but are now on the rise because of cases in immuno-compromised patients. "Most patients die of opportunistic diseases and infections, including *Pneumocystis* pneumonia, *Toxoplasma*, *Cryptosporidia*, *Giardia*," he says. And, as mentioned before, he stresses that, "Lyme disease is becoming more important. There's a similar, tick-borne, malaria-like disease which we're seeing more and more of."

Andy Spielman, Ph.D., of Harvard University's School of Public Health, one of the nation's foremost tick-borne disease researchers, has been keeping his eye on this malaria-like disease, called babesiosis. "The first case was diagnosed in Nantucket in 1969," he says. Though the disease has been very rare, "now it is spreading like Lyme disease." The pathogen can be seen more readily than *Borrelia burgdorferi*, which causes Lyme disease, making a definitive diagnosis easier, but generally the infection is more harmful.

These parasites will live on—which is why sushi lovers, among everyone else on the planet, are still at risk. But maybe you'd prefer that instead of taking out your appendix after you show up at the hospital bent over with severe pain that mimics appendicitis, they find a cluster of small red worms, close you back up, and send you away with a bottle of pills. ∎

Guillermo Metz is a New York-based journalist specializing in health, medicine, and science.

The Life That Lives on Man

by
John S.
Marr,
M.D., M.P.H.

The veneer of civilization clings like a scab to *Homo sapiens*; urbanity is like the Emperor's new clothes that deludes us into believing we are clean, sophisticated and safe from filth. The patina is occasionally scrubbed off, and people shudder when they are presented with the truth. Today, we are no less immune or impervious to microscopic fellow travelers than our powder-wigged forebearers. The urban animal is much filthier than Rousseau's noble savage. But it was Jonathan Swift who first turned the knife.

After dealing with Lilliputians, Swift's Dr. Lemuel Gulliver traveled to another mysterious land. If the Land of Lilliput was meant to demonstrate the petty politics of European nations, this new land was populated by giants. Why giants? Earlier in the novel, Swift had increased the size of a good doctor for satirical reasons, allowing Gulliver to discover petty, political flaws in the body politic. In the new land, it was Gulliver who was the homunculus. His size allowed him to peer into a rotting tumor with microscopic precision. He realized that humans, even ostensibly tidy aristocrats, are odoriferous, filthy creatures. Had Swift used Anton von Leeuwenhoek's microscopes to discover a new world? Indeed, the microscope had become a popular toy in Europe at the time Swift was writing *Gulliver's Travels*. It could increase the naked eye's ability to examine small objects by over a hundred fold. The first "germ" ever seen by a scientist was *Giardia lamblia*, a protozoan parasite living in Leeuwenhoek's small bowel!

Had Swift used the primitive microscopes to greater advantage, he would have viewed landscapes never dreamed of in the pre-microbial world: A single hair might be a mountain to be climbed, the recesses of an eye lash's roots spelunked, a craggy fingernail to be traversed. The traveler could plummet into the ravines of a sebaceous gland, scale plaque along a gum line, swirl through stomach rugae bathed in acid, mire in intestinal chyle, and explore a teeming bacterial jungle which composes excrement. But Gulliver would have to be wary. The human body has always been seething with fauna and flora which feed off the body politic silently. These are not necessarily parasites nor infectious agents, although some do get a bit greedy. They are, for the most part, the routine life that lives on man.

Human skin is alive with viruses looking for homes, bacteria and fungi that live in concert with each other, and transient larger scavengers that can live freely, if necessary. Scrubbing the skin removes only a small fraction of these germs. Scouring and scratching will not dislodge other denizens that hide in deeper recesses: the pores, follicles and sweat glands. The inhabitants of the ecological niches are the most extraordinary microscopic life that feeds off human beings. These are arthropods—hundreds, perhaps thousands of small, insect-like ectoparasites

> "Face mites *(Demodex folliculorum* and *Demodex brevis)*—the good news is that they're microscopically small; the bad news is that they live exactly where their name implies."
> —Roger M. Knutson,
> *Furtive Fauna*

Photo: Bob Braine

Face mites.

that feast on discarded skin fragments (scarf) and dwell in the caves of sebaceous glands. A true fantastic voyage begins on the skin where these majestic dinosaurs roam, some on the surface, others in crags and caverns, drinking in sebum, waiting for prey, or upon occasion, piercing the soft dermis to withdraw serum and blood.

Human body mites are mighty arthropods armored with exoskeletons of chitin, using eight hairy legs to clamber over and through the epidermal landscape. Most of these mites are less than 1/4 millimeter in length. The *Tyrannosaurus rex* of mites is the organism causing scabies, *Sarcoptes scabei*. If left untreated, these burrowing scavengers cause a chronic condition—Beggar's itch or Vagabond's disease. If undiagnosed or untreated, scabies may also last for years, and is the origin for the term "seven year itch."

But most commensal mites are much, much smaller—they are the true raptors of an endless dermatological diorama. They can live in carpets and mattresses, feeding off shredded skin fragments, or on a variety of domestic animals, and on humans. Most of the time they consume exfoliated scales and skin, other times they descend into apocrine and exocrine glands to drink sebum where they sometimes extract nutrients. The more aggressive mites, like scabies, produce an allergic itch; the smarter ones feed quietly on discarded plates of scarf as if the scales were potato chips.

Demodex follicularum was discovered in ear wax in 1842, but its favorite haunt is sebaceous glands. Shaped like a Cuban cigar, each human eye lash supports a happy couple of *D. follicularum* breeding over 1,000 eggs monthly. The young move out to an adjacent lash or the slum of the upper cheeks and nose. The average clean face of an adult may contain thousands of these mites. It is only when they elicit an allergic reaction that one notices something amiss. A chronic allergic reaction produces rosacea, and in the long run a grog blossom nose.

Skin, nails and hair originate from keratinized layers in the epidermis. In animals, the same keratin forms hooves, horns, talons, scales, claws and armored plates. These dermal modifications are prey to superficial fungi which weave microscopic extensions in and through the layers of keratin. A fungus produces both magnificent fruiting bodies as well as root-like extensions, hyphae. The name given to one fungus—*Aspergillus*—comes from a religious tool used by priests—the aspergillum, an instrument used to dispense holy water. But it is the mass of interconnected snake-like hyphae that form carpets of interlaced filaments—the mycelia that does the damage. These matted accumulations disrupt the integrity of the skin causing plates of skin to drop off. Dandruff falls like snowflakes to floor surfaces where other free-living mites feed on the blessings from above as if manna.

Fungi which invade hair cause the tangled fibrils connected to each other to unwind. Fungal enzymes dissolve interconnections between fibrils, slicing through the cable-like hair, weakening proteinaceous bonds, until like mighty trees, the shaft falls off, leaving a naked hole. A similar phenomenon occurs in nails, causing them to become rippled, disfigured and discolored. More aggressive fungi penetrate past the outermost layer of skin into the dermis where they cause cracking, fissuring and fetid odors, as they assimilate protein and fats.

Certain fungi enjoy the moisture, darkness and humidity of captive feet, especially when socks and shoes prevent aeration. *Candida albicans* (thrush, monilia, and "yeast") prefer a more tropical, almost rain forest, atmosphere of the groin, often invading deeper into the body—the mouth, throat, esophagus, rectum and vagina—if given the opportunity. The strands of fungal growths may even swim through the bloodstream seeding organs with mushroom-like growths. It is then that the commensal organism transforms into a parasite, and finally a pathological invader.

It was once felt that stomach acid provided a cleansing bath for foods with dubious provenance. The hydrochloric acid was thought to kill most microbes before the chewed bolus was propelled farther down the alimentary canal. Now a formidable organism, *Helicobacter pylori*, has recently been found to live freely in the acidic fluids of the stomach lining, and may be the cause of peptic disease, and perhaps stomach tumors. The spiral shaped bacillus, looking remarkably like a cork screw, drills through the acid-bathed mucosa of the stomach, causing single or multiple penetrating wounds—ulcers. It too produces a telltale gas, urea, which can be captured and measured in a burp. No one knows where this bacterium lives outside man. Its natural nidality awaits identification and eradication.

A newborn's intestinal tract is sterile. However, after mother's milk and formula, the solid diet of a toddler allows for entry of routine germs. They colonize the intestinal tract, acting as opportunistic bacteria, feeding off the liquid chyme as it traverses 20 odd feet of small intestine. Most anaerobic bacteria live in the large bowel, and are rapacious scavengers for the detritus of leftover juices that are delivered to the colon. Over 3/4 of stool is composed of bacteria which need no oxygen to grow. They ferment sugars, break down fats and lyse proteins. Their enzymatic factories emit the characteristic gases, the rich aromatic-ringed scatoles of flatus. The same bowel bacteria may also escape the intestine and colonize skin, especially below the belt line. All skin allows for bacterial growth. Bacteria enter and reside in the ear canals, mouth, throat and nasal passages, living commensally until foreign intrusions damage their ecosystems.

Shaped like a Cuban cigar, each human eye lash supports a happy couple of *D. follicularum* producing over 1,000 eggs monthly. The young move out to an adjacent lash or the slum of the upper cheeks and nose.

John S. Marr, M.D., M.P.H., is an epidemiologist and author.

The Woodpile

by
Jocko
Weyland

A former competitive skateboarder, Jocko Weyland is now a New York-based artist. As the son of a foreign correspondent, he spent his childhood in far-flung spots like Moscow, Caracas and Albany. From 1975 to 1983, his family settled in the middle of the Colorado wilderness, in a remote plot of land located at an altitude of 6,000 feet right next to the Rocky Mountain National Park. One of Jocko's first memories of his new rustic setting was of the family dog Max, a French poodle, getting attacked and mortally wounded by a pack of coyotes. However, many of his recollections centered around a woodpile his father built, which became a focal point for both the Weylands and the animals that lived near them.

Seven days a week at noon my father would go out into the forest with an ax and handsaw and he'd cut fallen dead trees—this is how the woodpile took shape. By the outset of our second year, after a full summer cutting wood, the woodpile had grown. It now stretched the length of the garage and was about five feet high. At its biggest, during our eight years there, the pile contained over 18 cords (a cord of wood is eight feet long, four feet high, and four feet wide). As time went on, the last two rows closest to the garage became permanent and weren't used. This became the nucleus of the animal habitat that flourished a few feet from our side door.

The amount of wildlife in this part of Colorado is staggering. In the nearby town of Estes Park, animals were highly visible—the school's football field was often covered in deer droppings, and elk-auto collisions were common. Animals were everywhere. When I built a skateboard ramp in a meadow not far from the house, elk used to graze nearby and watch me skate. And during the night, the elk as well as deer and coyote came close to our house, frequenting the salt lick my mother set up near the driveway. For the most part, though, the larger fauna kept their distance. The animals mostly at ease with us humans, were the smaller, friendlier, furry and winged creatures that lived side by side with us—those that benefited from our handouts. And it was the woodpile that drew them in, giving them a better environment than their natural one. It became an animal condominium complex, providing them with shelter, protection from predators, warmth, and a reprieve from the wind.

Our lives became one of interaction and familiarity with the animals. This could not have been possible without my mother's unflagging support of the woodpile colony. She put out suet and apples for the deer, seeds for the rabbits and birds and bread with peanut butter for the squirrels. It was a virtual zoo, and we were both the keepers and the watchers.

The most prevalent animals were rabbits, black squirrels, ground squirrels, chipmunks, and mice. Small birds like siskins and nuthatch-

Our lives became one of interaction and familiarity with the animals. This could not have been possible without my mother's unflagging support of the woodpile colony. She put out suet and apples for the deer, seeds for the rabbits and birds and bread with peanut butter for the squirrels. It was a virtual zoo, and we were both the keepers and the watchers.

es came too, attracted by a feeder. And there were untold multitudes of ants and beetles—many of them stowaways from the trees' previous life in the forest. The black squirrels and ground squirrels were the tamest of the animals. We would sit down on the doorstep with some peanuts and they would run up, get on their hind legs, and take the item directly out of our hands. One ground squirrel became very close with my sister. She named him Mr. Lee. She gave him so many peanuts that his cheeks would get stuffed and bloated to ridiculous proportions. One day, I accidentally stepped on the tail of a mother squirrel of whom I was particularly fond. The tail broke off at the base. I remember being very upset by what I had done, thinking that the squirrel would not be able to "navigate" without a tail; however, she was soon able to get around nicely.

Jocko Weyland and his woodpile (c. 1978).

On the perimeter of our house, and not members of the woodpile clan, were fiercer animals like great-horned owls and goshawks. I guess these predatory birds saw the woodpile as a place to get an easy meal. Every now and again, a hawk or owl would descend from the sky, and snatch one of the woodpile creatures, usually a squirrel or rabbit. And every summer, a weasel would show up to invade the woodpile. Weasels are one of the rare animals that kill for what we call sport. In other words, they would kill without eating their prey. The weasel's reign of terror would typically last a week or two, during which corpses of our woodpile animals would pile up. Then, the weasel would suddenly disappear and things would return to normal.

The woodpile and its animals were an integral part of our life. Winter after winter, it would shrink to the point that we'd make dire predictions that it wouldn't last through the season. Then in May, my father would drive the truck onto the property, coming home daily with diseased or dead wood that he had cut by hand. The woodpile would grow, and we would comment on how big it was getting.

The wood that had been alive and part of the forest, which had died from lightning strikes, beetle infestations or whatever, would spend time as part of the ever-changing, but permanent home for the animals. Different logs, same habitat. Then the logs would be consumed in the blazing fireplace, providing us with warmth. In the house, the fire burned. Outside, the smoke would curl out of the chimney and be caught by the howling winds. Close to the door, the scurrying of the small animals could be heard in the woodpile. Farther away, the moaning and howling of the coyotes. ■

The Enemy Within

by
Drake
Zimmerman

Wasn't malaria wiped out in the 40s or 50s? Almost, with DDT killing off all the mosquitoes. But when it was almost gone, people gave up on it and governments restructured. Meanwhile, several new strains of malaria have developed.

About 1/3 of the world's human bodies play unwitting hosts to a number of terrible diseases such as malaria, dengue fever and tuberculosis (TB). Even leprosy has not been eradicated completely, but it is down to only 1/2 million new cases every year. The key to this decrease is that leprosy is being identified, treated and thus neutralized. But not every disease is.

We are all familiar with the cliché of some killer virus arriving by plane or by monkey to upscale, urban America, only to be contained by the scientist-hero in a spacesuit. This picture of disease-containment is not entirely wrong. By and large, our public health efforts have done a rather good job. However, that does not mean that we will never get any diseases. It just means that we will probably not be at the forefront of disease development. Americans may not be the best incubators anyway, with only 250 million people living fairly close to public health departments. We may not be the best vaccinated (the U.S. has the second lowest vaccination rate of two-year olds in the West, barely above that of Haiti), but for now, we live around fewer diseases. Diseases have a lot more friends all around the world.

For example, the U.S. is seeing some TB, but only a fraction of the 8 million new cases per year that are occurring worldwide. One a second. Tick. Tick. Tick. One person with an active case of TB infects 10 to 15 people in one year's time. TickTickTick. In a decade, the estimated number of incubators will be 300 million. TickTickTickTickTick....

People spread diseases. Economics are the motor. Cement is the pathway. Drive the truck. Harvest the fruit. Mine the gold in the jungles of Brazil, Ghana or Papua New Guinea. Seek prosperity and wealth. Seek food for the family. Drive back home. Sate hunger. Diddle.

The coastal folks carry their diseases to the inland jungles and the urban pests go country. Country bugs go city and the cityboy job-hunters get rural parasites, like malaria; of course, they have no immunity and can die. If they survive, they take the bugs back to the city. Just being a good host, after all. The bugs adapt like college students to junk food. Malaria, the once rural disease, is now citified in most of sub-Saharan Africa and Asia.

Wasn't malaria wiped out in the 40s or 50s? Almost, with DDT killing off all the mosquitoes. But when it was almost gone, people gave up on it and governments restructured. Gone were the governmental departments that dealt with malaria control, as if they had been completely effective. Just try and reestablish a government agency in a new government after independence. And try to get through a bureaucracy without money for bribes. A new department for yesterday's problems? Priorities lie elsewhere. Besides, quinine drugs were dirt cheap, nearly free.

Meanwhile, several new strains of malaria have developed. The quinine-resistant strains spread across Africa in about 15 years. It turns out that quinine may have had an unusually long life-span as a drug. Some parasites now consistently outwit the second-line drugs. Vietnam had great drug supplies—anti-malarials, too—when the U.S. soldiers were there. But the drugs stimulated a wider response by the parasite. So some Southeast Asian varieties do not respond even to 3rd-line drugs.

There is a new drug on the market developed from an ancient Chinese herbal remedy: artemisinin. It is very effective now, but when that ceases working...? Some entrepreneur

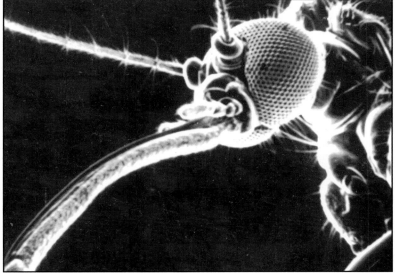

The stinger or proboscis of a mosquito may have felt this big as it penetrated your skin in order to suck blood.

might someday return from Southeast Asia to America with a little gift in his bloodstream. We have the right mosquitoes. We just don't have the human carriers to give malaria to these mosquitoes, who, by the way, do not pass the parasite on to their offspring. Then we could perversely hope for the headline "New Jersey Housewife Killed By Malaria," because, if she lived, she would be an incubator like millions around the world.

If TB is a drop a second, then malaria is a garden-hose on full blast. There are 300-500 million new cases of malaria a year. That comes to about one million a day. The death rate, as a percentage isn't too bad, only about 1%. One million a day. As many people die daily from malaria as contract TB. TB remains treatable, as does malaria. But give them both time; they've got the incubators.

Having said that, I am very hopeful about the efforts in place. We have had successes in the past. Smallpox was once a killer and has already been eradicated. Gone. 100%. The much larger and more difficult polio is on its way off the face of the Earth, thanks to concerted efforts by hundreds of agencies and governments.

The modern plague will probably not be caused by a disease that comes out of rural obscurity, like Ebola. The modern plagues are probably among us, right now. Humans are the most likely carriers, not rats or bugs. We may not be the enemy, but we sure do host a lot of them.

What we do know is that malaria can be dramatically slowed with some basic technology: education, nets and drugs. Use of mosquito nets impregnated with safe insecticides have dropped rates of infection and death by 30% to 90%. Rates also drop by simply making the appropriate drugs available. And by educating mothers as to the symptoms, causes, treatment and, above all, the prevention of malaria. Major initiatives have begun to prevent malaria and deal with it where it is worst: sub-Saharan Africa. What might come of malaria control is the development of a health-care and educational system that could slow the growth of a number of diseases.

Even with high-tech solutions and the best of world health-care and service organizations, disease-control still needs help. The roads are still there. The quest for subsistence and prosperity continues, and so carriers of disease travel more and more. The age-old scourges, like malaria and TB, may be the biggest threats, but we all get colds, even in the U.S., and colds are becoming nastier. Let us hope that medical science and other efforts will keep—or, just get—a step ahead of the bugs, before they reach you or me. ∎

Drake Zimmerman is an investment advisor and money manager and past President of the Rotary Club of Normal, Illinois. He is the U.S. Coordinator of Rotary Against Malaria (RAM) working to help build malaria control and basic health infrastructure in over 90 countries affected by malaria.

About 1/3 of the world's human bodies play unwitting hosts to a number of terrible diseases such as malaria, dengue fever and TB. Even leprosy has not been eradicated completely. People spread diseases. Economics are the motor. Cement is the pathway.

Illustration: Alexis Rockman

One day in South Florida, a woman was walking her small dog along a familiar route, a canal. In a flash and a splash, the rhinestone leash went limp.

The Healthy Body's Guests and Visitors

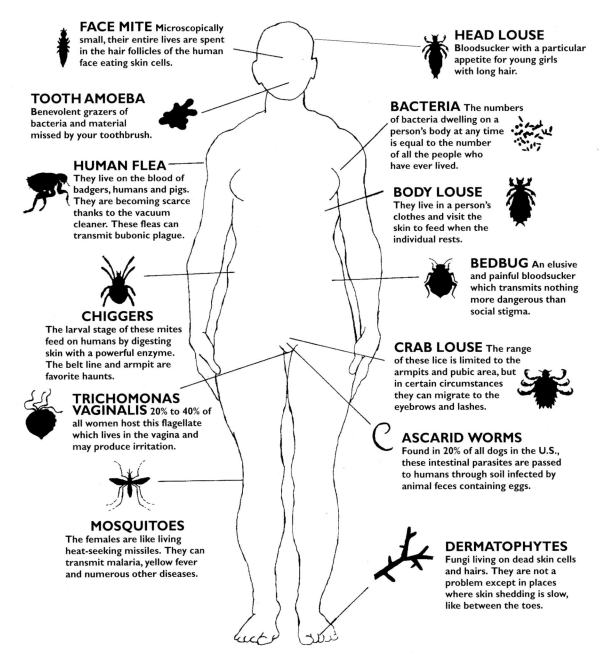

FACE MITE Microscopically small, their entire lives are spent in the hair follicles of the human face eating skin cells.

TOOTH AMOEBA Benevolent grazers of bacteria and material missed by your toothbrush.

HUMAN FLEA They live on the blood of badgers, humans and pigs. They are becoming scarce thanks to the vacuum cleaner. These fleas can transmit bubonic plague.

CHIGGERS The larval stage of these mites feed on humans by digesting skin with a powerful enzyme. The belt line and armpit are favorite haunts.

TRICHOMONAS VAGINALIS 20% to 40% of all women host this flagellate which lives in the vagina and may produce irritation.

MOSQUITOES The females are like living heat-seeking missiles. They can transmit malaria, yellow fever and numerous other diseases.

HEAD LOUSE Bloodsucker with a particular appetite for young girls with long hair.

BACTERIA The numbers of bacteria dwelling on a person's body at any time is equal to the number of all the people who have ever lived.

BODY LOUSE They live in a person's clothes and visit the skin to feed when the individual rests.

BEDBUG An elusive and painful bloodsucker which transmits nothing more dangerous than social stigma.

CRAB LOUSE The range of these lice is limited to the armpits and pubic area, but in certain circumstances they can migrate to the eyebrows and lashes.

ASCARID WORMS Found in 20% of all dogs in the U.S., these intestinal parasites are passed to humans through soil infected by animal feces containing eggs.

DERMATOPHYTES Fungi living on dead skin cells and hairs. They are not a problem except in places where skin shedding is slow, like between the toes.

Illustration and text: Mark Dion

149

The Diseased Host

 BOT FLY This neotropical pest lays its eggs on captured mosquitoes. When the mosquito later lands on a human, the egg instantly hatches and the maggot crawls into the bite wound. There it feeds until mature.

TRICHINA WORM A nematode responsible for the potentially lethal disease trichinosis. The larval cyst is transferred by eating under-cooked pork. Hogs often become infected by eating hosting rats.

HUMAN LIVER FLUKE The life cycle of this fluke is very complex. It must first develop in two intermediate hosts (snails and fishes). Adult flukes live in the bile passages and can cause "liver rot."

 BALANTIDIUM COLI This is the largest of all human protozoan parasites. In extreme cases it can cause ulcers of the large intestine or even fatal dysentery.

GUINEA WORM Found in tropical Africa and Asia, the female Guinea worm averages 3 to 4 feet in length. Infections result from swallowing a tiny crustacean host in drinking water.

 LEECHES These blood-sucking parasites are mostly freshwater dwellers, but some have adapted to terrestrial life. Tropical forest leeches are quick to attack humans and can be quite a nuisance. Some aquatic leeches are swallowed in drinking water and can be a problem on the pharynx and epiglottis.

CHIGOE Sometimes called a jigger, this tropical flea burrows under the toenails or between the toes. It can reach the size of a small pea and must be painfully dug out of the skin. It can be the cause of dangerous infections.

TSETSE FLY Found in Africa, this minute, bloodsucking fly transmits the parasitic protozoan that can cause sleeping sickness.

TICKS Female ticks need a blood meal before they can lay eggs (as many as 6,000 of them). Various species can carry over 20 human diseases.

CONGO FLOOR MAGGOT A highly mobile maggot which is totally dependent on humans who sleep on earthen floors.

TAPEWORM The most specialized of the flatworm parasites. Adults have no digestive system and must be bathed in nutrients found in their hosts intestines.

FILARIAL WORMS At least eight different species of these nematodes infect humans and some of these worms are major causes of disease (including elephantiasis). Some 250 million people in the tropics are infected with this scourge of the lymphatic system.

 ITCH MITE Microscopic mites cause mange or scabies. Itch mites burrow into skin and insert piercing mouth parts to draw blood and lymph. The itch results from the mite's feces.

HOOKWORM Only two species infest humans, but they are extremely widespread. The half-inch long adults live in the small intestine and nourish themselves on blood and tissue fluids. Hookworms produce between 5,000 and 10,000 eggs per day.

Illustration and text: Mark Dion

The Dead Host

EARWIGS Decaying organic matter is the primary food for earwigs, but some species are predatory. They may occur in large numbers on or under a corpse, particularly in wet conditions.

FLESH FLIES The maggots of the flesh fly look very similar to those of the blow fly. The larvae and adults of these flies are the predominant arthropod of the earliest stages of decomposition.

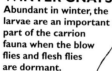

WINTER GNATS Abundant in winter, the larvae are an important part of the carrion fauna when the blow flies and flesh flies are dormant.

BLOWFISH This stout-bodied fly is often the first to arrive at a dead body. They deposit eggs in areas around natural body openings or wounds.

FLIES The order Diptera is made up of insects with one pair of full wings and a second pair that has transformed into rodlike stumps. Over 100,000 species are known to science. Many flies are carrion fauna, associated with the first stages of decomposition.

SILVERFISH A common household pest, the silverfish is not associated with fresh carrion. Rather, late in the stage of decomposition these primitive insects feed on the dried remains.

SPIDERS No instance of spiders feeding on carrion has ever been documented. However, they are often associated with decomposing remains as the predators of other arthrodpods.

ANTS Through maggot predation, ants may slow the decomposition process. They may also feed directly on the fluids and tissues of the corpse.

CARRION BEETLES The Silphidae are a group of insects which arrive in the early stages of decay. It seems that the immature beetles feed on remains while the adults hunt maggots and other insects.

Illustration and text: Mark Dion

Food Chain

written and photographed by Catherine Chalmers

The food chain begins with the fruit of a plant and steps through the door to the animal kingdom in accordance with popular ideas about what occurs in nature. Although they may resemble a natural ecosystem, these organisms are imported from many parts of the world. The tomato is imported from South America; the caterpillar is native to North America; the mantis is from China, and the tree frog is from the South Pacific. Each of these species were selected for the following reasons: appropriate behavior, commercial availability, convenience, inexpensiveness, hardiness and they look good. ■

Tomato

Name: The fleshy fruit of a solanaceous plant, *Solanum Lycopersicum* or *Lycopersicum esculentum*.
Origin: Tropical America.
Availability: Cultivated and available worldwide.
Characteristics: A very common ingredient in most Western diets.

Tobacco Hornworm Larvae

Name: Larva of the Manduca Sexta moth.
Origin: The Americas, up to Southern Canada, and the West Indies.
Availability: Wherever solanaceous plants are grown (eggplant, pepper, potato, tomato and tobacco). These caterpillars are pests and plague both the farmer and gardener. The eggs, larvae, and pupae can be purchased from Carolina Biological Supply and are very easy to raise.
Characteristics: Unlike many caterpillars, these are non-poisonous. They are bright turquoise with a red horn at the back end. The horn apparently leads a predator to attack the back leaving the front free to bite the attacker. The pupae and moths gained fame for starring in *The Silence of the Lambs*.

Praying Mantis

Name: *Tenodera aridifolia sinensis.*
Origin: Asian tropics and warmer regions.
Availability: Agricultural and biological supply catalogues offer praying mantis egg cases for sale that have been gathered from the wild. About 250 mantises hatch from one egg case. They are voracious predators and farmers and gardeners use them instead of pesticides.
Characteristics: Cannibalistic and infamous for their sexual habits. The female often eats the male after sex, or bites off his head during sex, or even eats him before he gets started.

White's Tree Frog

Name: *Litoria caerulea.*
Origin: Australia, Indonesia, New Guinea.
Availability: Pet stores throughout Europe and America. Most are captive bred.
Characteristics: Calm, hardy and easy to handle and keep.

Catherine Chalmers is an artist who lives in New York City. ∎

chapter 6

Trash

Concrete Jungle VI, Alexis Rockman (1996)

Ratville

by
Brian M.
Wiprud

Most people don't know what sewage looks like. They imagine it's a turd parade, some kind of subterranean BM regatta, with little Charmin sails carrying them out to sea on a methane breeze. In reality, the only flush-ables you see are the paper products swirling ghost-like in murky water. And the stink? Not too bad—you'd be surprised. Then again, think about how you use water every day. More than half is probably dedicated to washing. Sewers are pretty sudsy and tooth-pasty, especially first thing in the morning when the shower and shave tide rolls in.

As an inspector for the City of New York, I've gotten a good, close look at sewage. In order to decide if a sewer needs replacing, workers drag a video camera through the sewers to get a look at the pipe's con-dition. On occasion, I monitor these video shoots from the relative com-fort of a step van studio. The technician producing the show controls the camera and narrates at the same time, careful to note any deficiencies in the pipe structure. You have a rat's-eye view of the pipe and the sewage, as the camera trundles past house connections and drain pipes which poke into the main at all angles. You see a sudden gush from one of these pipes and try to figure out if it's one of those short-lived toilet surges or a rinse cycle deluge. Sometimes, of course, food shoots out. One time, while tooling along through a Fulton Street pipe, a house connec-tion vomited a mudslide of spaghetti all over the lens. The technicians are wary of connections that look like they hitch up to a restaurant and might slime the camera. You can tell restaurants from ordinary services by the grease shelves that form on the pipe wall opposite the connection; they're waxy, white, and covered with things like Band-Aids, Q-tips and Optimo butts. The biggest lard coagulation I've witnessed was in a pipe outside one of Brooklyn's notable Polish sausage mills. The camera couldn't squeeze by the protrusion of tallow, so the operator backed up the probe, and rammed the monster head-on, causing it to collapse on top of the camera.

Of course sitting there watching all this, you feel as if a giant wall of putrefied fat has just smothered you. Whenever there's a sag in the pipe and the camera starts to dive under the sewage, you find yourself raising your chin as you watch, trying to keep your mouth above the effluent.

When it comes to sewers, rats are what most people want to hear about, that and alligator yarns. Fact is, reptiles are almost as scarce as trolls. And you might be surprised to know that sightings of our furry friends are not very common either, largely because the video set-up often has a cleaning bell scouring the walls with water under 2000 pounds of pressure leading the way down the pipe. That sends the rats a-runnin'. However, some pipes are cleaned a day or so in advance of tap-ing, and the camera is not pulled by a cable, but driven through on a

Americans produce over 160 million tons of solid waste each year. That is about 13,000 pounds per person, 3.6 pounds per person per day. Eighty percent of U.S. solid waste ends up in landfills, 1/3 of which are expected to reach capacity in the next five years.

(Environmental Protection Agency)

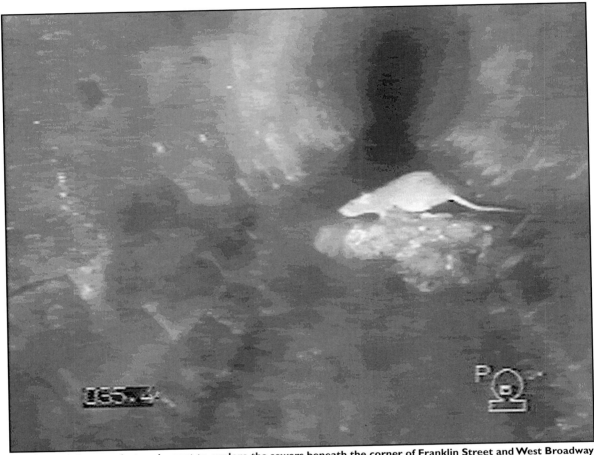

Video image from a robot probe sent to explore the sewers beneath the corner of Franklin Street and West Broadway in New York City.

In the U.S., we throw away enough glass bottles to fill the two towers of the World Trade Center every two weeks.

robot. That's when you get the stray, solitary rat coming out to check out what all the light and whirring is about. Invariably, the rat just watches disdainfully, like your garden variety coot sitting on his porch eyeing a newfangled roadster motor up the lane. At a recent taping, one of the little darlings was dining on the leftovers from TriBeCa Grill. The robot's approach didn't chase him from his salmon carpaccio. In fact, he deserted his meal to inspect the probe, smearing his cute, little, wuffling whiskered nose on the lens, sitting up on his haunches, sniffing at the lights, and scampering in circles around the camera. Not exactly the nasty *Ben*-type encounter you'd expect.

Frankly, as long as I don't have to get close and personal with them, rats don't bother me just to look at. Roaches are another matter. Not the little guys, but the greasy bruisers some lame-brain tagged with the euphemism *water bugs*. And as if the regulation black models weren't bad enough, the sewers have their own variety: white leviathans. Usually found on the inside walls of old brick manholes, these sebaceous, corpulent mutants' milky complexion really raises my short hairs. And the thing with roaches is, you don't usually just see a solitary bug, but whole seething broods. At a downtown location, we were popping the top on a sewer chamber. Not just opening the manhole cover, but digging down and using a crane to raise the entire concrete roof slab. Mind you, this is at an intersection with a restaurant on every corner, each with a disposal unit chumming the sewers with roach chow. At first, nothing seemed amiss as the lid jarred loose and sun began spilling into the chamber. But as the lid was pulled to the side, the crew cocked their heads. Something was odd about the chamber walls. Maybe it was the texture, or maybe it was the cumulative aura radiating from 100,000 insects. Anyway, when the crane dropped the lid to one side, the jolt started a stampede. Completely carpeted in "water bugs," the walls surged outward. A blanket of roaches spread from the hole like a death shadow, jolting a spasm of panic into onlookers. Civilians literally screamed, running for the nearest open doorway and scrambling onto car hoods. Workers cursed, jumping onto excavators and lamp posts like elephants fleeing mice. And I don't need to tell you where the roaches disappeared. While many funneled down catch basins back into the sewer, a huge number seized the opportunity and made for the restaurants, fluidly slipping under the doors by the thousands. The restauranteurs can be thankful it wasn't yet lunch hour. *Zagat's* raves not withstanding, the memory of that delightful event will find me seeking repast elsewhere.

What boggles me is the fact that people actually go down *into* the pipe. Over Houston Street, I had to watch these poor sons-of-bitches spend hours on their knees in a 4'0" x 2'8" brick sewer. Yeah, they wore chest waders and knee pads, and sandbags pretty much pooled the sewage upstream where a pump sent the effluent through a fire hose on a by-pass of the work zone. The sewer had just been cleaned, so what made these grunts' job hard wasn't wallowing in filth. They were guniting. Guniting is a process whereby the existing pipe is coated on the inside with a cementous mixture shot from a gun. To get the concrete to stick, you have to cover the inside of the pipe with chicken wire. You have to drag rolls of wire, a drill, and an extension cord down a narrow manhole, crawl with this stuff tucked in your armpits down a pipe, drill holes into the brick, insert fasteners, and hook the new wire section into the fasteners. Imagine doing all that in an egg-shaped crawl space that also has lights strung along the side. It's like trying to wallpaper the inside of a refrigerator as you're loaded with a case of beer and the door is closed. Finally, they have to shoot and trowel the concrete while backing out. Funny, but the crew didn't find crouching in a dank pipe all day much of a hardship, maybe because their back problems had yet to set

Half of the solid waste produced in New York City is paper. This paper trash is the single largest export through the Port of New York. New York City tax payers spend one million dollars each day to collect and dispose of more than 27,000 tons of garbage. The average New Yorker throws out four pounds of trash a day.

in. But Tony the foreman did take exception to rats.

"The day I see a rat in d'hole," Tony shook his head. "I quit, man."

"Five years, he not seen even a mouse," his Jamaican friend laughed. "Last year, downtown, I workin' when a rat goes zip right up over me back, mon, runnin' on down the pipe to Rat City."

The story—of which he'd doubtless had to suffer countless renditions —practically made rat-o-phobe Tony swoon. But now it was my turn. I had to go down and measure the thickness of the gunite, make sure the City was getting what it paid for. I donned the chest waders and went down for a look. Sure enough, claustrophobia, at the very notion of crawling into that pipe, twisted my vision. I asked Tony what his wife thought of his job.

He shrugged. "Didn't think nothin' of it. Until I brought home a video, coupla weeks back. She says, 'You don't actually go *in* there, do you?'" Tony looked skyward, shaking his head. "She doesn't wanna hear about it."

Tony's wife aside, the average citizen takes a keen interest in sewers, especially the open trench work where workers dig up, break out and replace a sewer pipe. During the work, raw sewage runs through the trench for all passersby to ogle. Countless rubber-neckers sidle up and ask: "Hey, that's not what I think it is, is it?" knowing full well that it was.

"It's a water main," I'd say.

They'd look at my deadpan expression, sniff and say "No, that's a sewer...isn't it?"

I'd smirk and nod.

"But, it's not like the stuff from toilets, right?"

"Of course not," I'd fib. "Just from showers and sinks. Toilets flush into a whole other system. Hey, you think we'd leave a trench open like this if there were doo-doo in it?" This they believed, probably because by the time they're standing over the trench on their way to work, shower, shave and shit time is long gone. Now, we're into laundry hours, the rippling brown water frosted in foam.

Despite all its many subtle charms and points of interest, I wouldn't recommend the sewer as a viable alternative to walking tours or museums for visiting relatives. Especially if you can't find any open trench work to admire. For one thing, many manholes don't have steps and require a rope ladder or spelunking gear. Uncle Bob may throw out his back helping you pop the manhole cover. I mean, they might never visit you again. Hmmm…. ■

Every year Americans discard enough unrecycled writing paper to build a wall 12 feet high stretching from New York to Los Angeles.

(Environmental Defense Fund)

Brian M. Wiprud is a Utility Infrastructure Analyst with over 12 years experience as a "manhole detective" and Project Supervisor and inspector for The RBA Group Consulting Engineers. He is also a writer and avid angler.

Public and Private Toilets

DIANA WALL: My name is Diana Wall, I'm an anthropologist specializing in archaeology. I'm on the faculty at City College and for the last
almost 20 years I've been digging in New York City. One of the types of
places that I've been excavating and spending most of my time in, is privy
pits from the 17th through the 19th century.

HELEN MOLESWORTH: My name is Helen Molesworth. I'm a graduate student in history, currently writing my dissertation about Duchamp.
Duchamp's most famous ready-made is an inverted urinal called
Fountain and in situating *Fountain* in its 1917 social context, I've done
a lot of research on the introduction of indoor plumbing in America.

TOM BURR: My name is Tom Burr and I'm an artist. I live in New York
and for the last decade or so I've been doing installations and site-relat-
ed projects relating to social and public spaces in general, specifically
in New York; many times and very often with regard to spaces like public rest rooms, public parks, and public buildings.

*ALEXIS ROCKMAN: What we want to talk a little bit about today is toi-
lets and their relationship to economics and archaeology.*

HM: I am interested in the way in which domestic spaces in this century are designed around what someone like Siegfried Gideon calls the

discussion with
Tom Burr, Helen
Molesworth and
Diana Wall,
led by Alexis
Rockman

Public rest room in New York City.

Photo: Tom Burr

"mechanical core," meaning the bathroom and kitchen. For instance, the standardization of plumbing fixtures and water availability structure the design of domestic space. This means that people develop particular relations to their bodies and machines. I'm particularly intrigued by the different relations to bodily functions and issues of privacy and publicness that are engendered by the use of a chamber pot, an outhouse, a communal hall toilet, or a private bathroom.

DW: One of the things that archaeologists have always been interested in is trying to look at when particular households or particular neighborhoods actually got access to indoor plumbing after the Croton water was first piped down to the city in the 1840s. There were a lot of people who lived in poorer neighborhoods with absentee landlords in New York, who didn't get access to this piped-in water till 40 or 50 years after it first began to be available. Even though there were pipes down under the street, individual landlords had to pay to have water piped into the houses and to have the plumbing. So the poor continued to use chamber pots and backyard privies long after the rich had access to indoor toilets. If it was a tenement building, there could be 60 people using one privy in the backyard. The impact on people's lives of having indoor plumbing, as opposed to hauling water up many flights of stairs and hauling wastes down again, was enormous.

TB: There then came a point where the chamber pot and the privy would then get connected.

DW: Right. Even in rural areas there was a combination of uses, because if it was quite cold outside you would use the chamber pot at night in the bedroom.

TB: And then just empty it in the morning.

DW: The thing that fascinates me is how movable chamber pots were throughout the house. There was not this idea of privacy that one went to the bathroom in a certain space. One went in the study, if that's where one had to go, you know.

HM: There are even records of chamber pots being in dining rooms.

DW: There was a very different way of thinking about what constitutes a private act.

TB: In my apartment which is a Lower East Side tenement, the bathroom and the kitchen are adjacent, which I believe shortly after that time could not occur.

HM: Because of housing codes?

TB: Yeah. My bathroom and my kitchen are very obviously one unit. If you go to the bathroom, you have to go through the kitchen, which in later apartments would rarely be the case. This may not be so much of a chronological development as much as it has to do with different building types housing different classes at different points in time. The whole idea of taking a chamber pot into the dining room, for instance, evokes various notions of privacy, but also breaches 20th

The white, porcelain bowl is, in large part, a 20th century response to hygiene anxiety created by the development of germ theory. Wood, fabric and other dark, hard-to-clean surfaces came to be seen as particularly dangerous. The pipes were left exposed in order to insure that germs and dirt wouldn't hide or fester. Hence, you have the rich proudly showing off their plumbing fixtures in the early 20th century.

Public rest room in New York City.

Photo: Tom Burr

century ideas of hygiene.

HM: The white, porcelain bowl is, in large part, a 20th century response to hygiene anxiety created by the development of germ theory. In the 19th century, the rich had incredibly ornate toilets, which were hidden in these very elaborate wooden cabinets. With the advent of germ theory in the late 19th century, wood, fabric and other dark, hard-to-clean surfaces came to be seen as particularly dangerous. There is a move toward porcelain, a hard, easy-to-clean surface, for bathroom fixtures. Additionally, when indoor plumbing is introduced, the pipes were left exposed in order to insure that germs and dirt wouldn't hide or fester. Hence, you have the rich proudly showing off their plumbing fixtures in the early 20th century.

DW: Archaeologists like to think that the ceramic shards that they find are from the dishes that people were actually using and broke and then threw away, as opposed to the dishes that they did not use and that therefore survived whole to end up in museum collections. When we dig privy pits, we often find pieces of the ceramic chamber pots that people dropped by mistake when they were emptying them. The shards show us that most of the chamber pots that people were using in the 19th century were plain white, too, in spite of the more elaborate cham-

Photo: Tom Burr

Public rest room in New York City.

ber pots that we see in museum collections.

HM: Was it about economics?

DW: No, it was about style.

AR: And standardization as well, right?

DW: Well no, because they were available in different patterns and people were choosing to buy the white ones. There is another thing that we've come across that I've always wondered about, something that we've learned from looking at architectural plans. Although there are very few architectural plans of outhouses from the 19th century, those that exist show that the outhouses were divided into two rooms, each with its own door. And the question is, what is the basis of that division? Is it gender or is it class?

HM: I was curious about that because the few privies that I've actually seen have had two or three seats in a row. Did people use outhouses simultaneously?

DW: Not that I've heard of, but I really don't know. But what I'm talking about is different compartments with an actual wall.

AR: A physical boundary.

HM: Were they meant to separate blacks from whites?

> I understand that more suicides take place in the bathroom than in any other room. It's the only private space we really have.

DW: Yes, it could have been class—one compartment for Irish domestics and the other for the enslavers in earlier times. But, on the other hand, one compartment could have been for men and the other for women, whatever their status in society.

HM: I read about a man who collects old bottles from privy pits. Apparently, men would use the privy as a place to sneak a drink, and then throw away or hide the bottle there.

DW: We just excavated a privy on Broome Street and we found a lot of medicine bottles. Women were not supposed to drink alcohol according to the temperance movements, but they were imbibing all these— what we consider controlled substances now. One of the bottles we found was labeled "Extract of Opium."

AR: So truly like a geological core sample of vertical evidence.

DW: Yeah, it's definitely a physical layer. We also tend to find domestic stuff—pieces of crockery, tumblers and wine glasses, and the remains of meals, animal bones, pig's feet—after they've abandoned the privy and start to fill it up.

AR: Landfill.

HM: In many ways, it prefigures the multiple functions of today's bathroom. Perhaps the bathroom is such a charged space because it affords such privacy.

AR: Right. Masturbation and suicide.

DW: I understand that more suicides take place in the bathroom than any other room. It's the only private space we really have.

TB: It's also the only door that always has a lock.

DW: It's interesting when you think about the 19th century in New York and you think about notions of privacy which were changing a lot at that time. Women, with their new notions of modesty, had to make the public statement of walking across the entire backyard to use the outhouse (the outhouses are always far away from the house, way out at the back property line for obvious reasons). There was research that a student of mine did where there was some mention of women making themselves ill by not using the outhouse during daylight hours. We're talking about the middle class obviously.

AR: The denial of humans as biological organisms.

TB: That's why I'm intrigued by this discourse that predates the turn of the century, specifically in public rest rooms in New York and other urban centers. They were trying to clean up and organize the working class in the city and trying to place facilities that paralleled the playground and educational movements at that time. There was already an incredible gender distinction in the 20th century, with "Comfort Stations" which would be located in department stores. And the saloon would be the domain of rest rooms for men. When Prohibition came along, there was a crisis in New York. Where were they to put these facilities?

HM: That's when those public ones were put up in the medians of Broadway?

TB: Exactly. The Parks Department put up a lot of them. Again, you have this space where other things occur. The fact that the first public facilities were in saloons is very intriguing; it parallels this idea of taking the drink into the toilet. This whole "men's club" thing. And then the eventual closing down of saloons prompted the emergence of new spaces, which had multiple functions as well, both intended and unintended. The discourses of vandalism, sexuality and hygiene converge into one big mess that the city never seems to be able to quite pick apart, so they eventually close down those places. Of course, this reflects a larger social preoccupation with collapsing the distinctions between crime, sexuality, dirt and cleanliness. Bryant Park is a good example of this preoccupation. There were heavily used rest rooms there. Bryant Park had become an extension of 42nd Street and Times Square, with a lot of drug traffic, prostitution and homelessness. The rest rooms were used by these different groups and were also used for gay cruising and sex. So,

The fact and fiction of crime surrounding the public rest room allowed the gay life to exist in terms of "tea rooms" which were used for gay connections. Not just gay sex, but also as a gay meeting place in a homophobic society.

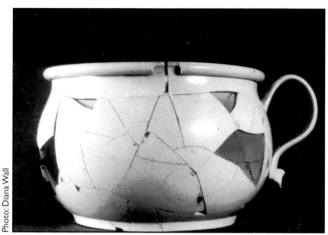

Photo: Diana Wall

Chamberpot made of white salt-glazed stoneware, c. 1780, found at the Barclay's Bank site at South Street Seaport Museum, NYC.

Archaeologists like to think that the ceramic shards that they find are from dishes but when we dig up privy pits, we often find pieces of the ceramic chamber pots that people dropped by mistake when they were emptying them.

it was eventually shut down, cleaned up and reopened. And I guess the rest rooms there are now functioning as they were intended to, with the other activities being kept in check.

DW: I'm just stunned when rest rooms in the park work and I feel that it's a real treat.

HM: In the New York City subway system, the women's rest rooms were closed long before the men's.

DW: It was discriminatory.

AR: *Well, there's physical contact too. Women tend to sit down and men can stand up.*

DW: I also think it's women being afraid to go into an uncontrolled space.

AR: *Women are more vulnerable. They could be locked in with someone else.*

DW: Sexuality and vulnerability put together in the same space. Where do the homeless go to the bathroom now? To put it euphemistically.

HM: The public library.

TB: Central Park still has some public rest rooms.

AR: *What's amazing is that you never see human fecal matter on the street.*

DW: I'm not sure I can tell. Dog or people.

AR: *Yeah. Carnivore.*

HM: It's as if the disgust we feel toward our bodily functions makes public rest rooms feel dangerous.

TB: And I think that it's that the whole fact and fiction of crime surrounding the public rest room that's allowed the gay life to exist in terms of "tea rooms" which were used for gay connections. Not just gay sex, but also as a gay meeting place in a homophobic society as early as the turn of the century. In the 20s and 30s, this network of meeting places and cruising zones enlarged rapidly, paralleling the growth of public rest rooms along highways, in parks, in bus and train stations. What's interesting to me is that on the one hand certainly homosexuality came to us through a criminal discourse anyway, and then also sort of took advantage of the fact that these spaces had a preexisting aura of criminality, providing a degree of safety from a hostile "general public." This is very different from the idea that trash attracts trash, or that dirty rest rooms are a natural habitat for dirty sex. Later, in the 1950s, the same rest rooms were used as sites of entrapment. Also, one would always hear stories about corporate America, where bugs would be planted in the bathrooms, the one place where people finally feel that they are out of view. Stall-to-stall conversations where authority can't reach you. It's this complex overlapping of certain acknowledgments of authority and the desire and attempts to be outside of that authority somehow.

AR: And that also goes back to being in high school and you can smoke in the boy's or girl's room or whatever and that would be the sanctuary from the official world, so to speak.

HM: Alexander Kira was the 1970s guru of the bathroom. He wrote a design and sociology book called *The Bathroom.* He wanted an open acknowledgment of the bathroom as a multi-use space and subsequently to make it more of a family room.

TB: Right. Like the kitchen opened up. The "swinging bathroom."

AR: There is a trend in recent history of bathrooms that are almost like play stations, where there's a hot tub and multi-angled shower heads, and a stereo and television.

DW: In California.

HM: The bathroom as site of pleasure.

DW: What about looking at the early 20th and late 19th century kitchen and the idea of having the bathing facility separate from the excretion facility? And many of these families had boarders living with them: how did you have a bath?

HM: There are 18th century accounts of French royalty receiving guests while using the bidet.

AR: The seat of power where you, as the guest, are powerless. It was a tradition of the rich.

TB: Isn't there some president who apparently was receiving his cabinet on the toilet?

DW: Lyndon B. Johnson.

AR: The one peculiar exception to America's fixation on hiding the toilet. It seems that in contemporary depictions of historical moments in film, art and literature, the French tend to show more than other cultures, images of the toilet as places of vital interaction. I am thinking of Danton and Bouchet's La Toilette.

HM: But it is extraordinary to realize that our contemporary bathroom is made possible due to the consolidation of water in one part of the house combined with the standardization of plumbing fixtures. For instance, they didn't figure out how to make a cheap mass-produced bathtub until around 1920.

AR: Another factor was just getting them up the stairs in terms of weight—I mean how many people would it take to carry a metal tub up to the sixth floor of a tenement building?

HM: Absolutely. You were lucky if you lived in a tenement and you had a bathtub. It's not really until tubs, sinks and toilets were mass-produced that the full indoor bathroom becomes available to the middle class.

DW: The impact on the quality of life is just amazing, amazing. ■

In 19th century New York, women, with their new notions of modesty, had to make the public statement of walking across the entire backyard to use the outhouse. There was some mention of women making themselves ill by not using the outhouse during daylight hours.

Interview with Mierle Laderman Ukeles
Artist for the New York Sanitation Department

interview by
Mark Dion
and
Anne Pasternak

Mierle Laderman Ukeles, the acclaimed artist-in-residence of New York's Department of Sanitation, has been a trailblazer in the field of public art for more than 20 years. Embracing what most would prefer to ignore—garbage, Ukeles has dug deep into our environmental, social, and cultural terrain. Through her art, Ukeles has made visible the creation, classification and relocation of our waste and called attention to those who are responsible for its handling. Subsequently, she has encouraged us to reflect on our own complex relationships to daily production, consumption, and refuse. Memorable projects have included Touch Sanitation *(1979), in which the artist thanked and shook the hands of all 8,500 Department of Sanitation workers;* Ballet Mechanique *(1983), a fleet of sanitation vehicles proudly parading down Madison Avenue;* The Social Mirror *(1983), a mirrored sanitation truck encouraging the public to reflect on its contribution to urban waste, and* Flow City *(1983–present), a plan designed to provide the public access to the 59th Street Marine Transfer Facility to witness firsthand the reallocation of the 13,000 tons of municipal refuse collected daily in Manhattan.*

To consider Ukeles' work only in terms of garbage, however, would be misleading as her art comunicates larger truths about public life and a profound understanding of our living world. Instead, it is through the example of refuse that Ukeles exposes compelling stories about each one of us and our interaction with our larger society. Her art makes us aware of the systems and attitudes that profoundly shape contemporary culture and encourages us to consider the impact of our individual actions on our collective welfare. Throughout our four-hour conversation, Mierle Laderman Ukeles leads us on a complex journey to consider the future; and, at the end faced with uncertainty and doubt, she reaffirmed our hope in the ability of artists and art to positively inform and impact our lives.

MIERLE LADERMAN UKELES: I'm not merely interested in the problems of urban waste, but I'm also intrigued with how art can be used to create a bridge and open people up to new ideas and a wider sense of community. That's what I learned through the piece *Touch Sanitation*, in which I visited every sanitation facility in New York City and spoke with each worker and shook their hands.

Of course, all these people were new to me; it was intimidating, but I talked to everyone. At the time, three or four different levels of city government "rat squads" had the sanitation workers under scrutiny, beside the usual hordes of social scientists, so it was vital to speak with these people and let them know my position as an artist. I needed to differentiate myself from the undercover surveillance people and the anthropologist types. My solution was to meet face to face with everyone and then to do the route with them and talk. You have to imagine what things are like for a sanitation worker. They did not have to do this. I asked them and no one ever asks them to participate in anything. It's a very rigid military-like system, totally hierarchical, with chiefs, foremen and other ranks.

ANNE PASTERNAK: The language used around the department is very militaristic. We hear of an "army" of sanitation workers and a fleet of dumptrucks and barges.

MLU: That's how people felt; this was a war against chaos. In the 70s, that was especially the mentality. Chaos was threatening to exterminate the city, how do you go to war against chaos—send in the marines. This was not a spit clean, proud army, but rather one neglected and kept under the worst possible conditions. Imagine a city department of 10,000 people without an allowance for their own furniture. Grown men had to sit in tiny children's seats that the schools had thrown out or wait until the cops got new furniture. There were not even doors in the toilet stalls. On any given day 65% of the equipment was broken down! This was two fiscal crises ago and things were bad. That was how people were treated and when I saw it, I was appalled. Then it was clear that the project would be about meeting people face to face because we had to start from the very beginning, start all over again.

So in I walk—the artist. I'm not their boss, I'm not from the union, I'm not there to make a specimen out of anybody, I'm not the press, so: Who the hell is this woman? I insisted on explaining my conception of this as an artwork. In this environment where you do what you're told, I invite them to participate. No one invites a sanitation worker to do anything.

Imagine: it's in the middle of the night or six o'clock in the morning and there I am making a fiery speech, dressed in my performance art uniform, not like their uniform. This is not a parody, and I'm standing in front of a floor to ceiling wall covered with pin—up crotch shots, the only women in the department those days. There I am talking about art. That was the deal and after I spoke, some guys would come up to me and say: "Does your husband

The Social Mirror, tempered glass and plexiglass mirrored New York City Department of Sanitation truck (1983).

Photo courtesy Ronald Feldman Fine Arts, New York

Fresh Kills Landfill, **Staten Island, New York, aerial view.**

let you do this?"

Nevertheless, after a full night out, doing the entire route, which is many streets, you could literally see people dropping their guards and making the decision to trust me. This is what I call the gates of acceptance, when a person relaxes the impulse to distrust and says, "Well after all, she is okay." The more I hung around, the more miles I put in, the more I refused to go away in disappointment, the more they allowed themselves to know me and the better I grasped their situation.

It was really a privilege to be working with the department, because many of the sanitation workers had an incredibly complex understanding of the city. Some of them see the city as a living entity. They know that they are part of the system that keeps the place alive. They are right in believing that the city will die if they stop doing their job or waste removal. So, imagine the anger they feel about being treated so badly. They had such complex ways of reading things about a neighborhood. They could tell if an area was safe or not, if it was in recovery or going down, just by the amount and type of trash that was there. In some abandoned places in the Bronx, a trash can made you want to applaud, because it meant someone was still hanging on. I respected the unique way sanitation workers understood the environment.

So when the workers dropped their guard and opened their hearts up to me, it represented one of the most powerful things that art can do. I want to explore this willingness to engage each other, because without that there is very little sense of community in this country. That some of these guys from the department still talk to me about how important the "touch sanitation" project was some 19 years later makes me proud somehow.

AP: This is going to sound really essentialist, but I'll go ahead anyway. When you speak of this idea of working to get people to open up their hearts to you, I can't help but think how important it is that you are an artist who is a woman and a mother. I know your intellectual and artistic formation comes from the 70s feminist movement which is a critical aspect of your development, but also important is that as a mother somehow the future means something different.

MLU: When I started out, I was a painter who only cared about my internal weather, which was pretty stormy, by the way. The outside world was not something to care about. When one becomes a mother, you can't help but rediscover the world. With every act, a child must invent; if they stand, it is the first discovery of the idea of standing. When a child succeeds, it is a moment of empowerment. Beyond that witnessing, the future becomes something tangible, you need it to be there for your child. You need a safe and clean environment for your child to live in. I always admire the Iroquois notion that any important decision you make must take into account how it will affect and benefit the tenth generation from today.

Our society could not be further from that sentiment. We have a peculiar form of brain damage. Take the example of Moscow, Idaho and one of the largest Superfund sites: The Kellogg Mine. Zinc, silver and lead were mined from one of the world's most inaccessible locations, and yet the construction engineers were so smart as to be able to transport expertise, raw materials and equipment to build a world-class refinery with 700-foot-high smokestacks. Imagine how ingenious these guys must be to construct the tools to exploit the metals' properties of differentiation. Mining science and architecture is awesome. So, tell me why does the curtain come down on all this creative genius when the mine is abandoned, leaving one of the worst toxic messes in history, with 95 feet of mercury tailings leaching into an important watershed and diminishing the future for everyone and everything in the area? The full stop our brain makes in situations like this is so visible as to be a wonder.

MARK DION: It's always around this issue of waste. Every organism must metabolize—take in food, transform it into energy for their needs and eliminate waste products. What is it that makes us so incapable of dealing with our own shit?

MLU: It's weird that we cannot handle the end of the cycle in the same powerful way we do the beginning. A lot of our physical response

---

FACTS ON FRESH KILLS
Staten Island's 3,000 acre landfill

In its 45-year history, the landfill has accumulated an estimated 100 million tons of garbage, making it the largest landfill on earth.

The height and volume of Fresh Kills rivals that of the largest of the Great Pyramids.

At the turn of the century when it closes, the landfill will have grown to 500 feet tall and will compete with the Great Wall as the world's largest man-made structure.

Fresh Kills contains enough accumulated refuse to fill the Panama Canal twice over.

When the landfill closes, it will be the tallest mountain on the Atlantic coast between Florida and Maine.

Fresh Kills is the host for over 40 bird species, many of which can be seen in no other part of New York City.

to decay and waste is an instinctive recognition of putrescence as something harmful. The body contracts, gags, turns away; that is a powerful response which I am certain is an adaptation against a potential threat. We cannot afford to get too close to our anaerobes. However, there are rational ways to react. We tend to turn away as if the problem did not exist. We have a strong desire for it to just go way.

MD: What does it mean to throw something "away?" "Away" is not limbo; it's always someplace.

AP: It's such a wonderful fantasy—I go "away" on vacation.

MLU: Here is another word for you: "trash." When the city chose a method to recycle, it took up the model of putting everything into one bag, thus collapsing all distinctions and demanding the least intellect and action from the people of the city. We need to be more complex and think about differentiation. These words, "trash" and "garbage," are masks for saying vastly different types of things are the same. What could be more different than hard or soft, wet or dry, small or large, yet it's all garbage. Once again, our creative brain has dried up. The psychology behind this thing is amazing. First, I desire an object and will do whatever I have to do to get it and make it a part of my larger self. People have spent millions of dollars to assure that I shall soon strip this object of its material qualities and here the lobotomy begins—I call it garbage. It's magic. Our senses dry up and the object's properties disappear.

MD: It's the opposite of alchemy.

AP: Of course, many of its desirable properties never existed in the first place. Maybe seeing it as garbage is seeing it for what it really is beyond a status-linked object.

MLU: Next comes the compounded fantasy that once it is garbage, it's someone else's responsibility to take it "away."

AP: I'd like to talk about the issue of time in your work. You have been working with the sanitation department for about two decades now. Flow City has been in production for 11 years. Most people think about politically-oriented art as something immediate, but you show the opposite tendency.

MLU: That's true, but frankly I'm bored and frustrated working on projects which rarely get finished because of the small-mindedness and bureaucracy of others. *Flow City* was a natural. A lot of people worked hard to make it happen; the building was constructed and zoned to make it happen. It should have been finished in 1989 and it was not. It was the easiest of a number of things I could have done. Think about how simple it is—a place where one can see sanitation workers bump up trash from the individual household to the mass of a city. The material flow mirrors the flow of the river. People see a process that they are contributors to. The ideas came quick; we worked hard to make it possible and then it just did not happen. I still feel that a lot of people in sanita-

Many of the sanitation workers had an incredibly complex understanding of the city. They could tell if an area was safe or not, if it was in recovery or going down, just by the amount and type of trash that was there. In some abandoned places in the Bronx, a trash can made you want to applaud, because it meant someone was still hanging on.

tion would rather people not understand the immensity of the issue.

Since 1977, I have been discussing the notion of the Fresh Kills landfill as a public place. Fresh Kills is amazing. It is the receiver of all the municipal waste produced by our entire city and yet for the people of Staten Island, it is a place just across the street. Over the past 48 years, the Department of Sanitation has operated on this site without a permit. The landfill's Director of Engineering, after almost two decades of awesome remediation catch–up work, has just finished the Herculean task of completing the permit application which is over 200,000 pages long. It is in itself a monument. It took 10 eight-hour days to truck the document to Albany. Staten Island has always, of course, wanted to close the landfill. After all, why should they get everyone's garbage? So what just happened? Our civic leaders, led by Staten Island, have just announced that Fresh Kills will close in six years. For Staten Island, this is terrific news. For New York City, I'm afraid it's a real crisis. Export out of town seems to be the only alternative being discussed; there are no other operating municipal landfills in New York City. Export is currently against city regulations. So the laws will have to be changed to allow an army of trucks, barges, and trains to take our waste "away." Where is each day's 13,000 tons of garbage to go?

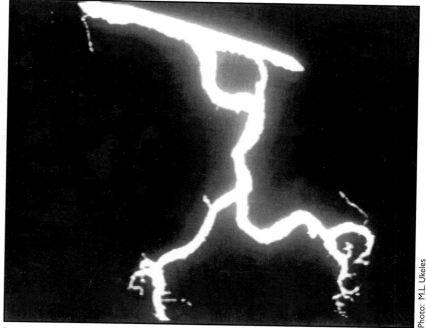

Image created on computer from aerial of waterway crisscrossing the landfill like a water creature racing across the landfill.

Photo: M.L. Ukeles

So to me there has never been a better time to make the things I've been speaking about real. Make sanitation visible so we can make informed decisions as to what to do about the problem. I'm not just interested in showing people the landfill after it's been capped and turned into some sort of park. The public should be aware of the process. Why can't we treat it like the valuable school of ecology that it is? It's so obvious and so valid. There are lessons there about population diversity of animals, about adaptation, about chemical waste, about energy. I'm certain that there is an intelligent and powerful role that art can have in a situation of complexity like this one, but it's just not happening. ∎

Mexico City Trashed

by
Joel
Simon

The first question most visitors ask when they arrive in Mexico City is: "Can I drink the water?" The second is often: "Can I breathe the air?" The answer, in both cases, is probably no. Like no other place in the world, Mexico City is condemned to live in its own waste.

The roots of Mexico City's environmental crisis lie in its unique geography. The city sits in a valley at 7,400 feet, surrounded by snow-covered mountains as high as 18,000 feet. Two million years ago, a volcanic eruption sealed off the valley's natural drainage in the south. Rainwater backed up, filling a series of five interconnected lakes, and creating a completely self-contained ecosystem.

In 1325, after wandering in the northern desert, the Aztecs arrived in the Valley of Mexico. They thought they had found paradise. Everything they needed for survival could be produced in a single valley. Pine forests rose on the slopes of the rain-drenched volcanoes, while cactus and maquey (used to make hemp clothing and an intoxicating drink called *pulque*) grew in the more arid north. Mountain creeks were diverted to irrigate the cornfields. The lakes themselves were not only a source of food, but in a country without horses or any other pack animals, they provided the basis for a transportation revolution. By the time of the Spanish Conquest, an estimated 200,000 canoes plied the waters, transporting food and other cargo long distances with astounding ease.

The Aztecs' reverence for their watery environment was so great that they built Tenochtitlan, their capital city, on an island in the middle of one of the lakes. There they raised an enormous pyramid to the water god Tlaloc. To show their reverence, they kept him sated with a steady stream of sacrificial victims whose still-beating hearts were ripped from their chests and offered in an act of pious devotion.

When the Spanish conquerors first set eyes on the Aztec capital in 1521, they were awed by its splendor. They compared it to Venice, but in truth, it was larger and grander than any city in Europe at the time. Although the Spaniards admired the beauty of the Aztec city, they were land-based people who preferred to travel on the horses they had brought from Spain, rather than in Indian canoes. Therefore, they filled in the canals which had crisscrossed the city, and dismantled the dikes and causeways which had protected it from floods.

The introduction of horses and iron axes also allowed the Spaniards to cut down huge tracts of forest. They used the lumber to build palaces and churches in the new city. The advent of grazing animals, unknown in the new world, unleashed an unprecedented wave of erosion. Also, winds blew the unprotected topsoil off the mountains. By the beginning of the 16th century, Mexico City has its first smog emergency as an enormous cloud of swirling dust called a *tolvanera* descended from the moun-

Because millions of people in Mexico City still lack indoor plumbing, the air is filled with more than a ton of fecal dust each day.

tains and covered the city. To this day, dust blown from the deforested hillsides remains a major source of air pollution.

The destruction of the forest also caused another unexpected problem. Rainwater, which used to gurgle down the mountain in small creeks, began to run off the exposed soil in a muddy torrent. As sediment washed into the lakes, the water level began to rise and Mexico City found itself battling more and more serious floods. The worst flood lasted from 1629 to 1634. The entire city was underwater and, as in Aztec times, the Spaniards were reduced to moving through the streets in canoes.

Rather than building dams to better control the flooding, the Spaniards declared war on the water. They decreed that the lakes, which still supported a large Indian population, would have to be destroyed. Thus began one of the most monumental projects of environmental engineering in human history—the draining of the Valley of Mexico. In 1608, the first phase of the project was completed. Sixty thousand Indians, under the supervision of Spanish authorities, completed a tunnel through the northern mountains, providing an outlet for the waters which had been trapped in the valley for 2 million years.

City dumps attract cattle egrets like this one.

Photo: AP/Wide World Photos

It took three centuries to finally drain the water from the Valley of Mexico. By the 18th century, the lakes had receded to the point where Mexico City was no longer on an island. A century later, all that was left of the lakes was a few stagnant, sewage-filled swamps.

If the lakes had not been drained, Mexico City would not have reached such mammoth proportions. It was on the dried-up lake beds where rural refugees, driven from the countryside, built urban slums. As the city grew from a relative backwater to an urban monstrosity, the ecological deterioration of the valley accelerated until it reached the point where the very survival of one of world's largest cities hangs in the balance.

Water is the biggest problem. By the 1840s, deforestation had reduced the springs. The same springs which once supplied drinking water for the city were only a trickle. Luckily, engineers discovered an enormous reserve of water in the aquifer which lay below the city. By the 1930s, thousands of wells had been dug. Authorities proudly announced the city's perennial water problems were over. There was only one problem: so much water was being pumped up from the aquifer that the

In Mexico City, you can get intestinal parasites—as well as typhoid and hepatitis—simply by breathing the air.

Photo: Bob Braine

Scientists have determined that toxins from the open air garbage dumps have migrated down to the water table.

ground was collapsing. The city was rapidly sinking. In 1951, the city sank nearly two feet. The downtown soon sunk below the level of the main sewage line and massive floods were the result. Today, a series of pumping stations move sewage uphill along a canal which once flowed downhill.

Despite the problems, 70% of the city's water supply continues to be pumped from the underground aquifer, and the city continues to sink at the rate of several inches a year. Another 30% of the water is pumped from neighboring valleys at enormous cost. Leaching from sewage lines is the main cause of contamination of the water supply, but there is growing concern that the aquifer itself could be in danger. Scientists have determined that toxins from the open air garbage dumps have migrated down to the water table.

Because Mexico City wants to revert to its natural state as a lake, the amount of rainwater which must be pumped out of the valley is enormous. Sewage lines are often overwhelmed and authorities are forced to store the sewage in dammed reservoirs. These sewage-filled lakes could eventually damage the drinking water supply. Because so much water has been pumped, the ground has cracked. These cracks provide a potential conduit for the sewage to leach into the aquifer.

The same factors which caused the city's water crisis—life in a high-altitude basin surrounded by mountains—are also the cause of the city's world record air pollution. It took 300 years and a series of tunnels to get the water out of the valley. However, the air has no escape (although blasting away a portion of the mountains has been proposed). Prevailing winds in the Valley of Mexico blow from north to south, trapping the 10,000 tons of toxic emissions produced each day against the southern mountains.

A good part of the haze which covers the city is produced by just plain dirt blown off the hillsides. The factories contribute their share as well, mostly in the form of sulphur dioxide. Meanwhile, cars dump thousands of tons of carbon monoxide into the air each day. In the winter, a thermal inversion often forms, pushing the contaminants down to street level. Then the sun goes to work, initiating a complex photochemical reaction which cooks the chemical haze into ozone, an irritant which may be carcinogenic. One 1987 study found levels of

By the beginning of the 16th century Mexico City has its first smog emergency as an enormous cloud of swirling dust called a *tolvanera* descended from the mountains and covered the city.

hydrocarbons and nitrogen dioxide in Mexico City were similar to those recorded in New York's Lincoln Tunnel. Because millions of people in Mexico City still lack indoor plumbing, the air is also filled with more than a ton of fecal dust each day. In Mexico City, you can get intestinal parasites—as well as typhoid and hepatitis—simply by breathing the air.

Air pollution has made Mexico City infamous, but it is only one of the environmental woes afflicting the city. Decisions made five centuries ago by the Spanish conquerors still reverberate today. Mexico City has completely destroyed all the natural cycles which once governed life in one of the world's most unique ecosystems. For as long as the city lasts, it will be paying the cost. ∎

This article has been adapted from Joel Simon's forthcoming book Endangered Mexico, An Environment on the Edge. *Joel Simon is a journalist specializing in Latin American and environmental issues; he can be contacted at JSimon@LANETA.APC.ORG.*

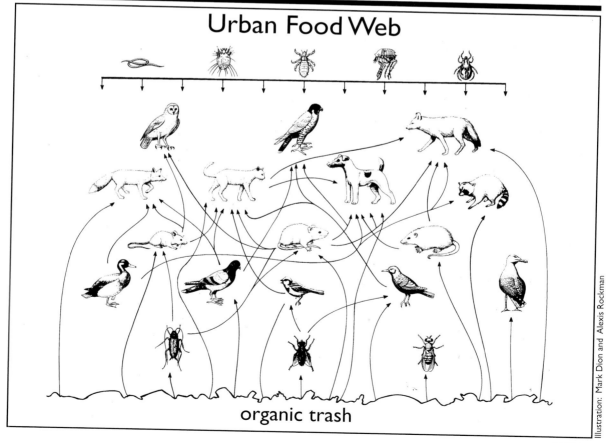

Urban Food Web

organic trash

Illustration: Mark Dion and Alexis Rockman

chapter 7

Road Kill

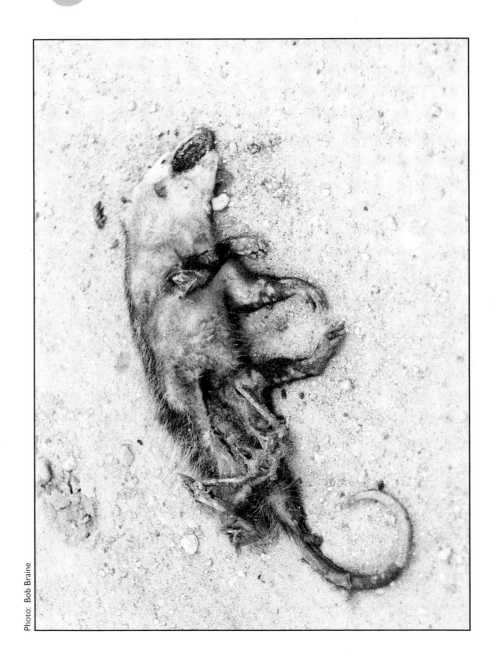

Photo: Bob Braine

This Car Stops for Road Kill

The Webster's Collegiate Dictionary has the word *roach clip* ("a metal clip that resembles tweezers and is used by marijuana smokers to hold a roach"), and the word *road hog* ("a driver of an automotive vehicle who obstructs others esp. by occupying part of another's traffic lane"), but it doesn't have the word *road kill*. The ubiquity of *road kill* (animals killed by moving automotive vehicles usually found on the sides of roads and highways) across the North American landscape makes this omission glaringly odd. *Roach clip* and *road hog* point to the fact that the oversight cannot be blamed on slang or the vernacular, so we must surmise that some other system of occlusion is at work.

    Bob Braine has been photographing road kill since 1986. The photographs are voluminous. Like the road, they go on and on. Their titles are consistently the location, position, and species of the dead animals they depict. This seemingly simple gesture is quite telling. For the titles speak to much more than morbid fascination. The sheer repetitiveness of the photographs, compounded by the titles, betray the systemic nature of road kill: on roads anywhere, at any time, any variety of dead animals can be found. The plethora points to much that

written by
Helen
Molesworth,
photo project by
Bob Braine

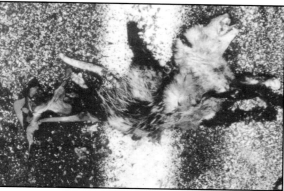

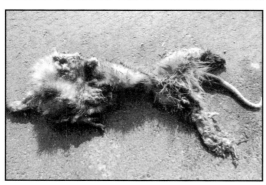

usually goes unnoticed.

To start with, there are the roads themselves. There is virtually no space in the United States that cannot be gotten to by car, given the thoroughness of the vascular system of interconnecting freeways, expressways, and local roads. These roads appear as if they were always already there, naturalized by their very expanse. The car, that greatest of American prosthetic inventions, propels us through spaces that exist as moving landscapes, blurs of well-tended medians and orange "Posted" signs nailed to trees. Braine's photographs of road kill freeze-frame these landscapes in a moment of bizarre time travel. They indelibly mark the present moment in which they were taken, but they also cannot help but evoke the time before the roads and the cars, before the advent of road kill. They remind us that the roads are far from a historical given; they cut through landscapes and habitats that we rarely think about, protected as we usually are from such thoughts by tape-decks, gas gauges, and cigarette lighters.

The road kill photographs offer the intimate intertwining of two historical forms of image-making, forensic and landscape. This mixture of "science" and "art" is part of what is compelling about Braine's work, for you can never simply talk about the photograph itself, you must always engage the process that goes into making it. The viewer, like the photographer, is positioned as some sort of perverse detective. How long ago was the animal hit? What is its level of decomposition? Was it sideswiped or did the car hit it with enough force to rip its leg from its body? However, there is another set of questions as well: what animal is this and what landscape can be seen by the side of the road? The important ecological question becomes: what is getting killed where? Once this dual set of questions is asked, the viewer has entered into the heart of Bob Braine's project.

Braine tells an extraordinary childhood anecdote, that unlike many artist's first-person narratives actually sheds some light on his work. As a little kid in the back seat of the family car, he would tell tall tales to his family about the passing landscape, "Look there's a black snake attacking a bird!" Laughing, he acknowledges that no one ever believed him, but what this story points to is the knowledge that something is always happening out there—in the woods, in the farm, on the landscaped median. What is dead on the side of the road does not only point to the brutality of the human relation to the landscape; it is also a clue as to what is living, even thriving, in our immediate surroundings.

The roads may shape, contour and inevitably dominate the landscape, but ultimately they are only part of the story. Nature, it appears, does not only exist in exclusively marked-off areas. It's true what they say: nature is all around us. But so too is culture. The glorious deadpan quality of Braine's photographs points to the banality that so many of us would rather ignore, the nature of everyday life. Opossums, seagulls, deer, mice, squirrels, rats, frogs, raccoons, dogs and cats, starlings, and skunks. These are animals that live near and with humans, yet they are the uncounted members of suburbia, the forgotten of urban parks, and the unmentionable of city streets.

Dead animals on the side of the road mark the beginning of Bob Braine's naturalist project. They are evidence that the landscape is more than an imagistic blur, more than just "trees" or an abandoned lot. The nature that surrounds us is as highly developed a system as the freeways we have laid down through it. The trees become more interesting when you know their names; a starling is fascinating when you are able to place it within its dynamic exchanges with other animals and the landscape. Essentially, road kill are the (forensic) evidence of our daily ecosystems. Road kill are as important as endangered species, for in death, in the transformation of one element of a system, the system itself becomes exposed.

The systems of interest to Braine have been the ones in which urbanization plays a crucial role. Instead of romanticizing the Sahara and the jungle (although Braine has made several naturalist trips to the latter), Braine feels that he catalogues the evidence of common animal life in accessible areas, such as roadways, fields and streams. It is here where the childhood anecdote becomes so telling and poignant. If you grow up in the suburbs, you fantasize about faraway places, but you are also surrounded by a level of complexity in your backyard that far outstrips in interest the ridicu-

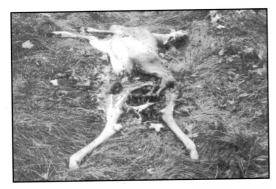

lousness of those pre-fab houses and cul-de-sac driveways. In this scenario, you can take the skunk's late night appearance as a nuisance, another indication of business as usual. Or you can view the skunk with a sense of wonderment. Or then again you could become analytical in your approach: where does the skunk live, what does it eat, what is its relation to the raccoon, how does it make that smell...? To talk with Bob Braine is to realize that he has all of these responses.

Bob Braine's work is deceptive for it looks simple, but it isn't. This may be the result of his work straddling two disciplines or modes of thought, the scientific tradition of the naturalist and the art tradition of documentary and landscape photography. On one hand, the forensic style of the photographs comes out of the pathological concerns of science. Through death much can be learned about the processes of life, not in small part because death is a process of life. (Hence there is no sentimentality in Braine's photographs.) On the other hand, in the tradition of documentary photography, Braine's work is true to the idea of the series. It is only in the photographs' accumulation that their meaning becomes contextualized and clear. This is particularly important with regards to their status as photographs of landscapes. For a singular road kill image does not convey the aspect of landscape given by an accumulation of the images. The reason behind this is two-fold. It takes a while to see past the explicit content of the images and the images are far from traditional landscapes. Rarely containing any sky, these are photographs of the ground, another area of daily life so often overlooked.

Many of us are used to a rhetoric that privileges the overlooked, claiming that more truth can be found at the margins than at the center of any given debate. Bob Braine's practice is neither that idealistic nor that programmatic. Rather, his work examines not so much what is overlooked, but what is all around us, seeing it from the double perspective of art and science, image and process, landscape and ecosystem. Perhaps when this stereo vision is more prevalent, *road kill* will make it into the dictionary. ∎

Helen Molesworth is a graduate student in history currently writing her dissertation on Duchamp.

Road Kill, Road Eats

Road kill. I know it sounds gross, but how many times have you ordered an aged steak or Peking Duck? They aren't far from a nice slab of road kill meat, flesh or, as I like to put it, carrion (nothing better than a little aged meat). Look around and you'll notice, excluding cats and dogs, (unless you have a craving for Rover Roast or Feline Fricassee), that there's plenty of meat for absolutely free!

Tips on finding and preparing good road kill: Look for head injury. This is key because minimal tissue trauma will have occurred to the part you intend to eat. This is especially important in small animals. For larger animals, like deer, just avoid ones that have been hit by trucks. If you get your road kill just after death, you're good to go, and in the winter you have longer, so long as the temperature has stayed below 30°.

It is also important to clean your road kill as soon as possible. I carry a skiing knife at all times; you never know when you might find a fresh kill (although I don't recommend doing this on a date). When you spot your road kill, approach slowly, as it might still be alive (be humane: club it if it is still alive). A wounded animal is very dangerous. If you can smell it 10 feet away, leave it where it lies. It's too far gone to eat unless you like maggots as a side dish (not recommended for the novice road kill eater). If the animal is completely flat, you know it's been run over 30 or 300 times, so forget it.

Now that your meal has met the above-mentioned criteria, split it open from neck to anus. This is your cue to reach in and pull every thing out. Wrap a plastic bag around your hands so you don't get blood and guts all over everything. Next, remove the head. Leave the skin or feathers on for now; just think of them as nature's shopping bag.

Now you're home. What to do? Skin the animal first; this means taking a knife blade and making small semicircular cuts between the skin and the muscle. This will work for birds also, but it's better to pluck them. Plucking is achieved by placing your fowl in hot water, then cold, and pulling out all the feathers.

Now that you have the skin and/or feathers off, look for bruises and large red spots; this is where blood has been trapped in the muscle. Cut it out like you would the eye of potato. Remove any visibly broken bones.

Now you're ready to try one of my recipes.

I was sitting in Tompkins Square Park eating a bag of popcorn. Needless to say, I was surrounded by 50 pigeons before I even got the bag open. I began to wonder what I could do with a few pigeons? Then I remembered a recipe. I lead my little flock to Avenue A and waited for a speeding truck to approach. I tossed a handful of popcorn into its path. I bet you can guess what happened. (Dinner!)

by
James Eckle
with recipes

Road kill. I know it sounds gross, but how many times have you ordered an aged steak or Peking Duck?

Pigeon with just a little garlic

(makes 3-4 servings)
3-4 pigeons (cleaned and plucked)
40 cloves of garlic (unpeeled)
3/4 cup of white wine (I like Thunderbird)
Salt and pepper to taste

Preheat oven to 450°. Pluck and gut pigeons. Wash thoroughly, making sure you get all the gravel out. Crush one clove of garlic and rub the inside and outside of each pigeon. Salt and pepper. Place pigeons in a Dutch oven and arrange remaining cloves of garlic around the pan. Place in oven and reduce heat to 350°. After about 10 minutes, pour the wine over the pigeons and baste every 10 minutes. Roast for a total of 45 minutes. This will also work well with chicken, game hens, blah, blah, blah.

Traveling through Pennsylvania on I-80 (I hereby dub Pennsylvania the Road Kill State), one can't help but notice the number of dead deer. Not being one to pass up a good meal, I found myself pulling over to get something for later (which would, incidentally, also feed 100 of my closest friends). Here's the tasty recipe I got from an Irishman who found himself displaced in Pennsylvania Dutch country. Being a good Irishman, he makes it with Guinness.

SOME OF MY MOTTOES:

The road is a banquet and most poor sons-of-bitches are starving.

Waste not want not.

Bambi in Guinness (makes 3-4 servings)

1 bottle of Guinness
3/4 pound of venison
4 carrots
1 large Spanish onion, or better still, 12 small pearl onions
2 teaspoons of sugar
Salt and pepper
5 or 6 small new potatoes, peeled
7 cloves of garlic, freshly peeled

Skin and wash Bambi thoroughly, making sure you get all the gravel out (the hind shank is the best). Cut everything (leave potatoes and garlic whole) into thick chunks: meat, carrots, onions (or leave pearls whole). Put all ingredients together in a large pot, add water to cover. Simmer for 1-1/2 hours. Add 1/2 teaspoon corn starch mixed with water to thicken, if needed. Adjust seasoning to taste. This will also work well with beef, lamb, blah, blah, blah.

Now for a little North African flavor. I got this recipe from a guy who lives just outside Casablanca on a dirt road—wait, ain't most of them dirt? You'll know his home by all the squirrel tails tacked on the door. His favorites are Stuyvesant Town black squirrels. I FedEx him some every time I get a chance.

Squirrels: you know those funny little guys running around every park in NYC. They run out into the street for oncoming traffic to maim and kill them. I say, why let all that meat go to waste? Pick up your new little friend and give him a name. Let's start. I named my squirrel Humphrey.

Couscous with Squirrel Squirrel (makes 3-4 servings)

1 onion chopped coarsely
1 green pepper chopped coarsely
8 cloves of garlic chopped coarsely
3 stalks of celery chopped coarsely
3 carrots chopped coarsely
2 small zucchini chopped coarsely
1 squirrel skinned and cleaned, cut into quarters
1/4 cup chopped parsley
12 cardamom pods
1/2 cup raisins
1 large can tomatoes
1 package of couscous
1 teaspoon chili powder
3/4 teaspoon fennel
Black pepper to taste

Skin and wash Humphrey thoroughly, making sure you get all the gravel out. In a pan, cover bottom with olive oil, then the first layer of onions, then garlic, peppers, celery, carrots, zucchini and squirrel. Add parsley, pods, raisins and fennel. Pour tomatoes over all of it, add water to cover, then stick a lid on it. Simmer over a very low heat for a good hour. Prepare couscous as directed on package and serve stew on top.

This will also work well with chicken, lamb, blah, blah, blah.

Traveling through South Carolina on State Route 25, I passed a sign for a small diner. I had to back up to see what it said: Gichies Soul Food and Lawn Mower Repair. Well, needless to say, I turned the wheel left and pulled in. I opened the screen door and sat at one of the three tables. Fay asked what I needed. My reply was a set of piston rings for a Briggs and Stratton 3/4 HP engine with a horizontal shaft and Today's Blue Plate Special: opossum.

Opossum Ambrosia (makes 6-8 servings)

1 opossum 5-10 lbs
4 carrots
2 large Spanish onions
2 cups red wine (Mad Dog is recommended)
1 cup of okra
2 green apples
1/2 cup of white vinegar
9 small new potatoes, unpeeled
3 cloves of garlic, peeled
1/2 tablespoon rosemary
1 tablespoon sage
Salt and pepper

Opossums are immune to the toxins of all venemous snakes in North America. This would lead one to suspect that poisonous baits have a dubious effect on their control.

Skin and wash your opossum thoroughly, making sure you get all the gravel out. Coarsely cut carrots, Spanish onions, apples and okra. Put opossum back down in Dutch oven. Split that sucker from jaw to belly. Place veggies in open chest cavity. Pour in wine and vinegar, sprinkle with spices. Cover and bake at 400° for 1–1/2 to 2 hours. Adjust seasonings to taste. This will also work well with birds, pigs and little baby cows, blah, blah, blah.

I'm sure you're aware that Groundhog Day was February 2nd and that the little bastard went back into his hole. Well, I have a little recipe to make us all feel a bit better. Groundhog Roast to keep you warm for the next 6 weeks of winter that the little son-of-a-bitch bequeathed us.

Groundhog Roasted In Its Hole (makes 5-7 servings)

6-8 pounds of groundhog meat cut from the bone
1/4 cup of olive oil
1/4 cup of balsamic vinegar

2 cloves of garlic, crushed
1/2 tablespoon rosemary
Salt and pepper to taste

Skin and wash your groundhog thoroughly, making sure you get all the gravel out. Cut meat from the bone and hammer with a mallet. In a glass bowl, place the groundhog, olive oil, and balsamic vinegar. Marinate for 6 hours. Place groundhog on a rack. Rub with salt, pepper, rosemary and garlic. Bake at 325° for about 1 hour. Baste with the marinade about every 10 minutes. Adjust seasoning to taste. This will also work well with pork, beef, lamb, blah, blah, blah.

I was up in the wilds of 125th street of NYC, walking the railroad tracks and I came upon a little shack. I knocked on the door and no one answered, so I peeked into the mail box to see if there was a key in it. All I found was a copy of the Unabomber's Manifesto and this recipe. How much wood can a woodchuck chuck? Better yet, how many woodchucks can you chuck?

Upchucked Woodchuck (woodchuck stew makes 5-7 servings)
10 to 12 woodchucks
2 cups Boone's Farm strawberry wine
4 tablespoons of olive oil
2 yellow onions, peeled and sliced
1 cup chicken stock
2 tomatoes diced
2 bay leaves
2 cloves of garlic, crushed
1/2 tablespoon rosemary
1/2 teaspoon thyme
1 lemon peel
Salt and pepper to taste

Skin and wash your woodchucks thoroughly, making sure you get all the gravel out. Place the woodchucks in a bowl, add wine and cover. Marinate overnight. Remove woodchucks from marinade and pat dry with paper towels. Heat a frying pan and add the oil and garlic. Sauté the woodchucks until brown on all sides, remove and place in a Dutch oven. Sauté the onions in the frying pan and add to the Dutch oven. Deglaze the pan with a little of the marinade and put that in the Dutch oven. Then add the chicken stock and simmer for a 1/2 hour. Add the wine, marinade, tomatoes, seasonings and lemon peel. Cover and cook for about 25 minutes more. Adjust seasoning to taste. This will also work well with beef, lamb, blah, blah, blah.

Not too long ago I was in Louisiana and met an old Cajun woman (she had to be 100). She loved rabbit baked, broiled, poached and fried. My favorite recipe follows.

Bunny Bathed In Fire
(makes 3-4 servings)

 1 rabbit cut into eighths
 3 tablespoons of Tabasco sauce
 1 cup of flour
 2 tablespoons of garlic powder
 1 tablespoon of thyme
 1/2 tablespoon of red pepper
 Salt and pepper
 Peanut oil for pan-frying

Skin and wash your bunny thoroughly, making sure you get all the gravel out. Place the rabbit pieces in a bowl and add the Tabasco (you can also add 1/2 cup of whiskey for a little more flavor). Mix well and let marinate for a half hour. Mix the flour, thyme, salt and pepper together in a paper sack. Dip the rabbit in the flour and spice mixture and pan fry in hot oil. Brown both sides evenly on moderate heat, uncovered. This should take about 20 minutes to cook. This will also work well with chicken, lamb, blah, blah, blah.

I realize that some of these animals are difficult to find in NYC, so I've decided to use something a little more available. What is it? Bones! You can find them in your favorite dumpster. Personally, I like to go over to the Meat Market at 14th and Washington Street—plenty of bones there!

Bone Broth (makes 5-7 servings)
2 or 3 bones (about 5 lbs of large beef bones)
3 cups Boone's Farm raspberry wine
3 tablespoons of olive oil
2 yellow onions, peeled and sliced
1 cup beef stock
2 tomatoes diced
2 tablespoons tomato paste

1 bay leaf
4 cloves of garlic, crushed
1/2 teaspoon rosemary
1/2 teaspoon thyme
3 celery stalks, sliced
Salt and pepper to taste

Wash your bones thoroughly, making sure you get all the garbage off. Crack each bone into three pieces and place in a bowl. Put all ingredients, except the olive oil and tomato paste, into the bowl. Cover with wine and let marinate over night in refrigerator.

Dump everything from the bowl into a Dutch oven and add olive oil and tomato paste. Cover and place in oven at 350° for 1-1/2 to 2 hours. Remove the pieces of bone and any splinters and serve. Adjust seasoning to taste. This recipe will work well with just the meat too. Try lamb, blah, blah, blah.

This recipe is for all my veggie friends since it has plenty of protein from a non-animal source. Why does it have so much protein you ask? Some kind of beans, nuts, what? OK. Roaches. Now, you have to admit there are plenty to go around and you can find them just about anywhere. Catching roaches is like catching flies. I like to put some honey on a plate and before long I have just what I need.

Squatter Pilaf (makes 5-6 servings)

50 –100 roaches
2 cups white rice
2 cloves garlic, minced
2 bay leaves
2 tablespoons olive oil
1 large onion, chopped
2 cups steamed green vegetables
1–1/2 cups stewed tomatoes
1/2 cup tomato paste
2 teaspoons hot sauce
2 teaspoons chili power
1 teaspoon cumin
1/4 teaspoon mustard
1 teaspoon oregano
Salt and pepper to taste

Bring 4 cups of water to a boil. Pour rice into boiling water and reduce heat and simmer for 25 minutes. Stir rice and simmer uncovered until done. Drain off any excess liquid.

Blanch roaches by putting them into a colander and pouring hot water over them. This makes them easier to handle. Next, heat oil in a large frying pan. Add the onion and sauté until brown on the edges. Add all remaining ingredients including roaches. Stir and simmer over low heat for 8–10 minutes. This also works well with lentils, fish, blah, blah, blah.

In China, many restaurants carry an entree that goes by the name of Super Deer, i.e., rat meat. Walking through any park in NYC, you'll notice an abundance of this free meat. My favorites are the Norwegian rats (sewer rats). One is enough to make a meal. So here's a recipe I got from an old Greek man in Astoria.

Rat with Olives (makes 3-4 servings)

3–4 rats, cut into 4 pieces (or one Norwegian rat)
1 cup white vinegar
3 tablespoons olive oil
1 yellow onion, peeled and diced
2 garlic cloves, crushed
5 very ripe tomatoes, chopped
2 tablespoons chopped parsley
1 cup Mogen David (Mad Dog)
1 teaspoon oregano
1 cup green olives, stuffed with pimentos
Salt and pepper to taste

Wash your rats thoroughly, making sure you get all the gravel out. Place rats in a bowl and cover with white vinegar and let marinate for two hours in the refrigerator. Remove from bowl and pat dry with a paper towel. Salt and pepper the rat pieces and place them on a broiling pan and roast in a 400° degree oven for 20 minutes or until they begin to brown.

While the rat is baking, prepare the sauce. Heat a frying pan and add the olive oil, the onion, and the garlic. Sauté until transparent. Add the remaining ingredients, except the olives. Simmer, uncovered, for about 20 minutes, or until the tomatoes have collapsed. Place the rat pieces in a Dutch oven with a lid. Rinse off the olives and add to the sauce. Pour the sauce over the rat, cover, and simmer until the rat is tender, about 1 hour. This also works well with duck, lamb, blah, blah, blah. ∎

James Eckle grew up in the midwest and ran away to a carnival. He is now publisher of the New York Hangover, *a source of unnecessary information. For further details, write to P.O. Box 20005, West Village Station, 527 Hudson Street, New York, NY 10014, fax 212-243-7252 or e-mail hangover@bigmagic.com or nyhangover@aol.com.*

Photo: AP/Wide World Photos

Fuo Ye Xia, an itinerant rat killer, sells packets of home-brewed poison in a free market in Shijiazhuang, China. Satisfied customers return the tails of rats and Fuo proudly displays them in a mountain said to contain 60,000 rodent tails.

chapter 8

Zoos, Museums & Other Fictions

Zoo Timeline

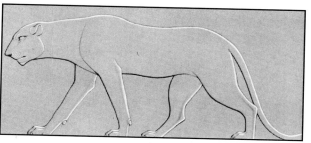

■ 2800 to 2250 B.C.

The royalty of the Egyptian Old Kingdom attempts to domesticate or acclimatize an extraordinary number of different species. Some are maintained as sacred animals, while others are kept as experiments in husbandry.

■ 1100 or 1000 B.C.

Chinese Emperor Wen Wang establishes the Ling-Yu, or "Garden of Intelligence," a 900-acre walled park which exhibits animals collected from the end of his vast empire.

■ 300 B.C.

Aristotle makes use of the Greek city-state's extensive menageries when writing his *History of Animals*. His commitment to zoology is passed on to his student, Alexander the Great, who makes the collecting of animals one of the priorities of his eastern campaign.

■ ROMAN EMPIRE

The passion for games and spectacles based on animal combat is so pervasive as to cause numerous local extinctions and change the ecology of parts of Africa and Europe. During Caligula's inauguration, 400 bears and 400 African beasts were put to death in the games, and hundreds of birds were sacrificed in his honor.

■ 8th CENTURY

Emperor Charlemagne keeps three menageries. Many of the animals received as diplomatic gifts are used for sport.

■ 9th CENTURY

The monastery of Saint Gallen in Switzerland becomes one of Europe's principal intellectual centers. It hosts a small but systematic collection of exotic animals.

■ 13th CENTURY

Princely menageries flourish in France, Portugal, Naples and Florence. The naturalist, Holy Roman Emperor Frederick II, maintains not only three large animal collections, but also a menagerie of elephants, big cats, monkeys and camels, which accompanies him on his travels. Marco Polo describes visiting the court of Kublai Khan. Khan kept a vast gathering of animals in a 16 square mile walled-in park. Polo reports seeing rhinoceros, elephants, tigers, civets, leopards and enough falcons to employ 10,000 men.

■ HIGH RENAISSANCE
Artists are employed to render the residents of the zoological collections which now exist in many monarchies and principalities. Da Vinci draws zoo animals in Milan; Dürer draws in Ghent.

■ 1519
Hernando Cortés reports an enormous menagerie kept by Montezuma. It consists of a huge aviary, mammal cages, luxurious down and feather lined serpent enclosures and a collection of various sorts of deformed people.

JANUARY 20, 1583 ■
After a nightmare of being devoured by animals, Henry III kills the entire population of the zoo at the Louvre with his haque-bus. The collection included bears, lions, monkeys and parakeets.

16th and 17th CENTURIES ■
In the European, Arab and Turkish worlds, menageries flourish. Exotic wild animals continue to have the role of high-status diplomatic gifts. Most collections at this time are little more than walled-in park lands. Contact with the new worlds provokes a zoological interest. Animals in culture stimulate curiosity. They also signify prestige, domestic control and far-reaching influence.

1640–1715 ■
Developed by over 50 designers, sculptors, painters and architects, Louis XIV's zoo at Versailles may be considered the first proper zoological garden. The animal enclosures are arranged like spokes on a wheel, around an octagonal pavilion attached to a residence. The animals can be observed from any single point. When the king is not present, the bourgeoisie and the poor are allowed to tour the zoo.

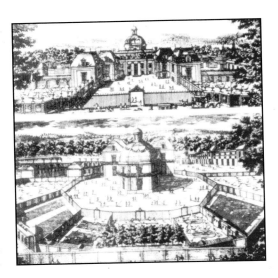

■ 1759
Austria's Schonbrunn Zoo is the oldest zoo which survives today. Based on the Versailles design, a central octagonal rococo pavilion is constructed as Queen Marie Theresa's breakfast room. From this point, the enclosures radiate out. Her son opens the zoo to the public in 1765.

■ 1789
A revolutionary group marches on the Versailles zoo to state: "In the name of the people and in the name of nature, we demand that the beings that had freely come out of the hands of the Creator and have been improperly detained by the pride and pomp of tyrants, must be set free." The dangerous animals remain caged, some beasts are freed and many are sent to the slaughterhouse.

■ 1793
The Musée National d'Histoire Naturelle de Paris in the Jardin des Plantes becomes the first national zoo. It is established as "a place set aside for the study of nature in the interest of science and the liberal arts, for scientists and for artists." Cuvier and Lamarck are just two of a score of celebrated scientists who use the institution.

■ 1827
The Zoological Gardens in Regent's Park in London opens to fellows of the Society. Its purpose is for "...animals to be brought from every part of the globe to be applied either to some useful purpose, or as objects of scientific research, not vulgar admiration." It opens to the public a year later.

MID–19th CENTURY ■

Most zoos view their role as that of "rational entertainment." Zoo architecture of this period places exotic animals in exotic buildings.

1864 ■

New York's Central Park Zoo becomes the first menagerie in the U.S.

■ 1866

Wild animal dealer Carl Hagenbeck revolutionizes zoo architecture and showmanship. In his animal park in Hamburg, Hagenbeck constructs enormous naturalistic environments consisting of mountains, lakes and caves. He develops enclosures which utilize moats rather than bars to separate animals from spectators. Hagenbeck also achieves wonders in animal acclimatization and breeding. In bizarre ethnographic encampments, Hagenbeck displays non-European people.

■ 1871

Yellowstone National Park dedicated.

1895 ■

The pugnacious William T. Hornaday becomes the director of the Bronx Zoo. Over the next four decades, he uses the zoo as a platform for wildlife conservation activism. Hornaday's successes include saving the bison from extinction, ending market hunting, providing protection for marine mammals and having the first wild bird conservation act.

EARLY 20th CENTURY ■

Most zoos consist of "postage stamp" type collections. Each collection tries to represent as many animals as possible. Zoo design and architecture take the natural history museum's taxonomic displays as a model.

W.W. II ■

European zoos post a 24-hour guard around the cages of dangerous animals in case bomb explosions free the beasts.

Photo: ©NYZS/Wildlife Conservation Society

■ 1950s

Around 300 zoos exist worldwide; most of these still view entertainment as their reason for being. Animal shows like the chimpanzee tea party are common. In zoo architecture, sanitation and animal hygiene become the rage.

■ 1968–1972

The safari park, in which the public drive cars through spacious paddocks, attracts a new generation of zoo-goers, who have become accustomed to seeing animal programs on television. In Africa, large scale eco-tourism becomes a serious economic factor in some countries.

■ 1970s

Zoological societies strengthen ties with international wildlife conservation efforts. Zoo exhibits become more concept oriented, focusing on ideas such as the nocturnal world or particular habitats, rather than taxonomy. Exterior zoo architecture becomes almost invisible.

1980s ■

Zoological societies identify themselves as cultural institutions on par with galleries and museums. The zoo's mission is largely defined as an educational one. The public's knowledge of ecology, animal behavior and conservation is eagerly challenged at the increasingly didactic zoo. Direct wildlife conservation efforts through captive breeding and reintroduction are developed further than ever before. Zoo architecture becomes the masterful hyper-real replication of specific habitats.

■ 1990s

The trends of education and wildlife conservation activism continue to dominate the zoo's agenda. Zoos explore and develop their role as endangered species breeders. It becomes increasingly clear that many animals will become extinct in the wild and will survive only as zoo denizens.

You Want a Northern Spotted Owl With That?
The American Museum of Natural History

by
D. Scott
Gregory

In 1951, Holden Caufield described the American Museum of Natural History as a place where "everything always stayed right where it was." 1995 saw great changes for the museum in an effort to bring it to the 21st century. The mission to modernize the museum has, in part, meant revising out-of-date exhibition halls to reflect changes in scientific study and exhibition design, but it has also meant the planning of a series of blockbuster exhibitions, which have broken records in both attendance and sales.

The most successful of these exhibitions have all capitalized on the recent popularization of natural history in science fiction/action films such as *Star Trek, Jurassic Park,* and *Raiders of the Lost Ark.* Indeed, gift shop sales associated with both "The Dinosaurs of Jurassic Park and "Expeditions" reached an all-time high, and "Orion Rendezvous: A Star Trek Voyage of Discovery" earned the highest ticket revenue of any show in the planetarium's history.

The trend towards the commodification of natural history—and more generally of educational institutions using "edutainment" to maintain a bottom line—is not singular to the American Museum of Natural History. Such moves are not surprising given our ever-shrinking government funding for culture and education.

That the museum has chosen the popular route of edutainment, revising old material in a jazzed-up technologized form, should not be surprising given the history of the museum itself. In his history of the American Museum of Natural History *Dinosaurs in the Attic*, Douglas J. Preston describes in the 19th century, how the early scientific pursuits of founder Professor Albert S. Bicker, with his esoteric interest in fossil invertebrates, almost drove the museum to financial ruin in a short 10 years. The museum was saved by the new president Morris K. Jesup, who had been commissioned to do a report on the then-failing institution. Jesup astutely perceived that collections of fossil invertebrates would not draw big crowds and that the museum should instead look to lions and other big mammals to draw public interest. He also refocused the mission of the institution to reflect an audience largely uneducated in science. As he often repeated, "I am a plain, unscientific man; I want the exhibits to be labeled so I can understand them,

The American Museum of Natural History.

Photo: Mark Dion

As spectacular as it is speculative, the mother barosaurus towers above visitors at the Natural History Museum. The installation was intended to be scientifically provocative.

Photo: Mark Dion

and then I shall feel sure that others can understand."

Jesup's populist view of the future of the museum was perhaps influenced by the enormous commercial success of P.T. Barnum's 19th century scientific side shows. While Barnum banked on the authority of science to boost his enterprise, advertising it as a "Zoological Garden," a "Polytechnic Institute," and a "Colosseum of Natural History and Art," he had first made a name for himself as "The Prince of Humbug," exhibiting hoaxes—or humbugs—a popular form of entertainment in America in the 1830s. From his first major success with Joice Heath, the alleged 161-year-old former nurse of George Washington, Barnum was irresistibly drawn to the entertaining lure of the "exotic" and opened the American Museum in New York in 1841. Barnum also understood that it was the parody that was entertaining. Trying too hard to convince wasn't funny: "the public appears to be amused even while they are conscious of being deceived," he observed of his particular take on the art of humbug. Barnum's early humbugs spoofing evolution still took the idea for granted. For Barnum, "every sham shows there is a reality," and he looked down on true conmen.

The relationship between Barnum's "hoaxes" and the life-like dioramas which would appear from the hands of Carl Akeley at the American Museum Natural History 20 years later seem inextricably linked. In fact, it was through the "Jumbo" accident that Akeley first acquired the fame which eventually led him to the American Museum Natural History. In 1882, Barnum acquired Jumbo the elephant from the Royal Zoological Gardens in London. At the time of his acquisition, Jumbo was already world-renowned for his extraordinary size, reportedly consuming each day, "two hundred pounds of hay, two bushels of oats, a barrel of potatoes, several quarts of onions, and ten to fifteen loaves of bread." But, alas, Jumbo's successful tour of America with P.T. Barnum's circus was only to last three years before he was killed in a head-on collision with a freight train. Always the publicity man, Barnum sent the body to Henry Ward's Natural Science Establishment in Rochester, New York, to have it preserved and mounted. Akeley, a young taxidermist, was given the job and managed to increase the animal's size by a foot in its final form.

After achieving fame for his work with Jumbo, Akeley spent several years at the Field Museum in Chicago, which sent him on his first expedition to Africa in 1909. He was so impressed by the African wildlife, which he saw as being endangered by the spread of civilization, that upon his return, he approached the American Museum of Natural History with a proposal to reconstruct their African exhibitions. The new "Hall of Africa" would include samples of African mammals in their original environments presented at an extreme scale and level of realism. The museum needed little persuasion—this proposal was exactly in keeping with the direction of the museum established by Jesup. Soon thereafter, Akeley joined the staff of the American Museum of Natural History. One might think that the diorama was the more scientifically relevant form of exhibition, accurately representing nature in a way that allowed viewers to observe and study specimens and artifacts, but, as Barnum himself knew, the hoax relied more on engaging the imagination of the viewer, while the diorama depended on the innovation of the scientist. As Donna Haraway has pointed out, "hoax assumed greater confidence in the active intelligence of the audience than did the more reverent television nature special. The relation of hoax and popular natural history is unnervingly close...." It was precisely this relationship between exhibition and audience which led Charles Wilson Peale, whose sons had donated a large part of the collection of Barnum's American Museum, to describe Barnum's shows as "rational amusement." Barnum's American Museum was destroyed by fire in 1865, never to be rebuilt. Nearly ten years later the American Museum of Natural History opened its doors. Barnum had a brief retirement before getting back into the circus business.

The American Museum of Natural History had somewhat of a symbiotic relationship with Barnum from the start, occasionally receiving animals which died at the circus to be taxidermied and displayed at the museum. When the newly-chartered American Museum of Natural History opened in New York in 1874, Barnum promised that, "If any of our animals die, we will present them to your institution with pleasure." He also made the same promise to the Smithsonian, which eventually sparked an acrimonious battle between the museums for the greatest

Photo: Mark Dion

Ornithologist Frank Chapman wowed the public in 1911 with diorama "habitat groups" of North American birds. This exhibit displays the passenger pigeon, one of the most plentiful birds to have ever lived. It was hunted to extinction by 1914.

specimens from the "Greatest Show on Earth."

Within the world of science exhibition and education, museums are increasingly faced with what could be called the "Jurassic Park" phenomenon—competition from theme parks which provide an uneven mixture of "edutainment" facilities—drive-through safaris, thrill-seeking rides, and interactive exhibits. To cope with the increasing competition from these highly-commercialized, edutainment mall-like (epi-)centers, the Museum has devised a variety of solutions—ranging from savvy to absurd—to reinvigorate the dinosaurs and bring the crowds back in.

A fascinating case study of the Museum's attempt to juggle popular attraction with science is the awesome fossil mount of an allosaurus attacking an adult and baby barosaurus. This is the first exhibition to greet the visitor in the Museum's Theodore Roosevelt Memorial Hall. Through a series of Roosevelt quotations, the museum orients visitors to its early goals. The entrance hall has been characterized by Donna Haraway as "...a space that sacralizes democracy, Protestant Christianity, adventure, science and commerce."

The mounted barosaurus stands on its hind legs, looming some 60 feet over the tourists' heads, in an attempt to fend off the attack on its offspring. As spectacular as it is speculative, the exhibition was con-

Photo: Mark Dion

The Akeley method of taxidermy stretches a preserved animal skin over a sculpted form for astoundingly lifelike effects. The Hall of African Mammals (completed after Akeley's death) is the pinnacle of diorama art (c. 1936).

structed intentionally to be scientifically provocative, as the spearhead of the $45 million reorganization of the fossil halls (completed in 1996). While the Museum curators were vocal in condemning other Natural History institutions for hosting gimmicky robotic dinosaurs, which amuse the public by fleshing out bones with color and sound (the precise bits of information which elude paleontologists), it responded with the most ambitious single fossil mount ever attempted, based largely on physiological and behavioral conjecture. Whether the titanic Jurassic herbivore could have stood erect on its hind legs and whether or not it cared for its young are issues of pure guess work. Where hard information was missing, the designers opted for the most spectacular aesthetic solution, while at the same time monumentalizing protective motherhood. The controversy around the barosauruses secured the museum a great deal of publicity and flocks of eager viewers.

The value of spectacle is not new to the museum and if one wished to characterize the most salient trend in the institution over the past decade, it would not be the interplay of entertainment and education. The Natural History Museum has learned an important lesson from its better endowed sister across the park (The Metropolitan Museum of Art): the value of the gift shop. With over half a dozen stores, the Museum is one of New York's more marketable cultural institutions. Many of the gift stores are theme-related such as the Dinostore and the F.A.O. Schwartz franchise, which displays all the neocolonial charm of an Indiana Jones film. While the commercialization of the museum may be regrettable, it must be understood in the context of the last 15 years of government cutbacks and the general financial underdevelopment of cultural institutions. However, with exhibition-linked stores such as the Amber gift shop located at the exhibit exit, pulling in as much $55,000 during the first week, it is not difficult to imagine that commerce will join entertainment as a significant pressure on curators and designers.

This leads us to questions regarding the forthcoming permanent exhibition hall slated to open in 1998, tentatively-titled: "Biodiversity: The Crisis of Life." While perhaps less of a public attention grabber than dinosaur exhibits, Biodiversity does capitalize on one of the most powerful icons of environmentalism: the tropical rainforest. The exhibition is to replace the current outdated and confusing Invertebrate Hall which featured large-scale conceptual models. These abstract attempts at demonstrating insect evolution and diversity proved uncompelling and visually and conceptually too baffling for the general public.

The new hall will showcase multiple levels of the diversity of life from variation among individuals to species diversity, to how organisms relate and support one another (socially and instinctually). A series of interactive walk-through "biome" dioramas educating the public on the destruction of ecosystems by humans will be a central feature of the hall. The new diorama will attempt to engage hearing, touch and smell,

The building [the American Museum of Natural History] presents itself in many visible faces. It is at once a Greek temple, a bank, a scientific research institution, a popular museum, a neoclassical theater. One is entering a space that sacralizes democracy, Protestant Christianity, adventure, Science, and commerce.
—Donna Haraway, "Teddy Bear Patriarchy," *Primate Visions*

Photos: Mark Dion

Some of the many gift shops at the American Museum of Natural History: the F.A.O. Schwarz gift shop (top) and the Museum Shop (bottom).

senses usually excluded in diorama art. While being the most Disney-like of the museum's exhibits, the Biodiversity Hall is clearly a response to pressure from both inside and outside of the institution to be more responsive to critical issues facing the natural world at the twilight of the millennium. Over the past decades the museum has side-stepped some of the more critical ecological debates. The Biodiversity hall will be the first hall to negotiate the political debates around wildlife conservation.

The American Museum of Natural History is one of the most important sites of the "official story" of what gets to stand for "Nature" at a particular time for a particular group of people. The exhibition halls have always been encoded with the social relations of the period of their construction. In the past, that has embraced conservation, eugenics, the cult of utopian futurism, and a variety of dubious notions regarding gender, class and race. This is no less true today. Indeed the exhibition halls of today with their souped-up techno-aesthetic remind us of current assumptions of what information has to look like for the Nintendo generation. The challenge facing the museum is a crisis of the wider culture: not only how to negotiate popular culture and scientific education, but also how the pressing need and obvious success of the commodification of nature and natural history affect that mixture. The institutional forays into popular culture might signal a positive effort to engage a wider audience and place science in a larger cultural context or it may simply signal taking advantage of a marketing situation. In either case, the result of exhibitions like "The Dinosaurs of Jurassic Park" and "Star Trek" at the Hayden Planetarium foreground the fictitious. It becomes increasingly difficult to distinguish between stories, real and imaginary, and science based on fiction versus fiction based on science. In the museum, fantasy provides the escape from our lived social problems to a hyperrealized world ordered by a revised myth of nature. Coming soon: "Biodiversity: The Crisis of Life." ∎

D. Scott Gregory is a multi-media sculpture installation artist, writer, and poet living in Brooklyn, NY, who recently resigned from his position as a Senior Preparator in the Exhibition Department of the American Museum of Natural History.

Magic in Plain Sight: The Art and Science of Diorama Display

by
J. Willard
Whitson

As I write this essay, NASA has just reported that the evidence of life on Mars may have been preserved in a meteorite; that with the aid of new, improved electron microscopy scientists may have found fossils of organisms that lived as long as 4.5 billion years ago on what is now a lifeless planet. If proved to be true, it will be the first time that we know with certainty that we are not alone; that life itself has existed elsewhere in the solar system; and that, by logical inference, if life exists not only on Earth in what is a relatively small galaxy, then the odds of life existing in countless other places in the universe increase exponentially.

However, while this meteorite may be stunning evidence for abundant life in the universe, it also offers dramatic evidence that life on a heavenly body can be extinguished. Indeed, a living planet can become a lifeless orb. The implications for our own planet are clear. Biological and environmental scientists today believe that our own planet is on the threshold of, or is in the midst of, a mass extinction episode, one that may spell our own demise. There have been five great extinction events in the Earth's 3.5 billion year history of life. All of these episodes have occurred without human intervention. However, the crisis that the living world faces today is the direct result of human activity in the environment. Through habitat destruction and alteration, we are threatening the web of infinite complexity that sustains all life. This biodiversity crisis is the single most pressing problem that humanity faces.

The crisis is being addressed in many arenas. Scientists are studying the living world with an unprecedented urgency; schools are increasingly stressing environmental science in their programs; the news media communicates a constant stream of news bites expressing the need for concern; governments and non-governmental organizations are taking a more and more sophisticated approach to studying and finding solutions to this problem. And organizations with which I am personally very familiar, natural history museums, are beginning to create exhibitions and design educational programs to heighten public awareness of this rapidly escalating crisis. How and why this concern is being communicated in museum exhibitions (specifically dioramas) is the subject of this essay.

At a recent art fair held at the Gramercy Hotel in New York City, one piece particularly struck me. It was very simple, and part of its impact was due to its simplicity and undisguised artifice. A plain, transparent jar contained a frosted piece of glass or acrylic. Behind the jar, a small video camera projected a continuous tape loop depicting a butterfly flapping its wings. The effect was mesmerizing. All of the means by which the illusion of the butterfly in a jar was created were readily apparent. There were no concealing tricks. And yet what was witnessed was magic. Magic in plain sight. At the American Museum of Natural

Unfavorable comparisons with zoos arise, being primarily that museum animals are dead and stuffed, and that zoo animals are alive, but captive, and miserably deprived of their natural environment. I firmly believe that these negative assessments have something to do with the success (or lack of success) of both types of institutions to create illusions, the sleight of hand that makes for good magic.

History and at natural history museums around the world, this kind of magic is performed every day in countless exhibits. I am referring to the three-dimensional depictions of natural scenes known as dioramas. As defined in the museum setting, a diorama is a display consisting of a constructed foreground with fabricated or preserved elements (plants, rocks, water, etc.) and (usually) taxidermied (or modeled) fauna. The constructed foreground is blended seamlessly into a realistically painted background, which then illusorily extends the vista to the horizon. The background wall is ideally a semicircle topped by a quarter hemisphere. Thus, the field of view contains no sharp angles, straight surfaces, or corners. Of course, architectural realities such as low ceilings or unfortunately eccentric spaces—as well as a lack of understanding of the diorama art form itself—often preclude having the ideal circumstances.

In reality, exhibitions for natural history museums are rooted in art and magic—in the service of science or, more accurately, in the service of science education. Creating the illusion of pristine nature is a concept that dates back before the creation of natural history museums themselves. In the late 18th century, public displays called "panoramas" were invented as a form of mass entertainment. Huge circular paintings surrounded audiences sitting on platforms with the scene filling their

Neg. #317571, Courtesy Dept. of Library Services, American Museum of Natural History

Akeley African Hall. Hyaena-Jackal-Vulture group (c. 1936).

view. Louis Daguerre (inventor of the daguerreotype) was one of the artists who painted these panoramas. He later improved on the technique by adding a number of semi-transparent foreground scrims that provided the opportunity to create various lighting effects, thus enlivening the scene depicted. While the audience sat on the stationary platform, the images changed as the scrims were moved and altered. Daguerre called his improved displays "dioramas." The only true similarity between the traditional natural history displays and Daguerre's invention is the use of a realistically painted curved background. By the mid–19th century, dioramas and panoramas went into decline—mainly due to the invention of photography, which was felt to present a more realistic depiction of nature.

It was not until the beginning of the 20th century that the diorama was employed as an exhibition technique in a natural history museum. Frank Chapman, an ornithologist at the American Museum of Natural History, created a series of bird dioramas which he called "habitat groups." As he stated: "The habitat group does not copy nature slavishly, even though an actual scene forms the background; it aims to give a broad and graphic presentation of the conditions under which certain assemblages of bird life are found to bring home to the observer the atmosphere and vegetation of some typical part of the country." The presentation of specimens in such a natural setting was, in fact, controversial at the time and was not universally accepted by the museum's curatorial staff as an appropriate way to communicate science. Fortunately, his technique proved popular and the creation of a dramatic visual context for specimens once viewed in systematic isolation eventually became an accepted approach to exhibition in natural history museums. Chapman was not alone in this innovative technique. In 1911, in Sweden, the taxidermist Olof Gylling began creating similar displays and, in fact, was the first person to use the term "diorama" to describe this technique in a museum setting.

The diorama has proven to be an enduring medium for natural history museums. However, not all dioramas are created equal. The success of the diorama can be measured in the satisfied gazes of visitors as they ponder the seemingly distant vista and marvel at the illusion. I have had numerous conversations with our visitors regarding what they most like about the dioramas. The answers inevitably have to do with the appearance of reality: "It looks so real!" I have also had conversations that reveal that some visitors think of these displays as akin to wax-museum creations. The illusion is not convincing. It is often during these conversations that the unfavorable comparisons with zoos arise—the difference between the two types of institutions being primarily that our animals are dead and stuffed, and that zoo animals are alive, but captive, and miserably deprived of their natural environment. Neither observation is especially flattering. I firmly believe that these negative assess-

Are natural history museums the anachronistic artifacts of a turn-of-the-century illusion that we could literally capture nature and put it on display, and in so doing somehow project our dominion over it? In the U.S., the origins of natural history museums are linked to the spirit of the Victorian sportsman who were often condemned for their rapacious slaughter of wildlife in pursuit of trophies and glory, but abundantly aware of the ever-diminishing "nature pristine" from which they derived such great pleasure.

ments have something to do with the success (or lack of success) of both types of institutions to create illusions, to artfully employ the sleight of hand that makes for good magic. If the trick is a good one, people will enjoy the illusion. And if the magician has something meaningful to convey beyond his skill at *legerdemain*...well, he's got their attention.

The magic employed in the making of the foreground materials is based on two things: research and skill. The artists involved must have a comprehensive knowledge of what they are attempting to reproduce. For the scenic foreground artist, this usually means that careful observations in the field are made and recorded through sketches and models of the environmental elements to be created. Molds of leaves and trees are made for eventual casting and modeling in the museum studios. Color notes are made. Measurements are taken. Eventually, casts and models are created and assembled in the diorama shell.

The background painter must make similar observations and notes. If photographic reference is to be used, the artist must take into account not only the inherent distortions of the curved background surface, but

Neg. #281097, Courtesy Dept. of Library Services, American Museum of Natural History

The African buffalo group in preparation in the Akeley Hall (completed c. 1936).

also the distortions produced by the camera lens itself. There is no such thing as an undistorted view through a camera lens, regardless of how superior the optics may be. The undisputed master of the arcane art of diorama background painting was James Perry Wilson, many of whose finest efforts grace and enrich the Halls of African and North American mammals at the American Museum of Natural History. Wilson, an architect by training, was a self-taught painter, who in his 40s was "discovered" by a vacationing museum employee. Wilson was painting outdoors while vacationing in Maine when the chance encounter took place. Thanks to his background in architecture, his natural abilities as a painter, and his love and knowledge of mathematics, Wilson developed a most precise system for contending with the aforementioned distortions and transforming his photographic reference material to the background surface.

Of course, the other three-dimensional elements—the mounted specimens—are the players on the diorama stage. Contrary to a commonly-held belief, the familiar animals in natural history museum dioramas are not "stuffed." They are animal sculptures that have been covered with preserved animal hides (or feathers or scales.) These specimens appear life-like due as much to the sculptor's artistry as to their covering. The best known of the museum taxidermists was Carl Akeley. A gifted artist and naturalist, Akeley developed a method of creating a sculptural papier-maché hollow cast that provided a dimensionally stable structure for the faunal mounts. Although Akeley was an innovator who produced incredibly realistic animals, he was not the first to develop a method of truly sculptural specimen mounting. That distinction belongs to William Hornaday of the American Museum of Natural History. He was the first to do away with the old straw-and-rag method of stuffing in favor of a realistically sculpted clay mannequin formed over an armature. The art of sculptural taxidermy reached its apex in the American Museum's Hall of African Mammals, completed in 1938. This spectacular exhibition hall was Akeley's vision and his triumph. Tragically, he did not see it completed. He died in 1926 while on expedition in Africa doing research for the exhibition.

Magic does occur in natural history museums, but to what end? What do natural history museums have to say? Are they the anachronistic artifacts of a turn-of-the-century delusion that we could literally capture nature and put it on display, and in so doing somehow project our dominion over it? The answer must in part be "yes." Certainly in the U.S., the origins of natural history museums are linked to the spirit of the Victorian sportsman. There was a grand tradition of hunting that was a backlash to industrialism. As Karen Wonders says in her excellent book, *Habitat Dioramas*, hunting was a "romantic way to engage in adventure, travel, and recreation and at the same time study indigenous natural history." Indeed, these wealthy Victorian hunters, who are often condemned for their rapacious slaughter of wildlife in pursuit of trophies and glory, were abundantly aware of the ever-diminishing "nature pristine" from which they derived such great pleasure. In spite of the irony of filling exhibition space (the purpose of which is to celebrate life) with vast numbers of dead animals, the institutional mission of most natural history museums—and of the American Museum of Natural History in particular—was, and is, conservation and preservation. There is a great tradition of conducting "naked-eye" science in the U.S., a view that nature is best studied in the field rather than in the laboratory. The many diorama-type exhibits that fill natural history museums are an attempt to bring the act of field observation to as wide an audience as possible.

Continuing the mission of educating the public about the need for preserving and understanding the natural world, the American Museum of Natural History is developing a hall of biodiversity. In a sense, this exhibition will serve as an orientation to the entire museum's educational displays. The intention is for this hall to be a place where visitors will be able to apprehend the "state of the living world." The content of the exhibition is organized around three themes.

First, biodiversity is described, and the importance of the diversity of the living world is explained in terms of mutual dependency and survival. Throughout the exhibition the role of humans as both victim and victimizer will be discussed.

Second, this biological diversity is threatened by conversion of naturally diverse habitats to agricultural, industrial, or residential use; pollution of the environment; the (human) introduction of non-native or alien species; outright extermination of species, war, and countless other activities. Of course, these are proximal causes for the loss of biodiversity. The root causes can be found in overpopulation, unequal distribution of wealth and resources, and a general lack of understanding of the biological world.

The remainder of the hall deals with what is being done and what can be done to confront the biodiversity crisis. While this exhibition is continuing the same educational mission of all natural history museums, the means by which this message is expressed represents a departure from our traditional approach to exhibition. Rather than making the case for preservation by presenting the ideal, this hall will directly depict the current, non-idealized state of the biological world.

The centerpiece for the exhibition is a large (100 feet long by 30 feet wide by 18 feet high) representation of the Dzanga Sangha tropical rainforest in the Central African Republic. This particular site is an island of relatively pristine rainforest that is protected as a national park on a continent that is rapidly losing its natural splendor. It is emblematic of the biodiversity crisis.

This dramatic habitat reconstruction preserves elements of the con-

Visitors will not be fooled into thinking they are anywhere other than at the museum, but they will be treated to a grand illusion. It is the magic the museum visitors come to see.

ventional museum diorama, and it includes a number of innovations. Although we are keeping the meticulously crafted foreground, we are not using the traditional curved painted background. The magic of the background vista is enhanced by the use of rear-projection video animation, merged with digitized photographic backgrounds. Through these images, the habitat is animated with the illusion of living fauna. By orchestrating the occurrence and activities of these images, the element of time is introduced. Visitors passing through this space will see different things with each "walk through the forest." Effects such as changing temperature, humidity, and lighting in conjunction with directional and ambient sounds aid in creating an immersive environment. This forest will be a constructed environment, but the effect will be to simulate the randomness of a true encounter with nature. The theatrical proscenium of the traditional diorama, which implicitly proscribes the proper view of a frozen moment in time, is replaced by a dynamic encounter with an ever-changing environment. Visitors will not be fooled into thinking they are anywhere other than at the museum, but they will be treated to a grand illusion. If we are successful, the butterfly in the jar will be rendered on an immense scale and the art and magic will continue to serve science.

Photo: Bob Braine

The American Museum of Natural History's new exhibition on the biodiversity crisis will feature a 100-foot long by 30-foot wide by 18-foot high tropical rainforest. While these endangered forests cover only 7% of the earth's surface, they contain more than half of its species.

It is the magic the museum visitors come to see. And through that magic, we tell the wonderful and terrifying story of the state of this living world. ∎

J. Willard Whitson is the Senior Exhibition Developer at the American Museum of Natural History.

Imaginary Interview in the Future

Ian Foxglove, the CEO for a multinational entertainment empire during its period of greatest expansion, retired in 2013. Recently, he agreed to grant Concrete Jungle *an interview. The following is an excerpt.*

CONCRETE JUNGLE: Can you tell us, why zoos? The theme parks and television networks were extremely profitable in the late 20th Century. Was it financial trend surfing?

IAN FOXGLOVE: Well, to a certain degree, yes. The corporation's early investments in technology were viewed with skepticism at first, and so there was a need to diversify our holdings. Many of us within the company also felt our clientele sought greater authenticity, and at that time, animals represented to many people the greatest sort of purity because they came from the wild, untainted by culture. There was also a historic parallel that internally we took great pride in—the London Zoological Gardens. It was established at the end of the 19th century as an imperialistic showcase for the exotic fauna found throughout the British Empire. We all found it odd that often the company was accused of not having respect for history, just because of the suggested locations for some of the theme parks. Anyway, a great deal of resources were spent on creating natural habitats which simulated the original landscape for the animals, and we hired the best and the brightest young scientists to manage the animal populations within global species survival plans.

CJ: And so your visitors who came to see the animals in their natural-looking habitats in the zoo felt they were getting the "real thing," were on safari or going up the Amazon, just like they believed they were in the Wild West or outer space?

IF: I don't know if they believed they were there, but it was closer to their fantasy. That's what they were looking for, so we tried to make a place where their dreams could come true.

CJ: And was entertainment then ultimately the reason the virtual zoo replaced the live animal zoo?

IF: Many factors resulted in that decision. Visitors to zoos have always had very limited interaction with the animals, especially the more exotic and dangerous ones, which are the most desirable to interact with, of course. We tried some prototype virtual exhibits with lions, polar bears and chimpanzees. Obviously, the thrill of interacting with these creatures without any of the danger made these the most popular exhibits in the park. Plus these animals didn't throw their feces at the visitors unless they asked for it. The live animals' behaviors always had some element of unpredictability no matter how much research or time was devoted to studying them. Ultimately they were very difficult to manage—worse than the pirates of the Caribbean.

CJ: You certainly have a distinctive way of speaking. I mean, there

Disney's Animal Kingdom will be magical, fanciful and fun in the tradition of all of our theme parks, yet it will incorporate a new dimension of reality with live animals in their natural habitat. With a combination of thrilling rides, exotic landscapes and close encounters with wild animals, we are creating an entirely new experience for our guests.
—Michael D. Eisner, chairman and chief executive officer of the Walt Disney Co. speaking about their upcoming live-action adventure park

weren't actually pirates, it was just a ride.

IF: What do you mean?

CJ: Um…never mind. Let's get back to the virtual zoo. Was it your idea?

IF: No, it was brought to my attention by one of our marketing directors who claimed the idea was hers. I heard a rumor many years later that it was really the idea of a lazy zoo keeper who was tired of cleaning the waste from a stall one day and he had facetiously suggested a virtual zoo, for obvious reasons.

CJ: What ever happened to him?

IF: He was fired. So were all the zoo keepers and most of the curators. We needed programmers, not animal people.

CJ: What happened to the animals?

IF: Once we shot the footage we needed for use in the virtual zoo, we donated the animals to other zoos around the world. It was a brilliant PR move.

CJ: You said you retained some of the animal curators?

IF: Of course. It was necessary to use their knowledge about animal behaviors to create the parameters for the computer programs. Also, there was still the need to retrain the public to forget their original fears and interact with the wildlife. Once they realized it was safe family fun, we couldn't build virtual zoos fast enough.

CJ: So why do you think the zoo profession didn't respond well?

IF: Jealousy, I guess.

CJ: Really. What about the public—do they ever complain about the virtual zoo not having real animals?

IF: They are real to the visitors. Perception is reality. ■

Wild Illusions

by
Thane
Maynard

Henry David Thoreau, the great American troublemaker, taught us that "in wildness is the preservation of the world." He, as in most things, was right about this. Nature and the natural systemic flow of water, air and energy all make life possible on this lonely planet. But Thoreau, who himself said, "I hate museums," might be surprised by the modern urban idiom that "in zoos, museums, and documentaries are the preservation of the wild."

As David Brower, noted archdruid and builder of the Sierra Club and Friends of the Earth, put it, "wild species are 2% flesh and bone and 98% place." By their very nature, zoos, museums and films present wildlife out of context. Thus, there are bound to be substantive problems.

Today's zoos, as oft-stated in their promotional materials, are not like zoos in the days of old. Wild creatures are not captive just for the entertainment of zoo visitors; they are not caged behind bars and bred randomly with brothers and sisters. No sir, zoos and aquariums are dedicated to two things: conservation and education. The problem is the public has been led to believe that breeding endangered species in captivity is conservation, leading directly to the reintroduction of those tigers and gorillas back into the forests of Asia and Africa. But the harsh truth is that these creatures are not, will not and *cannot* be "born free" like the fictitious Elsa, the lioness. Noah's Ark makes a great legend, but bad ecology. Zoos are not modern-day arks.

> As David Brower put it, "wild species are 2% flesh and bone and 98% place." By their very nature, zoos, museums and films present wildlife out of context. Thus, there are bound to be substantive problems.

The pre-existing selective pressures on most wild populations renders the release of a captive-bred animal into their ecosystem too complex, too expensive and too often more of a detriment than a benefit. Captive breeding for reintroduction is a feel-good solution, but an ineffective one.

In 1979, zoos across the U.S. (and now around the world) began to cooperate in an organized breeding project called the Species Survival Plan (SSP). The objectives were solid: genetic diversity of captive populations must be maximized if we hope to display elephants, orangutans, reticulated pythons and other species 200 years from now. But since babies are cute and very popular with zoo visitors and Associated Press photographers, and we're always eager for the quick fix, people began to equate these babies with the act of protecting endangered wildlife.

Today, many zoo professionals recognize that captive breeding is not a panacea for wildlife, but it is essential to the future of zoos—much like maintaining the collection at a museum. Rather than defining the effort in the lofty (and misleading) terms Species Survival Plan, many refer to captive breeding in what Bill Conway, Director of the Bronx Zoo and guru of the zoo world, describes with the same acronym, SSP—Self-Sustaining Populations.

Photo: Bob Braine

Exploring the jungle the safe way: In the 1980s, elaborate tropical rainforest exhibitions become a magnet for the urban public, whose curiosity was fed by reports of the jungle's disappearance.

In the 1980s, the high-tech age of assisted reproduction was ushered in at zoos. By using techniques from the cattle and sheep industries, zoos were now able to electro-ejaculate, *in vitro* fertilize and embryo transfer animals who had never even seen each other. Some were not of the same species, but heh, it's science! Appropriate technology can be of help, even for wildlife, but it is expensive and experimental.

The new "frozen zoo" concept is just such an endeavor. By cryogenically storing eggs, sperm and fertilized embryos, scientists are making claims of preserving wildlife for the future. Placing cells in liquid nitrogen at -385°F is the equivalent of throwing the Earth's biodiversity in the freezer with the leftovers. You may get around to them eventually, but they'll have a hell of a freezer burn.

Natural history museums have also undergone a comparable sea change over the last two decades. In an attempt to attract more members and a larger audience, many museums no longer celebrate the depth and diversity of their collection, opting instead for more of a video arcade atmosphere. Lots of action, lots of color, but relatively content-free. The same could be said of the local shopping mall; but, the organizations probably have differing mission statements.

Museums of natural history's strength is in their programs. As urban phenomena, they offer ways to better understand evolutionary biology (including human culture) and the way nature works. Museums and zoos are principally interpretive centers, otherwise they could simply be research programs closed to visitors. Despite the varying quality of their exhibits, museums usually have a first-rate staff who are often willing to demonstrate how science is applied in the real world.

Nature shows try to do the same thing, often with the same pitfalls. Documenting nature is what wildlife films are for. They serve nature up in digestible bites. In the process, we have become a culture with an Attention Deficit Disorder (ADD) toward nature. Often people spoon-fed on *Wild Kingdom* and The Discovery Channel initially lack the patience required for birdwatching, hunting, and fishing. Only over extended periods of time outdoors do they realize the patience and understanding of an ecosystem necessary to observe natural animal behavior.

The compressed pace of action in nature films is not merely the result of modern digital editing. Many of the scenes are staged. Food is often provided to draw animals in. Trained animals are used in order to make filming possible. Otherwise, getting usable footage of a nocturnal jaguar in a South American tropical forest would be difficult and dangerous.

What nature shows can and should do well is to document the context of the wildness that remains. As Edward Wilson of Harvard, put it, "The dreams of scientists come to this: *ex situ* conservation is not enough and will never be enough." We run the risk at Century's end of becoming one big scoop of vanilla in a politically correct world grown too tame. (My favorite bumper sticker is the one I

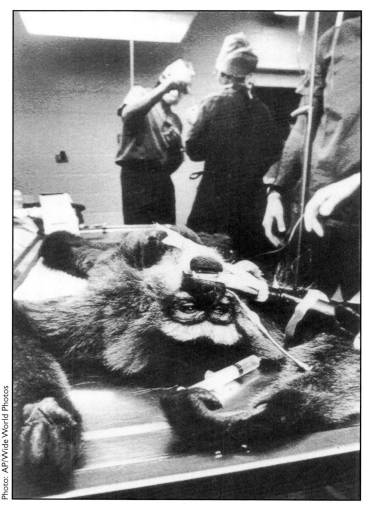

Photo: AP/Wide World Photos

PRESERVATION OF THE WILD: Doctors prepare to operate on Bebe, a rare grey gibbon, in an attempt to restore sight to her right eye (1983). Bebe went blind three years ago and had a $300 prosthetic lens implanted in her cataract-clouded right eye.

saw recently that said, "Save the tsetse fly!") Rather than staged animal behavior, nature shows can document the sheer, raw beauty of wildness.

Kentucky poet Wendell Berry, who is sometimes called the "last thinking man in America" has said: "The real work of planet-saving will be small, humble, and humbling." Modern nature institutions celebrate the Earth's biodiversity, but they are huge, lumbering organizations. Together,

Evolution of Zoos

Conservation
Center

Zoological
Park

Menagerie

21st century
20th century
19th century

Environmental Resource Center

Theme	Environmental
Subjects	Ecosystems
	Survival of species
Concerns	Holistic conservation
	Organizational networks
Exhibitry	Immersion exhibits

Living Museum

Theme	Ecological
Subjects	Habitats of animals
	Behavioral biology
Concerns	Cooperative species management
	Professional development
Exhibitry	Dioramas

Living Natural History Cabinet

Theme	Taxonomic
Subjects	Diversity of species
	Adapatations for life
Concerns	Species husbandry
	Species propagation
Exhibitry	Cages

Source: Chicago Zoological Society, 1992

zoos, museums and wildlife films annually constitute more than a $3 billion industry. In order to achieve the aims of conservation and protection of wild areas which they tout, they would be better served by encouraging visitors and members to "unplug," get off the World Wide Web and experience nature. This requires getting wet, often muddy, and learning what moss feels like to lay on while staring up through the trees, but it is infinitely more amazing than a canned trip to Sea World.

In the end, the burden of zoos, aquariums, museums and even wildlife documentaries is not that of living and dead creatures caged in our limited, human-made structures. I do not weep for these animals. It is all of us who are caged. The crime is in leading subsequent generations to believe that nature can be catalogued, replicated, frozen and preserved in our cities.

One thing is certain—"nature" will continue, even with biodiversity falling fast. Ironically, people are the only ones who care. This is how it should be though, since it is in our own best interest to protect wild areas. Zoos, museums and documentaries should never cease to remind us of how valuable wild areas are. The message is simple: "wild places for wild species." The solution is extremely complex: we need less consumption of resources and less people. One way or another, we'll get there in the 21st century. ■

Thane Maynard is Director of Education at the Cincinnati Zoo and Botanical Gardens.

Documenting nature is what wildlife films are for. They serve nature up in digestible bites. In the process, we have become a culture with an Attention Deficit Disorder (ADD) toward nature. Often people spoon-fed on *Wild Kingdom* and The Discovery Channel initially lack the patience required for birdwatching, hunting, and fishing.

Bibliography

Aronowitz, Stanley. *Science as Power: Discourse and Ideology in Modern Society*. Minneapolis: University of Minnesota Press, 1988.

Baldwin, A. Dwight Jr., *Beyond Preservation: Restoring and Inventing Landscapes*. Minneapolis: University of Minneapolis Press, 1994.

Balouet, Jean-Christophe. *Extinct Species of the World*. New York: Barron's, 1989.

Barber, Lynn. *The Heyday of Natural History 1820-1870*. Garden City, NJ: Doubleday, 1980.

Barlow, Connie, ed. *Evolution Extended; Biological Debates on the Meaning of Life*. Cambridge, MA: MIT Press, 1992.

Barlow, Connie, ed. *From Gaia to Selfish Genes: Selected Writings in the Life Sciences*. Cambridge, MA: MIT Press, 1992.

Beard, Peter. *The End of the Game*. San Francisco: Chronicle Books, 1963.

Berger, John. "Why Look at Animals." *About Looking*. New York: Pantheon, 1980.

Brown, Tom. *Tom Brown's Field Guide to the Forgotten Wilderness*. New York: Berkeley Books, 1987.

Bynum, W.F. et al, eds. *Dictionary of the History of Science*. Princeton, NJ: Princeton University Press, 1981.

Cahill, Kevin M., M.D. and William O'Brien, M.D. *Tropical Medicine: A Clinical Text*. Oxford, UK: Heinemann Media Books, 1989.

Camus, Alfred. *The Plague*. New York: A.A.Knopf, 1948.

Carson, Rachel. *Silent Spring*. Boston: Houghton Mifflin, 1962.

Catts, Paul E. and Neal H. Haskell. *Entomology and Death: A Procedural Guide*. Clemson: Joyce's Print Shop Inc., 1990.

Clarens, Carlos. *An Illustrated History of the Horror Film*. New York: G.P. Putnam's Sons, 1967.

Crewdson, Michael and Margaret Mittelbach. *Wild New York*. New York: Crown, 1997.

Cronon, William. *Changes in the Land: Indians, Colonists, and the Ecology of New England*. New York: Hill and Wang, 1983.

Cronon, William, ed. *Uncommon Ground: Toward Reinventing Nature*. New York: W.W. Norton, 1995.

Crosby, Alfred. *Ecological Imperialism: The Biological Expansion of Europe, 900-1900*. Cambridge, UK: Cambridge University Press, 1986.

Dawkins, Richard. *The Selfish Gene*. New York: Oxford Press, 1976.

Day, David. *Vanished Species*. New York: Gallery Books, 1989.

Devall, Bill and George Sessions. *Deep Ecology: Living as if Nature Mattered*. Salt Lake City, UT: Peregrine Smith, 1985.

Dürer, Hans Peter. *Dreamtime: Concerning the Boundary Between Wilderness and Civilization*. Oxford, UK: Basil Blackwell, 1985 (1978).

Bibliography

Ehrlich, Anne and Paul. *Extinction: The Causes and Consequences of the Disappearance of Species*. New York: Ballantine Books Inc., 1981.

Ehrlich, Anne and Paul and Gretchen C. Daily. *The Stork and the Plow*. New York: G.P. Putnam's Sons, 1995.

Eisely, Loren. *The Immense Journey*. New York: Random House Inc., 1946.

Eldridge, Niles. *The Miner's Cannery*. Princeton, NJ: Princeton University Press, 1994.

Evernden, Neil. *The Natural Alien: Humankind and Environment*. Toronto: University of Toronto Press, 1985.

Foweler, Cary and Pat Mooney. *Shattering: Food, Politics and the Loss of Genetic Diversity*. Tucson, AZ: University of Arizona Press, 1990.

Glasgow, Vaughn L. *A Social History of the American Alligator: The Earth Trembles with his Thunder*. New York: St. Martin's Press, 1991.

Golding, Charles. *Rats: The New Plague*. London: Weidenfeld and Nicolson, 1990.

Gould, Stephen Jay. *The Flamingo's Smile*. New York: W.W. Norton, 1985.

Gould, Stephen Jay. *The Mismeasure of Man*. New York: W.W. Norton, 1981.

Gould, Stephen Jay. *Wonderful Life*. New York: W.W. Norton, 1989.

Greenway, James C., Jr. *Extinct and Vanishing Birds of the World*. New York: Dover Publications, 1967.

Griffin, Susan. *Woman and Nature: The Roaring Inside Her*. San Francisco: Harper and Row, 1978.

Halpern, Daniel, ed. *On Nature: Nature, Landscape and Natural History*. Berkeley, CA: North Point Press, 1986.

Haraway, Donna. *Primate Visions: Gender, Race and Nature in the World of Modern Science*. New York: Routledge, 1989.

Haraway, Donna. *Simians, Cyborgs and Women: The Reinvention of Nature*. New York: Routledge, 1991.

Hendrickson, Robert. *More Cunning Than Man: A Social History of Rats and Men*. New York: Dorset Press, 1983.

Hernstein, Richard J. and Charles Murray. *The Bell Curve: Intelligence and Class Structure in American Life*. New York: Free Press, 1994.

Herrero, Stephen. *Bear Attacks: Their Causes and Avoidance*. New York: Lyons and Burford, 1985.

Herrick, C. Judson. *Brains of Rats and Men: A Survey of the Origin and Biological Significance of the Cerebral Cortex*. Chicago: University of Chicago Press, 1926.

Hoage, R.J. ed. *Animal Extinction, What Everyone Should Know*. Washington, D.C.: Smithsonian Institution Press, 1985.

Hoage, R.J. *Perceptions of Animals in American Culture*. Washington, D.C.: Smithsonian Institution Press, 1989.

Holt, Nancy ed. *The Writing of Robert Smithson*. New York: New York University Press, 1979.

Hough, Michael. *City Form and Natural Process*. New York: Van Nostrand Reinhold, 1984.

Kaufman, Les and Mallory, eds. *The Last Extinction*. Cambridge, MA: MIT Press, 1987.

Kieran, John. *Natural History of New York City*. Boston: Houghton Mifflin Co., 1959.

Kneen, Brewster. *From Land to Mouth: Understanding the Food System*. Toronto: NC Press, 1989.

Knutson, Roger M. *Flattened Fauna*. Berkeley, CA: Ten Speed Press, 1987.

Knutson, Roger M. *Furtive Fauna: A Field Guide to the Creatures Who Live on You*. New York: Penguin Books, 1992.

Lamb, Robert. *World Without Trees: Dutch Elm Disease and Other Human Errors*. London: Wildwood House, 1979.

Laycock, George. *The Alien Animals: The Story of Imported Wildlife*. New York: Ballantine Books Inc., 1966.

Leahy, Michael P.T. *Against Liberation: Putting Animals In Perspective*. London: Routledge, 1991.

Leiss, William. *The Domination of Nature*. Boston: Beacon Press, 1972.

Leopold, Aldo. *A Sand County Almanac*. Oxford, UK: Oxford University Press, 1949.

Lepenies, Wolf. *The End of Natural History*. New York: Confucian Press Inc., 1980.

Lewontin, Richard, Steven Rose and Leon Kamin. *Not In Our Genes: Biology, Ideology and Human Nature*. New York: Pantheon, 1984.

Ley, Willy. *Exotic Zoology*. New York: Bonanza Books, reprint 1987.

Livingston, John A. *The Fallacy of Wildlife Conservation*. Toronto: McClelland and Stewart, 1981.

Lovejoy, Arthur O. *The Great Chain of Being*. Cambridge, MA: Harvard University Press, 1936.

Matilsky, Barbara. *Fragile Ecologies: Contemporary Artist's Interpretation and Solutions*. New York: Rizzoli, 1992.

Matthiessen, Peter. *Wildlife in America*. New York: Viking Press Inc., 1959.

McHarg, Ian. *Design With Nature*. Garden City, NJ: Doubleday/Natural History Press, 1969.

McLoughlin, John C. *The Animals Among Us: Wildlife in the City*. New York: Viking Press, 1978.

Merchant, Carolyn. *The Death of Nature: Woman, Ecology and the Scientific Revolution*. San Francisco: Harper and Row, 1980.

Merchant, Carolyn. *Ecological Revolutions: Nature, Gender, and Science in New England*. Chapel Hill, NC: University of North Carolina Press, 1989.

Midgley, Mary. *Animals and Why they Matter*. Athens, GA: University of Georgia Press, 1983.

Misrach, Richard. *Bravo 20: The Bombing of the American West*. Baltimore, MD: John Hopkins University Press, 1990.

Mullan, Bob and Garry Marvin. *Zoo Culture: A Book About Watching Man Watching Animals*. London: Weidenfeld and Nicholson, 1987.

Myers, Norman. "A Look at the Present Extinction Spasm and What it Means for the Future Evolution of Species." *Animal Extinction, What Everyone Should Know*. Hoage, R.J. ed. Washington, D.C.: Smithsonian Institution Press, 1985.

Myers, Norman. *The Primary Source: Tropical Forests and Our Future*. New York: W.W. Norton and Co., 1985.

Nash, Roderick. *Wilderness and the American Mind*. New Haven, CT: Yale University Press, 1982.

Novak, Barbara. *Nature and Culture*. New York: Oxford University Press, 1980.

Ordish, George. *The Living American House: The 350-Year Story of a Home—An Ecological History*. New York: William Morrow and Co. Inc., 1981.

Orwell, George. *1984*. New York: Chelsea House, 1987.

Pepper, David. *Eco-Socialism: From Deep Ecology to Social Justice*. New York: Routledge, 1993.

Peterson, Roger Tory. *A Field Guide To Eastern Birds*. Boston: Houghton Mifflin Co., 1980.

Plato, (translated by Benjamin Jowett). *Apology*. New York: P.F. Collier & Son, 1937.

Poe, Edgar Allan. *The Pit and the Pendulum*. Mankato, MN: Creative Education, 1980.

Polakowski, Kenneth J. *Zoo Design: The Reality of Wild Illusions*. Ann Arbor, MI: School of Natural Resources, University of Michigan, 1987.

Preston, Douglas J. *Dinosaurs in the Attic: An Excursion into the American Museum of Natural History*. New York: St. Martin's Press, 1986.

Quammen, David. *The Song of the Dodo: Island Biogeography in an Age of Extinction*. New York: Charles Scribner & Sons, 1996.

Quinn, John R. *Wildlife Survivors: The Flora and Fauna of Tomorrow*. Blue Ridge Summit: Tab Books, 1994.

Rackham, James. *Animal Bones*. London: The British Museum Press, 1994.

Rifkin, Jeremy. *Biosphere Politics: A Cultural Odyssey from the Middle Ages to the New Age*. New York: Harper Collins, 1991.

Rivito, Harriet. *The Animal Estate: The English and Other Creatures in the Victorian Age*. London: Harvard, 1987.

Rodale's All New Encyclopedia of Organic Gardening. New York: Rodale Press, 1992.

Roots, Clive. *Animal Invaders*. New York: Universe Books, 1976.

Ross, Andrew. *The Chicago Gangster Theory of Life: Nature's Debt to Society*. London: Verso, 1994.

Ross, Andrew. *Strange Weather: Culture, Science and Technology in the Age of Limits*. New York: Verso, 1991.

Rowe, J. Stan. *Home Place: Essay on Ecology*. Edmonton: Newest Books, 1990.

Sale, Kirkpatrick. *The Green Revolution: The American Environmental Movement 1962-1992*. New York: Hill and Wang, 1993.

Schwabe. Calvin W. *Unmentionable Cuisine*. Charlottesville, VA: University of Virginia Press, 1979.

Shepard, Paul. *Man in the Landscape: A Historic View of the Esthetics of Nature*. New York: Knopf, 1967.

Simon, Joel. *Endangered Mexico, An Environment on the Edge.* San Francisco: Sierra Club Books, forthcoming 1997.

Simon, Seymour. *What You Want to Know About Earthworms.* New York: Scholastic Book Services, 1969.

Singer, Peter. *Animal Liberation.* New York: Random House, 1990.

Singer, Peter. *In Defense of Animals.* Oxford, UK: Basil Blackwell, 1981.

Skal, David J. *Monster Show.* New York: Penguin Books, 1994.

Skinner, B.F. *Beyond Dignity and Freedom.* New York: Knopf, 1971.

Skolimowski, Henryk. *Eco-philosophy: Designing New Tactics for Living.* Boston: Marion Boyars, 1981.

Smith, Betty. *A Tree Grows in Brooklyn.* New York: Harper & Row, 1947.

Snyder, Gary. *The Practice of the Wild.* San Francisco: North Point Press, 1990.

Starhawk. *Dreaming the Dark: Magic, Sex and Politics.* Boston: Beacon Press, 1982.

Street, Philip. *Animal Partners and Parasites.* New York: Taplinger Publishing Co., 1975.

Swift, Jonathan. *Gulliver's Travels.* New York: Modern Library, 1996.

Thomas, Keith. *Man and the Natural World: A History of the Modern Sensibility.* New York: Pantheon, 1983.

Tuan, Yi-fu. *Topophilia: A Study of Environmental Perception, Attitudes and Values.* Englewood Cliffs: Prentice-Hall, 1974.

Tucker, William. *Progress and Privilege: America in the Age of Environmentalism.* Garden City, NJ: Doubleday/Anchor, 1982.

Turner, Frederick W. *Beyond Geography: The Western Spirit Against Wilderness.* New York: Viking Press, 1980.

Verne, Jules. *Mysterious Island.* New York: Airmont Publishing Co., Inc., 1965 (1874).

Verne, Jules. *20,000 Leagues Under The Sea.* New York: Bantam Books, Inc., 1962 (1870).

Ward, Peter Douglas. *The End of Evolution.* New York: Bantam Books, 1994.

Weigelt, Johannes. *Recent Vertebrate Carcasses and Their Paleobiological Implications.* Chicago: University of Chicago Press, 1989 (1927).

Weston, Joe, ed. *Red and Green: The New Politics of the Environment.* London: Pluto Press, 1986.

Williams, Raymond. *The Country and the City.* London: Chatto and Windus, 1973.

Williams, Raymond. *Keywords: A Vocabulary of Culture and Society.* London: Fontana, 1976.

Wilson, Alexander. *The Culture of Nature: North American Landscape from Disney to the Exxon Valdez.* Cambridge, MA: Blackwell, 1992.

Wells, H.G. *The Food of the Gods and How it Came to Earth.* New York: Charles Scribner's Sons, 1904.

Wells, H.G. *The Island of Dr. Moreau.* New York: Signet Classics, 1988.

Wonders, Karen. *Habitat Dioramas: Illusions of Wilderness in Museums of Natural History.* Stockholm, Sweden: Almquist Wiksell International, 1993.

Wyndham, John. *The Day of the Triffids.* New York: Doubleday and Co.

Inc., 1951.

Young, David. *The Discovery of Evolution*. London: Natural History Musuem Publications, 1992.

Zinsser, Hans. *Rats, Lice and History*. Boston: Little, Brown, 1963.

■ Stupid Nature Books ■

Barnard, Peggy. *Monkey in the House*. New York: Dutton, 1961. A primate makes an evolutionary leap.

Colby, Constance Taber. *A Skunk in the House*. New York: J.B. Lipincott Co., 1973. "Secret" the skunk lives mostly stench-free in the Colby household.

Drabble, Phil. *A Weasel in My Meatsafe*. Stamford, CT: Ulverscroft, 1980. Memoirs of a British weasel lover.

Durrell, Jacquie. *Beast in My Bed*. New York: Atheneum, 1967. Not satisfied with just having an animal in the house, French author Durrell invites a whole bevy of beasts into her boudoir. The menagerie includes "Cholmondeley" the chimp, "Sarah Huggersack" the anteater and "Claudius" the tapir. Jacquie's husband, Gerald is also responsible for the following titles: *Rosy is My Relative, The Talking Parcel, Catch Me a Colobus, Beasts in My Belfry, A Zoo in My Luggage* and *Two in the Bush*.

Fryson, Marna. *Stinkerbelle the Nark*. New York: Taplinger Publishing Co., 1976. Thai otter is forced to live in a London Cottage.

Hancock, Lyn. *There's a Seal in My Sleeping Bag*. New York: Knopf, 1972. Canadian author Hancock shares intimate sleeping quarters with "Sam the Domesticated Sea Lion." Other titles by Hancock include *There's a Raccoon in My Parka* and *Love Affair with a Cougar*.

Lingrad, Jeremy. *The Zoo in My Backyard*. New York: A.S. Barnes & Co., 1972. "Tiki" the tame weasel becomes the star player in Lingrad's suburban zoo.

McKenna, Virginia. *Some of My Friends Have Tails*. New York: Harcourt, Brace & Co., 1970. McKenna forges relationships with George the Snake and "Slowly" the elephant.

Rood, Ronald N. *The Loon in my Bathtub*. Brattleboro, VT: Stephen Green Press, 1964. The king of the Northern Lakes becomes acquainted with modern bathroom appliances. This book could have been called "On Golden Sink."

Rose, Stuart. *There's a Fox in the Spinney*. New York: Doubleday, 1967. Memoirs of a British fox hunter.

Sloan, Ethel B. *Kangaroo in the Kitchen*. Indianapolis: Bobbs-Merrill, 1978. A family moves down under and gets cooking tips from a marsupial.

Van Wormer, Joe. *There's a Marmot on the Telephone*. New York: Axton Printer, 1974. "Floogie" the marmot moves into Wormer's house and disrupts the phone line when Wormer is talking to a powerful New York City magazine editor. Wormer gets contract to write book anyway.

Wilsson, Lars. *My Beaver Colony*. New York: Doubleday, 1968. Swede adopts four young beavers.

catalog

Concrete Jungle

edited by Mark Dion and Alexis Rockman

A pop media investigation of death and survival in urban ecosystems

Concrete Jungle approaches the intersection of urban living and Nature in a contemporary fashion with dark-edged humor and complexity. The contributions, from a diverse group of noted scientists, writers, and artists—including Dr. Paul Ehrlich, theorist Andrew Ross, photographer William Wegman, and notorious road kill recipe writer James Eckle—range from the serious to the seriously funny, from the documentary to the imaginary, and beyond. There are interviews with the Head of Pest Control of NYC; the master exterminator who dealt with the Staten Island Ferry roach infestation; and an archaeologist who specializes in outhouses and toilets and the human behavior surrounding them. An eclectic assortment of essays includes topics such as how forensic pathologists read the decomposition of the human body for criminological clues; case studies of urban animals and alien invaders, and the history and future of natural history museums and zoos.

SPECIAL PRICE!!! regularly $24.95 **$18**

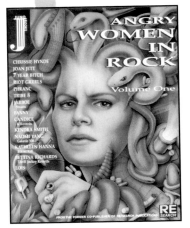

> "I always laugh at that question, "What's it like to be a woman in rock: I don't have any memory of being a man in rock, so I have nothing to compare it to!"
> —**Valerie Agnew, 7 Year Bitch**

Angry Women in Rock, Volume 1

edited by Andrea Juno

Angry Women in Rock, Volume 1 takes up where the best-selling *Angry Women*—a book that inspired a whole generation of young women who have redefined feminism for themselves—left off. Thirteen female musicians and producers, ranging in experience from the established to those of the young underground, discuss their views on politics, sexuality, creativity, violences, authority, feminism, corruption and exploitation in the music industry, and many other topics. *Angry Women in Rock, Volume I* is the first definitive map to a rapidly developing, but still wild, pop culture terrain. The women interviewed, with rare honesty and candor, cover such diverse topics that the book has tremendous appeal even to those who don't know or care much about rock music, and serves as an inspiration to both women and men.

FEATURING: Chrissie Hynde, Joan Jett, Kathleen Hanna (Bikini Kill)**, 7 Year Bitch, Jarboe** (Swans)**, Tribe 8** (the all-dyke punk band)**, Kendra Smith, Naomi Yang** (Galaxie 500)**, Phranc** (the "All-American Jewish Lesbian Folksinger")**, June Millington** (of Fanny, the '60s hard-rocking all-female band)**, Lois, and more!**

$18

CALL 1-800-758-5238 NOW TO ORDER!

Horror Hospital Unplugged

by Dennis Cooper and Keith Mayerson

In *Horror Hospital Unplugged*, well-known cutting-edge author Dennis Cooper and notorious artist Keith Mayerson collaborate to bring us the dark, but hilarious story of Trevor Machine: a twenty-something, gay-but-sexually-confused lead singer for an L.A. indy band on the road to fame and fortune. Inspired by the story "Horror Hospital" from Cooper's story collection *Wrong*, the book chronicles Trevor's adventures and struggles with love, sex and the music industry. Cooper's writing is packed with far-ranging cultural, artistic and literary references, and the book over-flows with biting commentary on trendy art, music and film communities as it explores young, punk sexuality.

Keith Mayerson's visually-stunning, intricate artwork takes us on this incredible voyage with many amazing stops including:

- ◆ **The band's debut at The Viper Room**
- ◆ **A psychedelic, spiritual visitation from the ghost of River Phoenix**
- ◆ **A gala event at David Geffen's fabulous party estate**
- ◆ **A debauched recording session with Courtney Love**

Mayerson's eye-popping artwork, which the *L.A. Times* praised as "post-slacker surrealism," is the perfect partner to Cooper at his best: engaging youth culture in a fresh, innovative style. While the story of Trevor Machine is a coming-out tale, it is also a GenX coming-of-age story, charting the fast drugs and slow climbs of stardom and beyond. *Horror Hospital Unplugged* is a cult classic.

"Dennis Cooper, God help him, is a born writer."

—William S. Burroughs

"Beautifully adapted into comics form, Cooper's themes have been wholly transformed by the brilliantly inventive, psychologically obsessive, black-and-white drawings of Mayerson."

—starred review *Publishers Weekly*

"Mayerson is a promising art brat of the first order."

—San Francisco Examiner

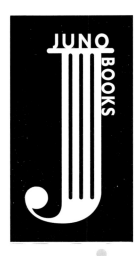

JUNO BOOKS

catalog

Angry Women

The critically acclaimed book that influenced a whole generation of women in which 16 cutting edge performance artists unleash their creative vision and cultural vengeances.

FEATURING: Kathy Acker ◆ Susie Bright ◆ Karen Finley ◆ Diamanda Galas ◆ bell hooks ◆ Avital Ronell Holly Hughes ◆ Sapphire ◆ Lina Montano ◆ Kerr & Malley ◆ Annie Sprinkle ◆ Wanda Coleman Valie Export ◆ Carolee Schneeman

"These women are definitely dangerous models of subversion!"
—Mondo 2000

$18

"This is hardly the nurturing, womanist vision espoused in the 1970s. The view here is largely pro-sex, pro-porn, and pro-choice. Art and activism are inseparable from life and being."
—The Village Voice

Incredibly Strange Music, Volume 2

"The bible of lounge music is *Incredibly Strange Music*."
—Newsweek

"Fans of ambient, acid jazz, even industrial rock, will find the leap back to these genres an easy one to make."
—Rolling Stone

CATEGORIES INCLUDE: Exotica-ploitation ◆ outer space Brazilian psychedelic ◆ singing truckdrivers ◆ yodeling sitar-rock ◆ religious ◆ ventriloquism ◆ moog ◆ theremin harmonica ◆ and much more!

$18

$13

**ALSO AVAILABLE...
Incredibly Strange Music,
Volume 2 CD**
for your listening pleasure

Bob Flanagan: Supermasochist

Flanagan grew up with Cystic Fibrosis and lived longer than any other person with CF. The physical pain of his childhood was alleviated by masturbation and sexual experimentation, resulting in his life long practice of extreme masochism. In deeply confessional interviews, he reveals his life story and sexual practices.

$15

"...the photos and lengthy question-and-answer sessions bring us as close as any outsider can be to the compulsions and the artistry of S-M thought and application."

—San Francisco Chronicle

The RE/Search Guide to Bodily Fluids

$16

by Paul Spinrad

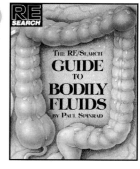

Bringing bodily functions out of the (water) closet into polite conversation

This guide sparks a radical rethinking of our relationship with our bodies and Nature, humorously (and seriously) spanning the gamut of everything you ever wanted to know about bodily functions and excreta. Each bodily function is discussed from a variety of viewpoints: scientific, anthropological, historical, mythological, sociological, and artistic.

TOPICS INCLUDE: mucus ◆ menstruation, saliva ◆ sweat ◆ earwax ◆ vomit ◆ urine flatus ◆ feces ◆ and much more!

SPECIAL OFFERS (includes shipping)

#1: SAVE $30 off bookstore prices!!!
Horror Hospital (reg. $24.95), Angry Women in Rock (reg. 19.95), and Concrete Jungle (reg. $24.95) for only **$40!**

#2: SAVE $10!!! ANGRY WOMEN SPECIAL Both Angry Women books (reg. $19.95 each) for only **$30!**

COMING IN 1997...

Sex, Stupidity and Greed: *The Underbelly of the American Movie Industry*

A revealing look at the tricks and tragedies of the American movie machine.

CALL 1-800-758-5238 NOW TO CHARGE BY PHONE!

ORDER BY MAIL OR PHONE
call 1-800-758-5238
or 212-807-7300
fax 212-807-7355
Juno Books
180 Varick Street, 10th Floor
New York, NY 10014
Please call M-F, 10am to 6pm, EST

NAME: _____
ADDRESS: _____
_____
PHONE: _____

Please indicate if you would like to be added to our mailing list, or send a SASE for a complete catalog

I am paying by:
☐ Check or money order (payable to Juno Books)
☐ Credit card (circle one): **VISA   MASTERCARD**

Visa/Mastercard #: _____   Expiration date: _____

Signature: _____

ORDER FORM

TITLE	PRICE	QUANTITY	TOTAL
Horror Hospital Unplugged	$18.00		
Angry Women in Rock, Volume 1	$18.00		
Angry Women	$18.00		
Concrete Jungle	$18.00		
Incredibly Strange Music, Volume 2	$18.00		
Incredibly Strange Music, Volume 2 CD	$13.00		
Guide to Bodily Fluids	$16.00		
Bob Flanagan: Supermasochist	$15.00		
SPECIAL OFFER #1: 3 Books!	$40.00		
SPECIAL OFFER #2: 2 Angry Women	$30.00		
		SUBTOTAL	
		NY Residents (add 8.25% sales tax)	
		Domestic Shipping & Handling (first item $4, each additional $1)	
		TOTAL DUE	

Payment in U.S. dollars only. Allow 6-8 weeks for delivery.

Take advantage of these mail-order discounts: lower than bookstore prices!!!

The End